THE ORDINATION
OF WOMEN
IN THE CATHOLIC CHURCH

THE ORDINATION
OF WOMEN
IN THE CATHOLIC CHURCH
Unmasking a Cuckoo's Egg Tradition

JOHN WIJNGAARDS

Continuum · New York

2001

The Continuum International Publishing Group Inc
370 Lexington Avenue, New York, NY 10017

Printed and bound in Great Britain

Library of Congress Cataloging-in-Publication Data
Wijngaards, J. N. M.
    The ordination of women in the Catholic Church / John Wijngaards
      p. cm.
    Includes bibliographical references.
    ISBN 0–8264–1339–0
    1. Ordination of women—Catholic Church. I. Title.
BX1912.2.W55 2001
262'.142'082—dc21

2001028739

Acknowledgements
My thanks go to the members of my Housetop team who have helped me write this
book: Roy Barton, Jackie Clackson, Deirdre Ford, Anne Miller and Barbara Paskins.
I am grateful to Professor Mary Grey, Professor van Eyden and Professor Peter Nissen
for reading the manuscript and sharing their comments and suggestions with me.

Designed by Sandie Boccacci
Phototypeset in 8.75/11.5pt Utopia by Intype London Ltd
Printed and bound in Great Britain by
The Cromwell Press, Trowbridge, Wiltshire

Contents

Contents

Part I
SETTING THE SCENE

'To the Pope yes, but to Conscience first!'

John Henry, Cardinal Newman,
in 1879 in reply to a toast
proposed to the Pope, at a dinner
in his honour when he had been created
a Cardinal.

1
The Discovery

On a lazy afternoon in November 1975 I walked down the long corridors of St John's Seminary in Hyderabad, India. The weather was hot and humid. I was casually dressed in a white *khurta* shirt over cotton trousers, slippers on my feet. As I entered the library I found it empty. It was the time for students to play football or to water the *thumma* trees in our garden. Nothing in the listless, easygoing, prosaic and sober setting prepared me for the life-changing discovery I was going to make.

In preparation for a nationwide research seminar on ministries in the Church, scheduled for June 1976 in Bangalore, I had been asked to study the ministries of women. The question intrigued me. In 1971, during the Bishops' Synod in Rome, Cardinal Flahiff, Archbishop of Winnipeg, had tabled the following intervention:

> In spite of an old tradition of many centuries against women's participation in the ministry, we believe that the signs of the times force us to carefully examine the present situation and the possibilities for the future. The clearest of these signs is that women are already successfully fulfilling pastoral tasks . . . This is the only recommendation which the Canadian Bishops submit to the Synod.[1]

Scripture being my area of expertise, I had made up my mind to focus on the scriptural objections against the ordination of women. The book I came across that afternoon was a seventeenth-century Latin commentary on 1 Timothy by my compatriot Cor van der Steen, professionally known by his Latin name as Cornelius a Lapide. The edition in our library, from Paris in 1868, almost fell to pieces. Its pages were browned with age and punctured by bookworms. But I could still read the Latin.

1 Timothy 2:12–14 says: 'I permit no woman to teach or to have authority over men. She is to keep silent. For Adam was formed first, then Eve. And Adam was not deceived, but the woman was deceived and sinned.' Cornelius weighs in with relish. Women may not teach in Church. And if they are not allowed to teach, how could they function

as priests? And the prohibition is absolute and universal, he says, for many reasons:

- It follows from a woman's nature.
- God subjected woman to man after the fall (Gen. 3:16).
- Silence in the presence of men agrees better with a woman's inferior status.
- A man's intelligence, judgement and discretion surpass that of a woman.
- By speaking in church a woman might lure men to sin.
- Women should remain ignorant of things they need not know.
- By asking stupid questions in church, a woman would give scandal to other women.[2]

As I translated the text, it was as if all the mindless and brutal medieval bias against women rolled out of the book and lay before me. So this is how theologians had interpreted Scripture! Prejudice had clouded their sense of judgement. I suddenly grasped that the implications were enormous.

From modern scholarship we know that the later Pauline letters, such as 1 Timothy, were written within the context of a Gnostic threat to which women were considered especially vulnerable. The Greek text itself and this context make clear that the injunction should be translated as: 'I am presently not allowing women to speak in the assembly';[3] 'I have decided that for the moment women are not to teach or have authority over men'.[4] The references to Adam and Eve are rationalisations, not inspired pronouncements, like the statement in Titus 1:12 that 'Cretans are always liars, evil beasts, lazy gluttons'. The prohibition for women to speak in the assembly was, therefore, clearly local and temporary, not a law for all time. This is also clear from the fact that in other church communities women did speak.[5]

To come back to Cornelius a Lapide: his commentary was for centuries a standard work and the obvious bias in his argumentation suddenly brought the central issue into focus. What we were dealing with, I realised, is not inspired Scripture, but a cultural interpretation imposed on Scripture. Was there really any valid *scriptural* basis for excluding women from the ordained ministries? It spurred me on to a period of intense research. I made the ten-hour train journey to Pune so that I could consult the library of the Papal Athenaeum. I ordered books and articles from Europe, some on microfilm. My studies led me to the conclusion that in total nine arguments from Scripture had been used to exclude women from ordination. None stood up to scrutiny.[6] In all cases it was cultural discrimination, not scriptural inspiration, that shored up the so-called tradition of not ordaining women.

It dawned on me that this was a serious matter. Cultural prejudice rather than God's will was responsible for relegating women to a purely passive role in the Church. Through this theological error, enormous damage had been inflicted on the faithful in previous centuries and the harm was still being done today. Cultural bigotry had invaded Christian beliefs and had succeeded in enthroning a pagan prejudice as if it were a genuine Christian practice. In other words, the opposition to women priests is a classic example of what I call a 'cuckoo's egg tradition' – of which there have been more in the Church!

Cuckoos not only lay their eggs surreptitiously in the nests of other birds; the eggs they lay cunningly imitate the eggs of the hosts. In Britain, for instance, cuckoos can variously lay eggs that resemble in spots and colours the eggs of dunnocks, redstarts, sparrows and warblers. The host bird remains unaware of the fact that a foreign egg has been added to the clutch. In a similar way we see how, in the Early Church, bias against women was presented in typically scriptural and Christian guises. But wait for what is to come!

The cuckoo chick has evolved a fiendish form of behaviour known as 'nest-mate eviction', to ensure that it does not have to compete with members of the foster brood for food. Within a few hours of hatching, the blind, naked, young cuckoo displays a strong urge to evict any objects, such as eggs or other nestlings, from the nest. It does this by working itself under the offending object and, aided by the presence of a depression between the shoulder blades, it heaves the object over the rim of the nest. Within about 24 hours of hatching, the young cuckoo has the nest and the attention of its foster parents to itself. Remarkable as it may seem, the spurious anti-woman tradition in the Christian Church acted in the same way. For many centuries women had served in a number of ministries, including the sacramental diaconate. It all went overboard. The priestly vocations of women were suppressed. Ancient practices that ran counter to the established prejudice, such as a devotion to Mary as priest, were suffocated. A cuckoo's egg tradition is a killer tradition. But the villainy does not stop even here.

When the cuckoo chick grows up, it usually exceeds its foster parents in size. However, the parent birds have now bonded to it and keep feeding it, in spite of the incongruity. They are firmly convinced this is their own chick. One can therefore see a tiny warbler offering newly caught insects to a cuckoo fledgling several times its size! The same happens in the Church with cuckoo's egg traditions. Those with teaching power are often blinded by the longstanding and seemingly ancient origins of the tradition, and will seek to defend its authenticity, even though the incongruity is obvious to impartial observers.

'Hold on,' you may say. 'These are just *your* opinions. How do we know that what you say is true? Rome holds the trump card. Women have not been ordained for two thousand years. You cannot dismiss such a long tradition out of hand!' You are right. I may not presume your agreement. Consider what I have said so far as the hypothesis that I will defend in the rest of this book. I maintain that opposition to the ordination of women does not come from Christ. It is not God who decreed the exclusion of women, but pagan sexist bigotry which squashed the true Christian tradition of women's call to ministry.

I presented my conclusions to the Seminar in Bangalore (2–7 June 1976), urging the Indian bishops to explore the possibilities of ordaining women to the diaconate and the priesthood. I pleaded for openness.

> What seems unacceptable at first may prove to be the will of Christ. What may seem unusual and strange may well be the demand of the Gospel in our own times. The pharisees rejected the carpenter from Nazareth. They refused to recognise him as their priest when they stood under his cross on Calvary. The idea that a woman could express the priesthood of Christ may seem equally upsetting – and our prejudice in this matter may be equally mistaken as that of Jesus' pious contemporaries. Only honest appraisal in the light of Christ's Spirit should decide the question of women's ministry; not convention or personal fancy. After all, it is *Christ's* priesthood, not ours, we are speaking about.[7]

Towards the end of June I was in London attending the General Chapter of the Mill Hill Missionaries to whom I belonged. To my dismay I was elected Vicar General of the Society, which implied a brutal uprooting from my various involvements in India. It was not to be the only shock for that year.

A few months later, in October 1976, the Roman Congregation for Doctrine, ignoring the advice of the Pontifical Biblical Commission, published its letter *Inter Insigniores*. While rejecting some of the old arguments against women priests, it reaffirmed the principal ones. Jesus Christ himself had excluded women, it maintained, and the Church had honoured this tradition. Women could not really represent Christ, who was a man. They could never be validly admitted to Holy Orders. I responded by writing *Did Christ Rule Out Women Priests?*[8] It was clear that the parent birds in Rome were still bolstering the cuckoo tradition, and the defence has become more clamorous ever since.

'But surely such a thing cannot happen in the Church?' you may argue. 'Surely the *magisterium* would not make such a colossal mistake?!' If this is what you believe, it will be instructive to study how the *magisterium* failed in discerning the true Christian teaching regarding slavery. It is the topic of the next chapter.

READINGS FROM THE WOMEN PRIESTS WEBSITE

Complementary information on the topics discussed in this book are available on www.womenpriests.org.

For background data on my life and work

http://www.womenpriests.org/wijnga~1/life.htm

On why I resigned from the active priestly ministry
in protest against the refusal to ordain women

http://www.womenpriests.org/wijnga~1/resign.htm

A bibliography of my books

http://www.womenpriests.org/wijnga~1/biblio.htm

The top priority in my life:'Meeting God in everyday loving'

http://www.womenpriests.org/wijnga~1/love.htm

2

Papal Teaching on Slavery

To SEE A CUCKOO'S EGG TRADITION in action we will analyse the Church's past teaching on slavery. For, believe it or not, for more than 1500 years Church leaders upheld as Catholic teaching that slavery was a legitimate institution. Worse than that, they argued that slavery was an institution actually willed by God!

In 1866, the Vicar Apostolic of the Galla region in southern Ethiopia asked the Congregation for Doctrine: 'Is slavery in harmony with Catholic doctrine?' It should be remembered that at the time slavery had already been abolished in Great Britain and all its dominions, in the USA, in Austria, France, Prussia, Russia, Chile, Ecuador, Argentina, Peru, Venezuela and most other civilized countries. In spite of this, the Congregation answered with an emphatic 'Yes'.

> Slavery itself, considered as such in its essential nature, *is not at all contrary to the natural and divine law,* and there can be several just titles of slavery and these are referred to by approved theologians and commentators of the sacred canons . . .

> *It is not contrary to the natural and divine law for a slave to be sold, bought, exchanged or given,* provided that in this sale, purchase, exchange or gift, the due conditions are strictly observed which the approved authors likewise describe and explain. Among these conditions the most important ones are that the purchaser should carefully examine whether the slave who is put up for sale has been justly or unjustly deprived of his liberty, and that the vendor should do nothing which might endanger the life, virtue or Catholic faith of the slave who is to be transferred to another's possession.[1]

In other words, though one should protect the life, virtue and faith of the slave, slavery as such is (a) in harmony with natural law – that is, human nature as created by God; and (b) in harmony with divine law – that is, with God's will as revealed in Scripture. The present teaching of the Church is – thanks be to God! – different. Vatican II declared every form of slavery as being 'contrary to God's intent'[2] and the Church endorses the Universal Declaration of Human Rights which rejects all slavery as contrary to human nature. The new official Catechism of the Catholic Church states the principle.

> The seventh commandment [you shall not steal] forbids acts or enterprises that for any reason – selfish or ideological, commercial or totalitarian – lead to the enslavement of human beings, to their being bought, sold and exchanged like merchandise, in disregard for their personal dignity. (no. 2414)

If this is Church teaching now, how did the endorsement of slavery retain a place in Catholic teaching till the end of the nineteenth century? The answer is: it was implanted as a cuckoo's egg.

Spotting the elusive parent cuckoo

The origin of the spurious tradition was in Greek philosophy and more specifically one of its prominent heroes – Aristotle (384–322 BC). Aristotle's ideas influenced the Church Fathers in a general sort of way. But it was in the Middle Ages above all that he was 'rediscovered' by the Church and his opinions were cast in concrete by Church law and doctrine.

Aristotle drew his conclusions from observations. He taught that slavery is natural because some people seem by nature destined to be slaves.

> That person is by nature a slave who can belong to another person and who only takes part in thinking by recognizing it, but not by possessing it. Other living beings [i.e. animals] cannot recognize thinking; they just obey feelings. However, there is little difference between using slaves and using tame animals: both provide bodily help to do necessary things.

Aristotle then proceeds to describe a slave's position and it is truly terrifying. A slave is no more than 'a tool of his master'. Together with the wife and the ox, a male or female slave is a householder's indispensable beast of burden. He or she should be kept well – for simple economic reasons. But slaves have no right to leisure or free time. They own nothing and can take no decisions. They have no part in enjoyment and happiness, and are not members of the community.[3]

For the same reason Aristotle also justifies wars to capture new slaves. For some people 'are by nature destined to be ruled, even though they resist it', like wild animals that need to be tamed. He even says that all foreigners to some extent belong to this category. 'That is why the poets say: "It is correct that Greeks rule Barbarians"; for by nature what is barbarian and what is slave are the same.'[4] It was also Aristotle, by the way, who taught that it is inherent in human nature for a woman to be dominated by a man. Slaves, tame animals and women fit in roughly similar categories.

> It is the best for all tame animals to be ruled by human beings. For this is how they are kept alive. In the same way, the relationship between the male and the female is by nature such that the male is higher, the female lower, that the male rules and the female is ruled.[5]

The prevailing cultural tradition saw society as layered in higher and lower forms of human being. Women were inferior to men by nature. Barbarians were inferior to Greeks by nature. Slaves were slaves because they were inferior by nature. The New Testament message contrasted sharply with this by a revolutionary new vision. 'There is neither Jew nor Greek, neither free nor slave, neither male nor female. For you are all one in Christ Jesus.'[6]

Unfortunately, this original Christian vision of universal equality and freedom was soon obscured by Christians themselves. What happened, to cut a long story short, is that Christians almost from the beginning lacked the spiritual enlightenment and will of character to break with the existing social systems. Instead of reaffirming people's new freedom in Christ, they gradually fell back into an acceptance of the pagan world views of their own culture.

Aristotle's teaching on slavery was quoted implicitly and explicitly by the Fathers of the Church. It did not stop there. Through the collection of laws known as the Decree of Gratian (Bologna 1140), it entered into the official law book of the Church. St Thomas Aquinas, the leading theologian of the Middle Ages, followed Aristotle. He agreed with all the pagan views, with just a dash of holy water. Slavery, he said, is 'natural' in the sense that it is the consequence of sin by a kind of 'second intention of nature'. He justified slavery in these circumstances: enslavement imposed as punishment; capture in conquest; people who sold themselves to pay off debts or who were sold by a court for that reason; children born of a slave mother.[7]

But surely the Fathers of the Church and the great theologians of the Middle Ages would not base Christian teaching on the writings of a pagan philosopher? The answer is: they did and they didn't. For the pagan arguments were presented under scriptural colours. Remember the cuckoo's trick of imitating eggs . . .?

Egg mimicry

Theologians were convinced that slavery belonged to Catholic doctrine. It was manifestly contained, they thought, in the Word of God. 'It is certainly a matter of *faith* that slavery in which a man serves his master as a slave, is altogether lawful. This can be proved from *Holy Scripture*.'[8] We can only uncover their misjudgement by looking at the texts they quoted.

The Old Testament took the institution of slavery for granted. Israelites could be enslaved by other Israelites as penalty for theft, to pay off debt, by purchase from a foreigner, and by sale of a daughter by her father. These kinds of text became the source on which canon lawyers and theologians constructed the four 'just titles of slavery' as mentioned in the instruction of the Holy Office quoted above: capture in war, just condemnation, purchase or exchange, and birth – the child of a slave mother was automatically a slave.[9] But such Old Testament laws are invalid now.

Paul had clearly shown that the Old Testament Law had been abolished. The principle of equality in Christ of Jew and Greek, slave and free, man and woman, had been clearly enunciated. The Old Testament arguments were really not scriptural at all; they were Greek cultural ideas disguised as biblical proofs!

But did Jesus not condone slavery? Did he not refer to slavery in more than one parable?

> Suppose one of you has a slave who returns from the fields after ploughing or minding the sheep, will the master say to him: 'Sit down now and have your meal'? Will he not more likely say: 'Get my supper ready. Tidy up and serve me while I eat and drink. You yourself can have your meal afterwards'? Will he be grateful to his slave for doing what he was told? In the same way, when you have done all you have been told to do, say: 'We are only slaves. We have done no more than our duty'.[10]

Fathers of the Church, theologians and popes have used such Gospel passages to prove that slavery is willed by God. Jesus himself, they said, accepted slavery. Jesus gave examples from slavery which show that he took the subordination of slaves for granted, they said. What is more, Jesus *admired* the service of submissive and humble slaves. Therefore, slavery is something beautiful that is not contrary to God's will.

Now here we have to be careful. Yes, Jesus at times pointed to the experience of slavery to make a point. Jesus based his parables on everyday life and slavery was a reality people were familiar with. But it is not legitimate to conclude from his alluding to slavery in a parable that he *endorsed* slavery. The examples which Jesus cites from everyday life often contain abuses that he does not condone: the unjust steward who cheats, the thief who breaks in at night, the man who finds a treasure in a field, then buys the field without disclosing its value, and so on.[11]

Again we find that the medieval acceptance of slavery was read into Jesus' words. To my knowledge, no one has ever claimed that tampering with one's boss's accounts is all right because Jesus praised the unjust steward. And no one has asserted that burglary is allowed when it is done at night. The egg of slavery, however, acquired the colouring of Jesus' teaching.

Then what about the Pastoral Letters? Don't they command slaves to be resigned to their condition?

> Slaves, obey in everything those who are your earthly masters, not with eye-service as just pleasing people, but in singleness of heart, pleasing the Lord. Whatever your task, work with commitment, as serving the Lord and not human beings.[12]

The argument is invalid because, in these letters, the authors address the immediate situation of their audiences, in which social slavery was a fact. Deducing general principles regarding slavery from the text goes beyond their intended scope. The authors do not discuss slavery as such, but only the practical question: 'How does a Christian behave in this particular context?'

'But were no voices raised in protest?' you may ask. There were. They were harshly squashed, however, by the brutal efficiency of the cuckoo chick.

Nest-mate eviction

In the Early Church Paul's principle of 'no free, no slave . . . we are one in Christ' was put into practice by some communities. St Gregory, Bishop of Nyssa in present-day Turkey, advocated the total abolition of slavery. 'To own people is to buy the image of God', he taught. He records that in his cathedral slaves were released from their bondage on the day of Easter 'according to the custom of the Church'.

Gregory (335–94) was a distinguished Church leader in his time. He took part in the Council of Antioch and wrote such famous books as *The Creation of Humankind, Great Catechesis* and the *Life of Macrina*. With regard to slaves, Gregory pleaded for Christians to listen to their consciences.

> You condemn a person to slavery who by nature is free and independent, and so you make laws opposed to God and to his natural law. For you have subjected to the yoke of slavery a person who was made precisely to be lord of the earth and whom the Creator intended to be a ruler, thus resisting and

rejecting his divine precept. Have you forgotten what limits were set to your authority? God limited your ownership to brute animals alone . . .[13]

Gregory gives many other arguments. Slaves can be seen to be equal to their masters as human beings. What price could ever buy human freedom? His prophetic voice and those of others were not heeded. The fat cuckoo hatchling of profitable cultural enslavement made sure it held the nest for itself.

Another chance for the genuine Catholic doctrine of human freedom came with the discovery of overseas colonies in the sixteenth century. The Catholic kings of Spain and Portugal had an important role to play in this. Again the question arose in the minds and hearts of some conscientious Christians: May we legitimately enslave these nations? Is slavery truly in harmony with God's will? The Dominican priest Bartolomé de las Casas, who had ministered to slaves in Peru, argued that slavery should on principle not be tolerated. He presented his case to the king, who organised a consultation. This resulted in debates at Valladolid, then the court of the Spanish king, in the years 1550 and 1551. On the side of slave hunters stood the traditional theologian Bishop Juan Ginés de Sepúlveda. On the side of the Indians was Bartolomé de las Casas.

Quoting Aristotle, Sepúlveda contended that the Spanish were engaged in a just war of conquest. Moreover, he said, the Indians are barbarians who deserve to become slaves. And Jesus himself approves of slavery and so does Paul.[14]

De las Casas, on the other hand, who had been a missionary in Peru, maintained that the Indians were human beings, as much created in God's image as Spaniards. They possessed a high culture, he said, and slavery was against the spirit of the Scriptures. He also rejected the authority of Aristotle, 'a gentile burning in hell, whose doctrine we do not need to follow except in so far as it conforms with Christian truth'. Here are some of de las Casas' pleadings:

> Our Christian religion is suitable for, and may be adapted to all the nations of the world, and all alike can receive it. No single person may be deprived of his liberty; or enslaved on the excuse that he is a natural slave . . . Are these Indians not people like us? Do they not have rational souls? Are we not obliged to love them as we love ourselves?[15]

Such appeals were not welcome to the slave traders and their colonial overlords. Small wonder that the slave traders won the day. The same happened to later Catholic theologians and bishops who fought for the true Catholic doctrine of freedom for all. In the eighteenth century they

13

included Abbé Raynal and Abbé Grégoire in France, and in the nineteenth century Johann Sailer, Bishop of Ratisbon in Germany.[16]

But what about the popes? Did they not steer the Church away from slavery? The answer is: they did not. They too believed and taught that slavery was part of Catholic doctrine.

Bonding by the foster parents

Understandably perhaps, popes consider themselves first and foremost guardians of tradition. And tradition is judged by what has been done in the Church throughout the centuries, without examining the credentials of the practice. It is as if Church leaders in this way become 'bonded' to the practice, not unlike host birds becoming bonded to the cuckoo chick.

In AD 362 a diocesan council at Gangra in present-day Turkey excommunicated whoever dared to encourage a slave to despise his master or escape from his service. Although this was a purely local event, it was a dangerous precedent. In AD 650, acting on this precedent, Pope Martin I condemned people who taught slaves about freedom or helped them escape.

A number of Church Councils imposed slavery as a form of punishment. It was used with a twisted sense of justice against priests who transgressed the new law of priestly celibacy. The ninth council of Toledo in Spain (AD 655) imposed permanent slavery on the children of priests – yet how could these poor boys and girls be held responsible for their father's violating a rule of Church discipline? The Synod of Melfi under Pope Urban II (AD 1089) inflicted unredeemable slavery on the wives of priests – again, a cruel form of misguided justice that betrayed every human right under the sun. But in terms of ecclesiastical bonding, it added weight to presumed tradition. The Church itself imposed slavery. So it can be done. Therefore it must be right!

The legitimacy of slavery was incorporated into official Church law from the first collection under Gratian (1140). Then in 1454, through the bull *Romanus Pontifex*, Pope Nicholas V authorised the king of Portugal to enslave all the Muslim and pagan nations his armies might conquer. Pope Alexander VI extended this licence to the king of Spain (1493), permitting him to enslave non-Christians of the Americas who were at war with Christian powers. The two major Catholic colonial empires thus acquired a blanket Church sanction for capturing the local natives and employing them on their estates as slaves.

When the facts of slave labour and especially the slave trade from Africa began to filter through to the Vatican chambers in Rome, popes began to express their concern. This was good. The popes began to criticise the exploitation of the native peoples. But unfortunately, they did not examine the principle of slavery itself. Thus Pope Paul III, in 1537, condemned the indiscriminate enslavement of Indians in South America. But when challenged, he confirmed ten years later that both clergy and laity had the right to own slaves. A century later, in 1639, Pope Urban VIII criticised unjust practices against the natives, but did not deny the four 'just titles' for owning slaves. Pope Benedict XIV condemned the wholesale enslavement of natives in Brazil – without denouncing slavery as such, nor the importation of slaves from Africa.[17]

This was to continue until 1866 when, as we have seen, the Holy Office under Pius IX still declared that slavery as such was not against human or divine law. What was wrong with these Church leaders? Were they heartless creatures who were not moved by the plight of helpless slaves in so many countries? The answer is that they were caught by their misguided awe for this solid 'tradition', which we know to be a cuckoo chick, but which they saw confirmed in the writings of the Fathers, the decrees of Church councils, the sanction of previous popes. They did not stop to think, 'What is the basis for all this?'

How could such an anomalous, un-Christian practice be tolerated in the Church in the first place? It seems that leaders were not prepared to listen to the prophetic voices raised by conscientious people in the Church.

Conclusion

The official Church, including the *magisterium*, has now – finally – come to the recognition that slavery is against basic human rights and 'contrary to God's intent'. It comes too late for the millions of slaves in previous centuries whose lot could have been alleviated by correct Christian teaching! But at least Church authorities should draw a number of lessons.

The so-called 'tradition' that was thought to endorse slavery and on which the *magisterium* based its justification of slavery, all those quotes from fathers and popes, proved, in fact, to have been spurious and contrary to the real tradition handed down from Christ. It had been a cuckoo's egg tradition. The true tradition that came down from Christ and the apostles was contained in the principle of fundamental equality for all, enshrined in the universal baptism of Christ applied to men and women, slave and free alike.[18] Only this valid tradition was truly biblical.

Church leaders claimed their position was scriptural. In fact, the biblical texts were quoted illegitimately. Their interpretation went beyond the inspired and intended sense. They were cuckoo's eggs masked by a biblical veneer.

If all the bishops of the world had been asked, two hundred years ago, whether slavery is allowed by God, 95 per cent of them, including the Pope, would have said, 'Yes, slavery is allowed'. Yet, in spite of their number, they would *all* have been wrong. Common opinion does not make informed, collective teaching.

But even if popes and their advisors can make mistakes, what right does it give me to challenge them in public?

READINGS FROM THE WOMEN PRIESTS WEBSITE

John Wijngaards

The true Tradition must be scriptural

http://www.womenpriests.org/traditio/biblical.htm

The Church made similar mistakes regarding the
taking of interest and the blanket condemnation of
homosexuality

http://www.womenpriests.org/traditio/informed.htm

The erroneous teachings of Pope Pius IX

http://www.womenpriests.org/teaching/piusix.htm

Aaron Milavec

'Jesus responds to John Paul II'

'What Peter might say to John Paul II'

http://www.womenpriests.org/teaching/jesus.htm
http://www.womenpriests.org/teaching/paul.htm

3

A Time for Speaking

SOME OF MY FRIENDS tell me that the ordination of women is an issue that can wait. 'Rome has decisively turned against it,' they say. 'Change may come, but only in the future – under another Pope, when the heat has died down.' They point to a vast majority of bishops and theologians who have decided to keep their mouths shut, even though they realise Rome is wrong. Tact is needed, they argue. There is a time for speaking and a time for silence . . .

I disagree. Yes, for years I too thought that wisdom would slowly prevail in the Church and that the issue of women priests would ripen in the course of time. That is why, until three years ago, I too had adopted a strategy of wait-and-see. But now I have changed my mind. For the Roman authorities force us to take sides. They impose their own view so strongly as *the truth*, that by keeping silent now, we would compromise our own consciences.

I am writing this book because I believe that for me, and for the Church, truth is more important than diplomacy.

The Holy Father, Pope John Paul II, and the Sacred Congregation for the Doctrine of the Faith have in recent years moved their rejection of priestly ordination for women into the realm of faith. They have declared that:

- the ban on women's ordination is to be held definitively as a doctrine belonging to the deposit of faith;
- though the Holy Father's interventions are not infallible declarations of doctrine in this instance, he bases his stand on what he perceives to be the infallible universal *magisterium* – that is, the collective teaching exercised by the international body of bishops;
- anyone who disagrees with the Holy Father is no longer in full communion with the Church.[1]

This Roman view is, moreover, imposed on bishops, theologians and parish priests by its incorporation in routine oaths of loyalty. It causes great anxiety to theologians who cannot admit the validity of Rome's arguments. 'I use mental restriction', one lecturer at a theological faculty told me. But are we allowed to compromise with truth? What if we *know* Rome is wrong? Does complicity with non-truth not undermine everything we are trying to do, as the community of Christ, as priests, as theologians? I believe it does.

I will argue my case for fearlessly speaking out on two grounds. The first one, for diplomatic reasons, looks at what the official Church itself has said about the duty of defending truth rather than toeing the party line. The message is clear: even within the establishment there is room for loyal public dissent. My second ground rests on even deeper pillars. It touches on personal integrity, on the Church's credibility, on not bartering away our most valuable assets.

The ministry of truth

By definition, it is our task as theologians to apply our human intelligence to revealed truth. Theologians stand in the service of *truth*. They owe their highest allegiance to truth in whatever form this may present itself. The First Vatican Council (1869–70) emphatically endorsed this search for truth and stated confidently that there could not be a clash between revealed truth and truth known through other channels. The reason is sound enough: God is the author of all truth and cannot contradict himself. If theologians are faithful to truth, they cannot fail to be loyal to God and to God's revelation.[2]

At the same time theologians also owe obedience to the Holy Father and the bishops to whom Christ entrusted his teaching authority. The correct attitude towards statements by the Holy Father has been described in these words by Vatican II:

> This loyal submission of the will and intellect must be given, in a special way, to the authentic teaching authority of the Roman Pontiff, even when he does not speak *ex cathedra* [i.e. infallibly], in such wise, indeed, that his supreme teaching authority be acknowledged with respect, and sincere assent be given to decisions made by him, conformably with his manifest mind and intention, which is made known principally by the character of the documents in question, or by the frequency by which a certain doctrine is proposed, or by the manner in which the doctrine is formulated.[3]

On the other hand, the possibility of conflict between a theologian's judgement and that of the *magisterium* [the teaching authority] has been acknowledged by those in charge. I quote from *Donum Veritatis*, a statement in 1990 by the Congregation of Doctrine on the vocation of a theologian.

> It can happen, however, that a theologian may, according to the case, raise questions regarding the timeliness, the form, or even the contents of magisterial interventions ... It could happen that some magisterial documents might not be free from all deficiencies.

> Even when collaboration takes place under the best conditions, the possibility cannot be excluded that tensions may arise between the theologian and the *magisterium*. The meaning attributed to such tensions and the spirit with which they are faced are not matters of indifference. If tensions do not spring from hostile and contrary feelings, they can become a dynamic factor, a stimulus to both the *magisterium* and theologians to fulfill their respective roles while practising dialogue.

> If, despite a loyal effort on the theologian's part, the difficulties persist, the theologian has the duty to make known to the magisterial authorities the problems raised by the teaching in itself, in the arguments proposed to justify it, or even in the manner in which it is presented. He should do this in an evangelical spirit and with a profound desire to resolve the difficulties. His objections could then contribute to real progress and provide a stimulus to the *magisterium* to propose the teaching of the Church in greater depth and with a clearer presentation of the arguments.[4]

'Public opinion' in the Church

We should be grateful that in our time the ancient practice of handing over dissenting theologians to the Inquisition has been discontinued. Today Church authorities have at their disposal more subtle forms of silencing opposition. These include putting pressure on bishops and religious superiors to subjugate priests or religious in their charge; sacking theologians from teaching posts at Church institutions; withdrawing financial support from centres that stand for freedom of expression; screening unwanted topics out of teaching schedules or congress programmes; blocking the publication of disgreeable books; selecting bishops only from candidates who subscribe to Rome's views. The ideology of the thumbscrew is not altogether dead.

During the Second Vatican Council the question of free theological discussion was incorporated into the Council statements.

> All the faithful, both clerical and lay, should be accorded a lawful freedom of

inquiry and of thought, and the freedom to express their minds humbly and courageously about those matters in which they enjoy competence.[5]

The Second Vatican Council also recognised the crucial role played by public opinion in today's society.

Public opinion exercises enormous influence nowadays over the lives, private or public, of all citizens, no matter what their walk in life. It is therefore necessary that all members of society meet the demands of justice and charity in this domain. They should help, through the means of social communication, in the formation and diffusion of sound public opinion.[6]

Public opinion, with freedom of expression as a necessary constituent, also plays a crucial part in the Church, as Pope Pius XII reminded Catholic journalists in an address on 17 February 1950:

Freedom of speech is a normal factor in the growth of public opinion which expresses the ideas and reactions of the more influential circles in a society.[7]

The same point is made in a follow-up document to Vatican II:

If public opinion is to emerge in the proper manner, it is absolutely essential that there be freedom to express ideas and attitudes. In accordance with the express teaching of the Second Vatican Council, it is necessary unequivocally to declare that freedom of speech for individuals and groups must be permitted so long as the common good and public morality not be endangered.[8]

Freedom of speech is, indeed, essential and does not contradict the spirit of theological obedience. When the Church demands 'a loyal submission of the will and intellect' she does not ask for a renunciation of one's own power to think. The Church demands a much more valuable service, namely the honest attempt to serve the faith with all one's intellectual powers.

When Vatican II speaks of obedience, it envisages a total commitment: 'They should bring their powers of intellect and will and their gifts of nature and grace to bear on the execution of commands and on the fulfilment of the tasks laid upon them.'[9] True loyalty to the Church implies loyalty to the truth. It requires willingness to question rather than readiness to conform. What may seem opposition and dissent at first, will eventually prove to be an active co-operation between the teaching authorities and the theologians towards the one aim of a better-formulated doctrine.

Theologians play an important role in the continual reformation 'of which the Church has always a need', a reformation that also concerns 'deficiencies in the way that Church teaching has been formulated'.[10]

Rather than speaking of a conflict between the *magisterium* and dissenting theological opinion, one should think of them as complementary elements in an ongoing search, both equally necessary for the Church's reformation.

Pope Paul VI described the interplay between the teaching authority and theological study in just such a positive way. In his address to a congress of theologians on 1 October 1966, he stated:

> The *magisterium* draws great benefit from fervid and industrious theological study and from the cordial collaboration of the theologians ... Without the help of theology the *magisterium* could undoubtedly preserve and teach the faith, but it would arrive only with difficulty at the lofty and full knowledge it needs to perform its task, since it is aware that it is not endowed with revelation or the charism of inspiration but only with the assistance of the Holy Spirit.[11]

Church documents, especially those of the present Congregation for Doctrine, are 'not entirely foreign to sanctimonious double-speak that smacks of self-promoting indoctrination', to quote a friend of mine. Yet even these documents urge theologians to speak out when they believe the *magisterium* is making a mistake. For me, though, there are more essential reasons for crying out my anguish in public and for revealing what I know to be true. These reasons live in my heart and my bones. I would die without them, and so would the Church.

If salt loses its saltiness . . .

To see my point of view, I would like you to take a step back and look at the world and the Church from a wider perspective. 'As soon as we lose our moral foundation, we cease to be religious. There is no such thing as religion over-riding morality. We cannot be untruthful and claim to have God on our side.' The author of these words was not a Christian, but Mohandas Karamchand Gandhi, a modern prophet popularly voted the most influential person of the twentieth century.

When I departed from Antwerp to take up my seminary post in India, missionaries still travelled the old-fashioned way – by boat. On Christmas Eve 1964 I boarded a German freighter that slowly made its way to Bombay, crisscrossing the Mediterranean, then the Red Sea, the Gulf of Aden and the Indian Ocean, picking up or discharging cargo in various ports. A journey which now takes ten hours took six long weeks then. But the leisurely pace also had its rewards. I saw the world.

At Porbandar in Gujarat our ship dropped anchor, to take on board loads of jute brought by barges. Porbandar, I knew, was the birthplace of Mahatma Gandhi. I managed to go ashore and eventually found the quarter of the town where Gandhi had lived as a boy. I had read his autobiography and remembered Gandhi's search. 'Morality is the basis of things and truth is the basis of morality.' India offers a bewildering palette of religious traditions, many weird and over-the-top, but as I was to find out from my friendship with Hindus, Muslims, Jains and Parsis, underlying the outgrowths there exists a healthy respect for the fundamental values. Sincerity, honesty and truth are highly regarded by all.

A few years later, when giving a scriptural course to priests and sisters in Ahmedabad, I visited the house where Gandhi had lived during the last part of his life. In my mind's eye I can still clearly see that simple Indian-style mansion. Four sparsely furnished rooms and a kitchen that encircled a courtyard. Here he had chosen to live the life of an ordinary peasant, wearing the loincloth and shawl of the rural Indian and subsisting on vegetables, fruit juices and goat's milk. Outside, a verandah that spanned the front of the house overlooked the banks of a river. Gandhi's mat was shown here and his spinning wheel. It was the spot where he had sat cross-legged, hand spinning cotton and weaving yards of cloth. The scene was breathtakingly plain and commonplace. And yet this had been the home of one of the most powerful political figures in India and a religious leader of international fame.

It was from this place that Gandhi started his famous salt march in 1930, a widely publicised walk to the coast of the Arabian Sea, where he began to manufacture salt in defiance of the British monopoly on salt. Gandhi himself and 60,000 of his followers were arrested on that occasion and during the peaceful protests that followed.

It was also in this house that Gandhi gave shelter to a number of *pariah* children. He shared his food with them and sent them to local schools. Though he belonged to the Vaishya (merchant) caste himself, Gandhi broke with age-old Hindu custom by treating the 'untouchables' as equals. Hindu prejudice considered the *pariahs* defiled persons, people born out of the accumulated sins of a previous life. Gandhi gave them a new name – *harijans*, which means 'people born of God' – and took some of their children into his home to ensure their education.[12] It was for this courageous act that attempts were made on his life. Eventually he was shot by a Hindu fanatic while visiting Bombay in 1948.

It is impossible to exaggerate the esteem in which Gandhi is held by fellow Indians. And it is not first and foremost because he championed Indian independence, as foreigners often think. People honour Gandhi's character, mainly his belief in non-violence and passion for truth. I realised quite early during my 14 years in India that, if people are to accept Christianity, it will not be because of our superior institutions, but because Jesus Christ is seen to contribute to primary values – authentic love, selfless service, ruthless honesty. 'Truth is my God', Gandhi had said. He was not a saint. He had many imperfections and shortcomings. But he was a man of integrity. He had also shown courage. He had stood up against colonial powers, but no less against patriots who favoured a path of violence. While he denounced Christian pretensions, he had not spared the bigotry of his fellow Hindus. It was this loyalty to conviction and truth that made Gandhi invincible.

> There are times when you have to obey a call that is the highest of all, that is: the voice of conscience, even though such obedience may cost many a bitter tear, and even more, separation from friends, from family, from the condition to which you may belong, from all that you have held as dear as life itself. For this obedience is the law of our being.[13]

Christianity had no hope in India, I knew, nor elsewhere in the world, if we were to lose those qualities. Didn't Jesus himself tell us not to corrupt values?

> You are the salt of the earth. But if salt loses its saltiness, what can make it salty again? It has become useless. It will be thrown out for people to trample on.[14]

For Jesus' contemporaries the value of salt lay not so much in its taste as in its perceived quality of preserving food. Salt was hard to come by. It was expensive. It was traded as a luxury good. On occasion, lumps of salt were used to pay soldiers: our word 'salary' (meaning 'portion of salt') derives from this. Salt losing its saltiness was worthless.

Across the centuries Jesus is warning us not to sell out our Christian values for money, or for power, convenience, harmony or anything else. If we tamper with truth, our testimony becomes useless, both inside and outside the Church. 'All compromise is based on give and take, but there can be no give and take on truth. Any compromise on truth is a surrender.' (Mahatma Gandhi)

As the followers of Jesus Christ, we will lose all credibility if we sell out on truth. Nor need we be ashamed in the Church itself of challenging authority on behalf of truth. When the first Pope, Simon Peter, re-introduced Jewish laws in Antioch even though the Council of Jerusalem had abrogated them, Paul challenged him in public. 'When Cephas came to Antioch I opposed him to his face since he stood manifestly condemned.'[15] Paul purposely calls Peter 'Cephas', referring to the fact that Jesus himself had given Peter that name, which means 'rock'. Even apostles can make mistakes and 'God has appointed in the Church first apostles, second prophets, third teachers . . . Are all apostles? Are all prophets? Are all teachers?'[16]

Regarding women priests, Church authorities have allowed a cuckoo's egg to hatch in the Church's nest. It is this intruder I am now going to expose.

READINGS FROM THE WOMEN PRIESTS WEBSITE

Main Roman documents on the ordination of women:

Inter Insigniores (15 October 1976)
http://www.womenpriests.org/church/interlet.htm

Commentary on Inter Insigniores (27 January 1977)
http://www.womenpriests.org/church/intercom.htm

Ordinatio Sacerdotalis (22 May 1994)
http://www.womenpriests.org/church/ordinati.htm

At times theologians have the duty to speak out
http://www.womenpriests.org/teaching/speaking.htm

René van Eyden
'Women priests: keeping mum or speaking out?'
http://www.womenpriest.org/teaching/eyden.htm

Mary McAleese, President of Ireland
'It Won't Wash With Women'
http://www.womenpriests.org/teaching/mcalees1.htmhtm
'Coping with a Christ who does not want women priests almost as much as He wants Ulster to remain British'
http://www.womenpriests.org/teaching/mcalees2.htm

Bernard Häring
'Letter to the Pope'
http://www.womenpriests.org/teaching/haering.htm

4

The Focus of This Book

As vicar general of the Mill Hill Missionaries it was my pleasant duty once a year to visit our communities and institutions in the USA. In 1978 I managed to arrange the visitation schedule in such a way that I could attend the National Women's Ordination Conference in Baltimore. It turned out to be an event I will never forget. I was excited by the range of speakers. I listened spellbound to theologians who have since achieved international acclaim, such as Mary Daly and Rosemary Radford Ruether. I took part in the demonstration march that carried a mile-long chain of cardboard links signifying bondage and I joined in triumphantly tearing it into pieces. But what impressed me most were the almost 2000 participants who crowded the central lecture hall and adjoining workshops. They consisted overwhelmingly of women, from a wide spectrum of professions – doctors, teachers, lawyers, business executives. There were religious sisters among them as well as married women. Commitment to the Catholic faith reigned supreme, notwithstanding common dismay at what Rome was doing.

Though in general I felt very welcome indeed and shared deep insights with wonderfully sensitive people, I also had sobering experiences that taught me a lesson or two. On one occasion I was bluntly refused entry into a workshop simply because I was *a man*. I remonstrated that I had just published a book defending the ordination of women. The answer was: 'So far you *men* have done all the talking in the Church. It is about time women had their say!' '*Touché*,' I thought, 'but can't I be a friend?' One campaigner maintained that, in order to celebrate the full sacramental Eucharist, ordination was not necessary at all. Another criticised my book for analysing the Roman arguments. By discussing the ordination of women *on Rome's terms* I had already lost half the battle. Another theologian, from my own native Holland, I am sad to report, persuaded me to part with a copy of my book, but then, two months later, published one of its chapters in the leading Dutch Catholic weekly *de Bazuin* without ever acknowledging her source.

Such negative incidents have not dented my overwhelmingly positive remembrance of Baltimore. I felt that I had met the enormous strength of thinking, caring, competent Catholic women. It filled me with hope. I *knew* then that the Church would never be able to stop this tide. The dedication, the quality, the Christian faith of women in the Church would win the day. But the confrontations also served a purpose. They prepared me for what was to come. I learnt that the issues surrounding women's ordination are highly complex, and subsequent developments have borne this out. Wounds need to be healed, ancient injustices undone. Women need to have the freedom to operate theology in their own way. Though men can be sympathetic to it, a real feminine and feminist contribution should come from women. Moreover, the ordination of women is embedded in wider questions, such as the nature of the Christian community and of Christian ministry themselves. The extreme, suppressive measures emanating from Rome under Pope John Paul II raise further questions of strategy. Should the power structures in the Church not be reformed first? In this arena it makes sense for me to say what I am trying to do in all this.

Early champions

It is indisputable that women theologians have changed the face of Catholic theology, especially since the Second Vatican Council (1962–65). It was when the Council began that women found their voice. As we review the historical record we can see how an age-old pain and anger at having been excluded now found expression in different parts of the Catholic community and all at once. As far as the ordination of women was concerned, there have been pioneers in many countries. I will briefly sketch some of their early work.

To start with England – since this is where I live at present – the St Joan's International Alliance had been active since its British foundation in 1911. It aimed to change the attitude of the Church towards women's rights – political votes for women, support for marginalised women, recognition for women in the apostolate. The exclusion of women from ordination became a pronounced issue in 1928.[1] Joan Morris, whom I was privileged to know personally and who left part of her library to me, studied archives all over Europe to document the involvement of women in Church ministries and jurisdiction in the early Middle Ages. After decades of research, it resulted in the classic *Against Nature and God.*[2]

The young German theologian Josefa Theresia Münch wrote letters to Pope Pius XII in 1953 and 1954 expressing her desire to be ordained a priest and protesting the invalidity of the official theological stand against it. When the Vatican Council was announced in 1960, she wrote to Rome to request the alteration of Canon 968, §1, to the effect that it should no longer read, 'Only a baptised *man* can validly receive priestly ordination' but, 'Only a baptised *person* can validly receive priestly ordination', adding her reasons. When the Council opened in October 1962, she travelled to Rome and during the first press conference of the Council caused a stir by asking, 'Why have *women* not been invited to the Council?' The question was dismissed by Bishop Kampe of Limburg, the official spokesman, but the issue received full attention in the press. A year later Cardinal Suenens of Brussels spoke up during a general session in the Council hall: 'Half of humanity is made up of women. In the Church too, at least half of it is made up of women; here at the Council, where are the women?' He received tremendous applause. It led to Paul VI appointing 16 women as *auditors* – among 2000 male participants.[3]

Meanwhile, the Swiss lawyer Gertrud Heinzelmann had been longing for the admission of women to the priesthood from an early age. 'Already when I had to make my first confession (in 1924), I felt a deep desire for a woman priest. I knew I would have revealed myself so much more easily to a woman than to a man since a man does not understand the fears and worries of a small girl . . . The woman whom I sought in my spiritual need did not exist.' Since official theological studies were not open to her, she pursued them privately, next to her legal career. So she was ready when the Council was announced. In May 1962, she submitted a well-documented proposal regarding women's ordination to the preparatory committee of the Second Vatican Council. It was the only proposal of its kind to make it into the official Council documentation. It detailed the untenable bias against women in traditional theology and called for a true equality for women in the Church, including openness to all ministries. Her writings attracted international attention.[4] In 1964 she published the explosive book *We Won't Keep Silence Any Longer. Women Speak out to Vatican Council II.*[5]

Since that time an avalanche of ground-breaking publications have appeared. The Dutchman Haye van der Meer, who had started revolutionary research under Karl Rahner even before the Council, exposed the flimsy basis of medieval reasonings.[6] Sister Vincent Hannon in England challenged the traditional stand.[7] Mary Daly, who had studied at Fribourg and who was the first American woman to obtain a doctorate in theology, wrote her initial feminist critique.[8] The German Ida Raming published a classic study that documented the origin of anti-feminine bias in Church law.[9] A 'select' bibliography on the ordination of women for 1965–75 lists 36 books and 175 articles.[10] The 1970s ushered in the golden period of Catholic feminist theology.

I can do no more than sketch developments at this point. The scandalous inequality between men and women, tolerated for so long, began now to be described and exposed in all areas of Catholic life: in worship and spirituality, in the parish and in the home, in theology as well as in law.[11] The roles of women in the Early Church, both during apostolic times and the house-church communities, were being re-examined and consequences from this drawn for New Testament exegesis.[12] Women's lives during various periods of the Church's history were studied in detail.[13] Much more clarity was gained from a woman's perspective on matters of language, imagery and church symbolism.[14] At the same time, and as a result of much of this research, it became clear that women's ordination could not be separated from other reforms needed in the Church.

The wider picture

The feminist impulse, no less than Rome's intransigence on women's ministries, served as a catalyst to unmask the underlying assumptions regarding the priesthood itself.

Since the Middle Ages, the priest had been conceived of as a 'sacred person', a *sacerdos*. In this view, a priest is raised to this status through the sacred rite of ordination that imprints an indelible character on him and that consecrates him to perform acts of ritual sacrifice. However, it is clear from Scripture that Jesus never saw himself in this light. Nor did he envision such a status for his disciples. The apostles 'laid hands' on their successors, whom they thereby commissioned to be 'elders' of the Christian communities, *presbyteroi*. Certainly, Jesus is called a 'high priest' in the letter to the Hebrews, but with no other purpose than to show how he abolished and transcended the system of 'sacred' priestly functions as understood in the Old Testament.[15]

The Second Vatican Council wanted to redress this balance by stressing again the *presbyter* function. 'Priests have as their primary duty the proclamation of the gospel of God to all. In this way they fulfil the Lord's command: "Go into the whole world and preach the gospel to every creature". (Mark 16:15) Thus they establish and build up the People of God.'[16] But the Roman *magisterium* has over the last three decades done all in its power to reinculcate the old concept of a cultic, sacrificial, sacralised, and therefore celibate, priesthood. 'It is the same priest, Jesus Christ, whose sacred person his minister truly represents. Now the minister, by reason of the sacerdotal consecration which he has received, is truly made like to the high priest and possesses the authority to act in the power and place of the person of Christ himself.'[17] In the revised *General Instruction on the Roman Missal* (August 2000) all the stress is on 'sacred things': the sacred sanctuary, sacred ambo, sacred altar, sacred vessels, sacred vestments and, of course, the sacred priest. Even the chair on which the 'consecrated minister' sits in the sanctuary shares in his sacredness. It has to be 'visibly distinguished from chairs used by others who are not clergy'.[18]

The Vatican Council struggled with two conflicting paradigms of the Church. The medieval model saw the Church as a clerical and hierarchical institution with sacred power percolating down from the top. An earlier, scriptural model, on the other hand, considered the Church rather as the People of God, with the stress on communion, co-responsibility, and Christian values such as grace and love. Though it could not free itself totally from the hierarchical model, the Second Vatican Council did attempt to promote the People of God concept.[19] The authorities in Rome, on the other hand, cling firmly to the hierarchical model and try to reinforce what has recently been called 'a very authoritarian, absolutist, completely un-Christian structure'.[20] It has become clear that an integration of the best in both models can be achieved only by a genuine *reform* in the way the Church operates.[21]

Many women who feel called to the priesthood are now searching for more communitarian models of ministry.[22] Positions are hardening. Many declare that they would not accept ordination to the present clerical, celibate, hierarchical priesthood. Women who insist on receiving such an ordination are ultimately condoning and confirming a system that, in fact, excluded women.[23]

My objective in this book

I share the view that the Church and its ministries urgently need to be reformed, according to the genuine vision of Vatican II and beyond it. I agree totally that the ordination of women should be seen as part of a much wider *aggiornamento* of Church structures. I am a member of various organisations: St Joan's International Alliance, Catholic Women's Ordination (UK) and 'We Are Church' (UK), all of which sponsor the admission of women to *reformed* ministries. But in this book I will limit myself to unnerving the traditional arguments against ordaining women.

Some theologians have already so utterly dismissed the traditional arguments that they consider it beneath their dignity even to discuss them. Though I share their feelings of distaste and impatience, I do not share their disdain of discussion. The traditional arguments against women priests are still the official arguments of the teaching authority in Rome. In various forms they are still republished in Catholic weeklies and supported by bishops, priests, religious and lay people. Reform will not come about without dialogue and discussion. I want to take all sections in the Catholic community seriously, including those who accept Rome's views uncritically because they feel it is their duty to do so, or others who cling to conservative views because the information they have is incomplete. To them I say: 'Look at the evidence. What Rome says is untenable even by traditional standards. Does true loyalty not demand that we speak the truth?'

Yes, there is a danger in dialogue *on Rome's terms*. I do not intend to sell out on my own principles in this book. I do not support antiquated views on priesthood or power-hungry clericalism. On the other hand, I will not throw out the baby with the bath water. I come from a Catholic family in the Netherlands that remained Catholic through four centuries of persecution. I do believe in the *sacramental* order in which Christ dispenses grace and love, and which pervades the whole Christian community. Within that sacramental order there is room for bishops and priests who guide, heal, and preside at the Eucharist. There is also room for real authority and the primacy of Peter's successor. The Second Vatican Council is a good basis for Church reform and our exasperation with the present leadership in the Church should not make us go 'over the top'. I passionately believe women should be ordained because it is the only truly *Catholic* response. If devotion to Mary is the hallmark of correct Christology, the full integration of women in all levels of the Church is the hallmark of genuine Catholic salvation.

Some of my priest colleagues have accused me of defending women priests 'because it is politically correct'. Others tell me Rome would not have reacted so fiercely if it had not been for the 'extremism of feminists'. In some ecclesiastical circles feminists are viewed as incurable men-haters who pursue a policy of Church subversion. This totally unfounded perception seems to be due to the harsh (but often true) language of some feminists, the wounded pride of their male audience and, I am sorry to say, spiteful slander by other women.[24] The unfortunate outcome is that quite a few people in the Church dismiss the ordination of women as 'just another cause pushed by fanatic feminists'. It is here that my contribution may be of use.

Though, with St Paul, I fully subscribe to women being treated on equal terms as men in the Church, I am not a feminist. I am a man, and I cannot speak from my Christian experience as a woman, nor judge issues from a specifically womanly perspective as women theologians do. Neither did I enter the field with a feminist agenda, as I narrated in the first chapter. I am approaching the question of women's ordination as a theologian. And like other theologians – both men and women – I have come to the clear recognition that the reasons for barring women from ordination cannot be substantiated from Scripture or tradition. Sacred Scripture leaves the question wide open. In so-called Catholic 'tradition', women were excluded from ministries because of social conditions and cultural prejudice. I will validate these claims in the next chapters. I am defending these conclusions as a man, as a professional theologian and as a Catholic.

READINGS FROM THE WOMEN PRIESTS WEBSITE

Ida Raming
Obituary of Gertrud Heinzelmann
http://www.womenpriests.org/called/heinzelm.htm
'Naissance et développement du mouvement pour
l'ordination des femmes dans l'Eglise catholique
romaine d'Europe'
http://www.womenpriests.org/fr/theology/raming07.htm
Iris Müller
'Katholische Theologinnen – unterdrückt, aber den-
noch angepaßt und ergeben'
http://www.womenpriests.org/de/called/muller02.htm
Marie-Thérèse van Lunen Chénu
'Marie-Thérèse is definitely not a "son" of the
Church!'
http://www.womenpriests.org/body/lunen2.htm

31

Part II

CLAIM AND COUNTER-CLAIM

It is not in the power of any creature, not even of the highest religious authority, to make statements true or false, otherwise than if of their own nature and in actual fact they are true or false.

It is surely harmful to the religious good of people if the authorities make it a heresy to believe what has been proved to be a fact.

Galileo Galilei
The Authority of Scripture
in Philosophical Controversies (1616)

Part II

CLAIM AND COUNTER CLAIM

5

The Mismatch in Vision

Howevер мисн а сискоо's egg may have looked like the other eggs in its foster nest, by the time the young cuckoo flies out it is clearly different from the parents that nurtured it. The contrast stands out. In the following three chapters I will show that the non-ordination of women carries so many intrinsic contradictions and anomalies that it can clearly be seen to be in the wrong nest. And, as in the case of birds, we could start by studying the overall image.

Why were women singled out for omission?

Pope John Paul II and the Congregation for Doctrine tell us that the exclusion of women from the ministerial priesthood goes back all the way to Jesus himself.

> In the light of tradition it seems that the essential reason moving the Church to call only men to the sacrament of order and to the strictly priestly ministry is her intention to remain faithful to the type of ordained ministry willed by the Lord Jesus Christ and carefully maintained by the apostles.[1]

Leaving the discussion of detailed arguments to further chapters, this then is the overall picture: Jesus himself decided that it would not be good for women to take part in the key ministry he left to his apostles. That is why he deliberately left women out when he picked the apostolic twelve. Yes, Jesus had some women among the group of disciples who followed him and he could easily have chosen one or two of them. But he did not do so. He was not influenced here by the social customs of his time, for when necessary he revolted against such customs.

> It has to be recognized that Jesus did not shrink from other 'imprudences', which did in fact stir up the hostility of his fellow citizens against him, especially his freedom with regard to the rabbinical interpretations of the Sabbath. With regard to women his attitude was a complete innovation: all

the commentators recognize that he went against many prejudices, and the facts that are noted add up to an impressive total.[2]

But when it came to choosing the twelve and commissioning them at the Last Supper, he pointedly omitted women. It must have been a deliberate decision by Jesus himself.

In calling only men as his apostles, Christ acted in a completely free and sovereign manner. In doing so, he exercised the same freedom with which, in all his behaviour, he emphasized the dignity and the vocation of women, without conforming to the prevailing customs and to the traditions sanctioned by the legislation of the time.[3]

This is, Rome claims, confirmed by tradition. The apostles laid their hands on worthy persons to succeed them and they found many excellent women among the new converts. The apostles never imposed their hands on women. The Early Church continued this practice. The Fathers of the Church criticise Gnostic sects in which women were given a variety of ministries. The Fathers of the Church point out that Jesus chose only men. In the Middle Ages this tradition became explicit. The medieval theologians state categorically that in not ordaining women, the Church follows the example of Christ. The conclusion is, therefore, inescapable:

Priestly ordination, which hands on the office entrusted by Christ to his apostles of teaching, sanctifying, and governing the faithful, has in the Catholic Church from the beginning always been reserved to men alone . . . The fundamental reasons for this include: the example recorded in the Sacred Scriptures of Christ choosing his apostles only from among men; the constant practice of the Church, which has imitated Christ in choosing only men; and her living teaching authority which has consistently held that the exclusion of women from the priesthood is in accordance with God's plan for his Church.[4]

In the same apostolic documents the Pope also maintains that the exclusion from the priestly ministry does not in any way minimise the role or status of women. 'The presence and the role of women in the life and mission of the Church, although not linked to the ministerial priesthood, remain absolutely necessary and irreplaceable.' 'The Church desires that Christian women should become fully aware of the greatness of their mission; today their role is of capital importance both for the renewal and humanization of society and for the rediscovery by believers of the true face of the Church.' 'By defending the dignity of women and their vocation, the Church has shown honour and gratitude for those women who – faithful to the Gospel – have shared in every age in the apostolic mission of the whole People of God. They are the holy martyrs, virgins, and the mothers of families, who bravely bore witness to their faith and passed on the Church's faith and tradition by bringing up their children in the spirit of the Gospel.'[5]

We can sum it up in these words: women share fully in the apostolic mission of the Church, but Christ did not want them to be ministerial priests. Does it make sense?

A ministry of 'people like you and me'

To understand the specific ministry established by Jesus Christ, we should note that he abolished the Old Testament priesthood based on so-called 'sacred' realities. He did away with the priesthood as understood in Old Testament terms. That priesthood rested on a philosophy that distinguished between the sacred and the profane. Some everyday realities, such as houses, cattle, eating and sleeping, doing business, and so on, were ordinary and 'profane'. God was not really directly present in these realities. Other realities of our world, however, were considered to have been penetrated with God's presence and to have become 'sacred' on that account. This is the origin of 'sacred' times (the Sabbath and feast days), 'sacred' places (mainly the Temple), 'sacred' objects (e.g. vessels used for worship) and 'sacred' persons (priests) consecrated to God. The Old Testament priest was separated from other people on the same basis as the Sabbath was considered holier than Monday, or the Temple was a more sacred place than the Pool of Bethzatha. The priest was the embodiment of a divine presence in a profane world.

Instead of substituting new holy realities for the old ones, Christ went further. He radically abrogated the distinction itself between the sacred and the profane. This may seem startling to some Christians who unconsciously continue to think along Old Testament lines. They may imagine the New Testament to be an updated version of the Old. They think our churches have taken the place of the Temple at Jerusalem, that our Sunday replaces the Sabbath, that our sacred vessels continue the Temple furniture and that the New Testament priest is a polished version of the Old Testament one. The cause of this misunderstanding is partly due to developments within the Church in the course of her history, partly in deference to the human necessity of having quasi-sacred realities like churches as part of an established religion. But basically the clinging to realities that are intrinsically 'sacred' is a regression and contrary to the teaching of the New Testament.

In the new kingdom of God Jesus came to establish, it was ordinary things that were turned into signs of God's presence and means of grace.

Plain water, used in baptism, makes people into children of God. The bread and wine of a family meal provide the matter for the Eucharist. The anointing with oil normally applied to wounds can come to signify God's healing and forgiveness. Jesus' humanity was a sacrament and the sacramental order he brought about sanctified ordinary things and ordinary people.

Jesus abolished the priesthood as a sacral institution. He himself did not belong to the priesthood of Aaron. As representative of all human beings, he abolished that priestly dignity which was linked to bodily descent. He established a new priesthood built on 'the power of indestructible life'.[6] The Old Testament notions of the priesthood were so alien to Christ that we never find him applying the term priest to himself or his followers.[7] Jesus called himself 'the son of man' which, in Aramaic, translates as 'an ordinary person', 'someone like you and me'.

The people Jesus chose to continue his ministry were not members of a privileged class, but ordinary people like himself – fishermen, tax collectors, farmers, craftsmen, businessmen. The ministry Jesus initiated was a ministry by ordinary people, not by sacred functionaries. If he abolished all the other categories, why would he have held on to the requirement of the male gender in future ministers? Would that not be odd and contradictory?[8]

The sons and daughters of God

The Gospel of John tells us: 'To all who accept him, he has given power to become children of God, to all who believe in his name, who are born not out of human stock, or urge of the flesh or human will, but of God himself.'[9] Note that no distinction is made between men and women here. All become God's children through baptism. And all receive a share in Jesus' priestly and prophetic ministry.

Every disciple, whether man or woman, carries his or her cross with Christ. Each of his followers has to bear witness to him even unto persecution and death. All worship the Father with Christ. All Christians thus participate in the royal priesthood of Christ.[10] All are called 'priests to his God and Father', 'priests of God and of Christ'. Both men and women constitute 'a kingdom and priesthood to our God'.[11]

> Christ the Lord, High Priest taken from among people, 'made a kingdom and priests to God his Father'. The baptized, by regeneration and the anointing of the Holy Spirit, are consecrated into a spiritual house and a holy priesthood.[12]

This common priesthood is given through the sacrament of baptism. We should note that this baptism is exactly the same for every single person. There is absolutely no difference in the baptism conferred on women. This was a revolutionary change that Jesus brought about, which dramatically transformed the position of women in religion. Whereas women had only belonged indirectly to the covenant of Moses, through baptism they were made children of God on an equal footing with men.

In the Old Testament, it was the men who were the immediate bearers of the covenant. It was only the male children who were circumcised when they were eight days old.[13] The covenant, therefore, was concluded directly with the men. Women belonged to it only through men – first as daughters of their fathers, then as wives of their husbands.

It was the men who were expected to offer sacrifices in the Temple. Three times a year, at the three major feasts, all the menfolk were to appear before Yahweh's face.[14] The women could come along and take part in the sacrificial meal, as did children, slaves and guests. But it was not really their own sacrifice. The principal reason was that the wives, like children, slaves and cattle, were, in fact, owned by their husbands. 'A good wife is the best of possessions.'[15] The husband could practically divorce his wife at will, but she could not divorce him. A religious vow by a woman was valid only if it was ratified by her father or her husband.[16]

In the Temple at Jerusalem, Jewish women were only admitted into a 'parlour' – the court of women. They were not allowed to proceed further. The men, on the other hand, could enter the court of Israel. It was this court that faced the altar of holocausts and it was there that the priests accepted the gifts for the sacrifice. Men had the principal seats in the synagogues; women looked on from an enclosure. Men could read from the Torah. Only males, ten of them, could form the quorum, *minyan*, required for public prayers. At the age of 13, boys were initiated into their adult religious duties by the *Bar Mitzvah* ceremony. No such thing existed for girls.

All these things changed through Christ. St Paul affirms that the baptism of Christ transcends and obliterates whatever social differences exist among humankind.

> It is through faith that all of you are God's children in union with Christ Jesus. For all who are baptised into the union of Christ have taken upon themselves the qualities of Christ himself. So there is no difference between Jews and Gentiles, between slaves and free persons, between men and women . . . You are all one in union with Christ Jesus.[17]

The ordination to the sacramental priesthood is an extension of the basic sacrificial and prophetic sharing that has already been given in baptism. Although the ministerial priesthood adds a new function to the powers received in baptism, it is at the same time intrinsically related to it.

> Though they differ essentially and not only in degree, the common priesthood of the faithful and the ministerial or hierarchical priesthood are none the less ordered one to the other; each in its own way shares in the one priesthood of Christ.[18]

When the Council says that the sharing in Christ's priesthood through the sacrament of Holy Orders is *essentially* different, it means that baptism by itself does not confer the commission to teach, rule and offer sacrifice in the name of Christ. It does not mean to say that for Holy Orders a different set of discriminating values would hold good.

A common dignity

Jesus made men and women equal children of God. The common priesthood men and women share with Christ is ordered towards the ministerial priesthood. Why then would the ministerial priesthood suddenly be restricted to men only? Whatever may be required for ordination to the ministry, it cannot be a reality that would make one person intrinsically superior to another. Vatican II is explicit on this.

> There is a common dignity of members deriving from their rebirth in Christ, a common grace as children, a common vocation to perfection, one salvation, one hope and undivided charity. In Christ and in the Church there is, then, no inequality arising from race or nationality, social condition or sex . . . Although by Christ's will some are established as teachers, dispensers of the mysteries and pastors for the others, there remains, nevertheless, a true equality between all with regard to the dignity and the activity that is common to all the faithful in the building up of the Body of Christ.[19]

Jesus abolished gender as a category in his kingdom. Men and women are equal as God's adopted children. Would it not be illogical to imply that discriminations wiped out by baptism should be revived in the sacramental priesthood?

The idea that Jesus, after abolishing the priesthood based on sacrality and founding a ministry of people like you and me, would rudely exclude women makes no sense. The presumption that Jesus who had wiped out the ancient bias against women in the common priesthood of the faithful, would reintroduce it in ministerial priesthood defies all logic. The contention that Jesus, who brought worship 'in spirit and in truth' and for whom love and service were the supreme characteristics of his ministry, would then introduce maleness as an essential requirement offends the inner consistency of the Gospel.

Even before we have looked at all the arguments in detail we can already discern that the tradition of excluding women, whatever its origin, cannot really go back to a 'deliberate decision of Jesus Christ'. It simply does not work. This tradition has all the plumage of a cuckoo hatchling. And even those who have not studied theology professionally can sense this, as we will see in the next chapter.

READINGS FROM THE WOMEN PRIESTS WEBSITE

Vatican II
Readings from *Lumen Gentium*

http://www.womenpriests.org/church/lumen.htm

John Wijngaards
The dominance of men was a reality in Jewish culture

http://www.womenpriests.org/scriptur/myth__ot.htm

The social perception of male superiority

http://www.womenpriests.org/scriptur/mythmale.htm

Jesus Christ and the fact of social male dominance

http:/www.womenpriests.org/scriptur/myth1.htm

Jesus showed great openness to women

http://www.womenpriests.org/scriptur/christop.htm

Mary exemplified the ministerial implications of the common priesthood of Christ enjoyed by all believers

http://www.womenpriests.org/scriptur/mary.htm

6

The Assessment of Believers

In the previous chapter I indicated some theological reasons for stating that the ban on women as priests does not sit well with the actions and priorities which Jesus established in the Gospel. This mismatch is becoming more and more obvious to members of the Catholic community as they grow in understanding and autonomy. I believe that thinking and praying Catholics all over the world *know* in their heart of hearts and in the depth of their Catholic faith that it is not Jesus who keeps women from being ordained.

Some time ago I was visiting a Catholic family and the question of women's ordination came up. The father is a bricklayer, yet he and his wife were managing to send four of their children to college.

'Of course, women should be ordained,' the father said.

'How can you be so sure?' I asked.

'I've got two daughters,' he said, 'and they are just as important to God as my sons. I'm sure that Jesus would not refuse ordination if one of them applied to him for it.'

Should we listen to a bricklayer to tell us what to believe? The answer, strangely enough, is yes. But before we analyse why, we should register the fact that many good and committed Catholics share the bricklayer's conviction. They too appeal to their instinctive knowledge of what agrees with Catholic faith and what does not.

> I hate the double standards that the Catholic Church produces. Our school is an all-girl school and we are encouraged to be strong women of the nineties. But the views of the Pope and the church just hold women back. Will the Pope ever understand the injustice that women have suffered? When will the law on women in the priesthood be changed? The church will never have my full support until women receive the equality they deserve.[1]

But such opinions of Catholic believers can hardly be used as an argument, you may say. What do ordinary people know about the contents of faith?

The sense of faith

Let me first explain the theological meaning of 'sense of faith' (*sensus fidei*). Other terms with slightly different meanings have been used throughout the centuries: the Gospel in the heart, the Catholic spirit (*sensus catholicus*), the ecclesiastical spirit (*phronema ekklesiastikon*), the mind of the Church (*ecclesiae catholicae sensus*), or sometimes the agreement of the Church (*consensus ecclesiae*) – in these last expressions 'Church' stands for the whole community of believers. For simplicity's sake I will just use the expression 'sense of faith'.[2]

The 'sense of faith' carried in the heart of believers implies fidelity to the core truths we believe in, combined with a growth in understanding. The beliefs which we, as the community of believers, received from Jesus Christ are not a dead parcel of stale doctrines, but *a living tradition*. The tradition lives because it manifests the growth through time of the truth entrusted to the Church, like the growth of a living plant. Tradition is living because it is carried by living minds – minds living in time. These minds meet with problems or acquire resources, in time, which lead them to endow tradition, or the truth it contains, with the reactions and characteristics of a living thing. It leads to adaptation, reaction, growth and fruitfulness. Tradition is living because it resides in minds that live by it, in a history which comprises activity, problems, doubts, opposition, new contributions, and questions that need answering.[3] In the issue of the ordination of women, the 'sense of faith' in the hearts of believers tests its conformity with the intentions of Christ.

The sense of the faith may also be understood in terms of 'awareness'. Tradition is the people of God's awareness, an ever renewed awareness. Its role in the Church is similar to that played by awareness in a person's life: comprehension and memory; gauge of identity; instinct of what is fitting; witness and expression of personality. The awareness in the heart of the faithful, however, is special, because this awareness comes from Christ, it holds data it has received as a deposit. The Church keeps and actualises the living memory of what she has received, and the Holy Spirit continually sustains and deepens that living memory in her. In a sense, this awareness possesses its object totally and integrally from the start, but it does not express it fully at each moment in its history.[4]

Ordinary believers know a lot about the contents of faith. In fact, they are the main carriers of the Church's gift of infallibility. Many Catholics think that the deposit of faith lies first and foremost with the hierarchy, with the Pope and the bishops. The model they have in mind is a top–down flow of knowledge and communication, like the commander-in-chief of an army and his staff who hold all the information, make the plans and pass them down to the ranks.

The true picture is different. The Church is more like a large family business in which the core of information is carried by all the family members jointly and individually, through a wide range of skill, experience and competence. The Pope and the bishops have the duty and the charism to articulate that knowledge as teachers of the Church. They can only do so by paying careful attention to the *sensus fidelium*, the faith that lives in the hearts of the faithful. This is how the Second Vatican Council put it:

> The body of the faithful as a whole, anointed as they are by the Holy One (cf. 1 John 2,20.27), cannot err in matters of belief. Thanks to a supernatural *sense of the faith* which characterizes the People as a whole, it manifests this unerring quality when 'from the bishops down to the last member of the laity', it shows universal agreement in matters of faith and morals. For, by this *sense of faith* which is aroused and sustained by the Spirit of truth, God's People accepts not the word of human beings, but the very Word of God (cf. 1 Thessalonians 2,13). It clings without fail to the faith once delivered to the saints, penetrates it more deeply by accurate insights, and applies it more thoroughly to life.[5]

The Pope and the college of bishops have a crucial role in articulating matters of faith and morals through their authoritative teaching. However, this exercise *is grounded in* the infallibility of the whole people of God, not the other way about. A proposed amendment during Vatican II that wanted to make the infallibility of the *magisterium* the source of the people's infallibility was rejected by the Council as being contrary to tradition.[6] The infallibility of the Church's teaching office has no other aim than to give explicit expression to what is already infallibly believed by the whole people of God. The infallible teachings of the Pope and the college of bishops do not need the approval of the faithful, but 'the assent of the church can never fail to be given to these definitions on account of the activity of the same Holy Spirit, by which the whole flock of Christ is preserved in the unity of faith'.[7]

The sense of faith in action

It is not always easy to pin down this sense of faith regarding a particular issue, especially when the issue is being reflected on, debated and researched, as is the case with the ordination of women. The sense of faith then needs to be carefully listened to in prayer. It needs to be discerned. We may not use it as a conclusive *proof* of something being right for the Church or not. On the other hand, neither may the strong testimony of believing and committed Catholics be dismissed out of hand. The body of infallible truth lies, after all, in the heart of the believers.

It is my conviction that, with regard to the ordination of women, the voices of lay people in our Catholic community may no longer be ignored. A very great number of them feel strongly that openness of holy orders to women is implied in our faith priorities. They sense unresolved contradictions in the official Church's present position. Just listen to what they have to say.[8]

My wife and I are Catholics of 67 years standing. One of the matters that deeply concerns us is that throughout that 67 years and all of the years before, our Church has been greatly impoverished. This impoverishment has arisen because every facet of the life of the Church has been dictated and viewed by and from the male perspective. The gifts, charisms and insights of 50 per cent of the church, the female 50 per cent, have been almost entirely ignored except for a few well-known exceptions, i.e. Teresa of Avila, Thérèse of Lisieux. Jesus clearly saw women and men as equal. It is only the male priesthood that sees them as inferior. The male priesthood has adopted a dreadful arrogance of righteousness which only serves to cover the impoverishment that they inflict on the whole church by their treatment of women. As lifelong Catholics we find it offensive and un-Christian to be told by the Pope that to be Catholic means that we must believe that Jesus does not want women to be ordained. If we take his words seriously we are surely excommunicated for our deeply held conviction that on this matter he is not speaking for Jesus Christ.

I have sometimes wondered whether this is not a logical deduction: the premise that it is impossible for women to be ordained implies ultimately that women cannot receive *salvation*. I think it would be possible to prove the connection – thus giving the lie to the premise as there have been many women saints.

I am not a priest or theologian, just a member of the laity – I hate that word because of its implicit reference to the hierarchy. The church is interfering with the work of the Holy Spirit amongst the people of God because of its narrow view of the role of women. I look forward to the day when the Catholic Church will accept the ordination of women.

My layman's logic would get to the heart of the matter in this way: How can the Church support gender equity everywhere except in the Church? How

45

can the Church baptise women into the priesthood of the faithful and then exclude them from the priesthood? How can the Church offer one less sacrament to half of humankind?

It has seemed to me for a long time that, apart from the theological and historical arguments, one of the most compelling arguments for the ordination of women is that the Church is impoverished by a single-sex priesthood. In the structure of the Catholic Church everything in the end is promulgated through the priesthood, it is the holder of all power and authority. If, then, the priesthood is chosen from only one sex, only one approach to life, spirituality, belief in Christ and the attaining of salvation is ever preached. All papal, episcopal and other pronouncements are made by men. In every Catholic church, every Sunday morning, all over the world, only a man preaches the word of God. In every confessional only a man offers guidance and comfort. Every time a priest is required for anything, it is always a man who undertakes that duty. In every facet of the Church's mission the male voice leads and directs. The quality of what these males do is not in question (at least not all of it!), what is in question is that the charism, wisdom, insight, perception, understanding and all the other gifts and abilities of women are lost to the Church. Women are different from men. God made people that way and gave us different male and female characteristics. Without women as priests, we are only half a Church. Such a Church is not the Church Jesus left with Peter. The Church we have now is a Vatican imitation of a truly Christian Church.

I am a California high school student and I am a confirmed Catholic as of last year. Anyway, I was assigned a research paper for my English class and I chose to investigate why on earth women can't be priests. I just want to say that after reading the official Church documents, I am absolutely shocked!!! I am not kidding – I dropped my jaw! I cannot understand why the Church would shy away from this topic, and I feel that women may be allowed to become priests in the future – maybe just not yet. But I had no idea that I'm potentially a heretic for believing this!

And it is not just a few people who think like this. Surveys in the USA show that two-thirds of Catholics support the ordination of women. Some 63% would accept women who are ordained priests if they remained celibate, 54% would accept them even if they are married. Additionally, 63% state that the laity should have a say in deciding the question of whether women should be ordained or not.[9]

Among Catholic college students in Australia, 62% believe priestly ordination should be open to women.[10] By the most recent statistics, Catholics in other 'Western' countries too favour women priests: Spain 74%,

Germany 71%, Portugal 71%, Ireland 67%, Italy 58%. At the Montreal Synod in Canada in 1998, 66% of participants voted in favour of women priests, 73% in favour of women deacons.[11]

The voices of committed Catholics may not always be articulate. They speak from that deep Gospel awareness that lives in their heart. But what they tell us is crystal clear: excluding women from priestly ordination is a mistake. It does not come from Jesus. It is an intrusion of anti-feminine prejudice from outside.

READINGS FROM THE WOMEN PRIESTS WEBSITE

John Wijngaards
On why the Church needs to be reformed in our time

http://www.womenpriests.org/teaching/godselv2.htm

On latent tradition

http://www.womenpriests.org/traditio/latent.htm

John Henry Newman (1801–90):
'The Theory of Developments in Religious Doctrine'

http://www.womenpriests.org/traditio/newman2.htm

Jeanne Pieper
'The Forbidden Subject: the Ordination of Women'

http://www.womenpriests.org/called/pieper1.htm

7

Naming the Culprit

MY MOTHER USED TO SAY jokingly at times that through the van Dits-huisens, from whom she was descended via her grandmother, she was distantly related to Alessandro Farnese, the Duke of Parma. Now, to Dutch ears, this is hardly something to be proud of. The Duke of Parma was the military governor in the Netherlands (1587–92) of Philip II of Spain. He is remembered for ruthlessly suppressing nationalist Dutch uprisings, while enjoying the amorous advances of local noble ladies. The duke was descended from an illegitimate son of Pope Paul III and an illegitimate daughter of the Habsburg Emperor Charles V. Tracing one's ancestry can uncover nasty surprises!

The custom of refusing priestly ordination to women does not easily fit what we know about Jesus' vision in the Gospel. Ordinary believers feel there is something wrong with blaming Jesus for the exclusion of women. But if the ban does not derive from Jesus, where did it come from? Research points to the anti-feminine cultural bias in the past. But we can be even more specific. The greatest culprit was ancient Roman law which the Church gradually made its own. How do we know this?

Geographic variations

Prejudices against women existed everywhere in the past. But in Christian countries that stood predominantly under Greek influence, the prejudices were less pronounced. I will give some examples.

The philosophy of Plato (427–347 BC), though partly overshadowed by Aristotle's, remained influential. And Plato's attitude to women was ambivalent. In some of his writings he ascribed the inferior status of women clearly to a degeneration from perfect human nature. In other writings he advocated a fairer deal for women. In his idealised *Republic* he foresaw an upper class of 'guardians' among whom the chattel status of woman would be abolished – that is, she would no longer be owned by her husband. Then women would receive equal education to men. This is a far cry from Aristotle's claim that women were inferior by nature.[1]

When we read the Greek-speaking Fathers of the Church, we are often surprised to find a greater openness than among the Latin-speaking Fathers. The Latin Fathers Tertullian, Augustine and Jerome routinely implied that women owed their 'state of punishment' to Eve. The Greek-speaking St Irenaeus (AD 140–203) presented a more even-handed interpretation of the Genesis account. He blamed the devil, rather than Adam and Eve. And he held Adam more responsible than Eve. He showed real empathy with women and regretted the unjust plight they were often made to suffer. St Ignatius too, another Greek Father (died AD 110), had no grudge against women. Yes, the fall came through one woman, Eve, he said, but redemption came through another woman, namely Mary.

In Latin-speaking circles there existed an abhorrence of menstruation. Women were told to stay at home, to abstain from receiving communion until they were cleansed, and so on. The third-century *Didascalia*, however, an instruction book composed in North Syria, presented a truly Christian response. Women should not think that their monthly periods were a time of evil during which they should keep away from prayer or the Eucharist. No, God has created the body and all its functions. They are all holy. 'And through baptism women receive the Holy Spirit, who is ever with those that work righteousness, and does not depart from them by reason of natural issues and the intercourse of marriage, but is ever and always with those who possess him.'[2]

The Greek Fathers of the Church spoke of Mary as a priest. Epiphanius II, a bishop in Cyprus who died in AD 680, composed a long hymn on Mary's priestly status, saying among other things: 'I call the Virgin both priest and altar, she, the "table-bearer" who has given us the Christ, the heavenly bread for the forgiveness of sins.'[3] The term 'table-bearer' was a title of the 'priestesses' of Pallas Athene.[4] We do not find this association between priesthood and women with the Latin Fathers.

For about nine centuries the Early Church had sacramentally ordained women deacons. They flourished in the Greek-speaking countries of the Byzantine Empire. In the Latin-speaking countries, however, they were only grudgingly tolerated. Soon local councils in North Africa and Gaul imposed local bans to stop the diaconate of women altogether.

There are tantalising traces of women having been ordained priests in the southernmost part of Italy among Greek-speaking colonies until the third or fourth century, when the practice was stamped out by Rome.

Although a bias against women existed everywhere, the most deep-seated prejudice was found in the Latin-speaking regions of the old

Roman Empire: central and northern Italy, Gaul (present-day France), northern Africa, Spain and Britain. Let me give some examples.

In Carthage, north Africa, lived Tertullian (c. AD 155–245), who exercised a great influence on the Latin Fathers who were to follow him. As the initiator of ecclesiastical Latin, he was instrumental in shaping the vocabulary and thought of Western Christianity for the next thousand years. Tertullian opposed any participation of women in Church ministries. 'It is not permitted to a woman to speak in the church; but neither may she teach, baptize, offer, claim for herself a share in any masculine role, certainly not in any priestly office.'[5] Tertullian's negative stand was followed by other Latin Fathers, such as Augustine (Hippo, north Africa), Jerome (Italy, Palestine) and Ambrosiaster (northern Italy).

The local synod at Carthage (345–419) forbade bishops, priests and deacons to touch women before eucharistic celebrations. The synod of Orange in Gaul (AD 441) abolished the ordination of women as deacons in its area. In the late fifth century, the priest Gennadius of Marseille in Gaul drew up a list of rules, known as the *Statuta Ecclesiae Antiqua*, that included restrictions against women. The synods of Epaon (517) and Auxerre (588), both in Gaul, reiterated the local abolition of the diaconate of women and forbade women to touch sacred objects or receive communion in the hand. Bishop Theodore of Canterbury in Britain (died AD 690) forbade women, whether lay or religious, to enter into church or receive communion during the time of menstruation.

From such examples we can establish that the rejection of women was strongest in the Latin tradition. And this was continued during the Middle Ages. The anti-woman code of church laws assembled by the monk Gratian in Bologna, Italy, in 1140, became the core of future Church legislation. The theologians and canon lawyers of the Latin-speaking universities of Italy, France, Spain and England carried on the same tradition of keeping women in submission and barring them from access to 'sacred things'.

What is behind all this? Why all this hostility in the territories of the ancient Roman Empire? What is the *Latin* connection?

Roman laws

No system of law has been so influential in the world as that which arose in the city of ancient Rome. Its thinking dominated the Roman Empire for more than a thousand years, and in the Byzantine Empire it remained in use until 1453. It formed the basis for the law codes of most Western countries. More important for us, it shaped much of Church law in the Catholic Church.

The great contribution of Roman legislation was its laying down of simple and clear principles. Roman law was detailed, specific, practical. It lent itself to resolving disputes. It was a form of law developed by people who were able administrators and efficient organisers. But organisation often hides structural prejudice, and this is what happened in the case of women. For Roman law was hostile to women.

Roman family law was based on the principle that the father of the family (*pater familias*) had complete authority both over the children and over his wife. This was defined as paternal power (*patria potestas*). The wife depended totally on her husband. She was his property and was completely subject to his disposition. He could punish her in any way, even kill her, or sell her as a slave – though this last punishment was forbidden after 100 BC. As far as family property was concerned, the wife herself did not own anything. Everything she or her children inherited belonged to her husband, including also the dowry which she brought with her on marriage.

In later times this absolute power of the husband was somewhat diminished, leading to what was known as a form of 'free marriage' which husband and wife could agree upon. However, even in this new situation, the husband had the right to make the final decisions in all questions concerning the family: for instance, the place of residence which the wife had to share with him, the education of the children, the exclusive rights on her wifely duties, while the husband himself could make love to other women with impunity.

The rights of women in general civil Roman law were not much better. Although the woman was considered a Roman citizen, she obtained her position only through her husband. Women could not carry their own name, just as slaves were prohibited to do so. Only men carried this distinct sign of their being a Roman citizen.

- The general principle was: 'In many sections of our law the condition of women is weaker than that of men.'
- Moreover, women were excluded from all public functions and rights: 'Women are excluded from all civil and public responsibility and therefore can neither be judges nor carry any civil authority.'
- A woman could not have charge of another person. 'Guardianship is a man's duty.' She could not have patronage of even her children or cousins, except in later Roman law.
- Women could not function as witnesses, whether at the drawing up of a last will, or in any other form of law. 'A woman is incapable of being a witness in any form of jurisprudence where witnesses are required.' Like minors, slaves, the dumb and criminals, women were reckoned to be incapable of being witnesses.
- Women could not enter a court case without being represented by a man. Women could not represent themselves in law 'because of the infirmity of their sex and because of their ignorance about matters pertaining to public life'.

In spite of a slight relaxation in laws, which offered more protection to women in the Roman Empire of the third and fourth centuries, the overall inferior status of women remained the same.[6]

If we understand that this was the condition of women *by law*, a law which everyone greatly respected, we can appreciate how this devaluation of women slipped into Church thinking. The inferior status of women was so much taken for granted that it determined the way Latin-speaking theologians and Church leaders would look on matters relating to women. Just listen to this reasoning by Ambrosiaster (fourth century) which is typical of the time:

> Women must cover their heads because they are not the image of God . . . How can anyone maintain that woman is the likeness of God when she is demonstrably subject to the dominion of man and has no kind of authority? For she can neither teach nor be a witness in a court nor exercise citizenship nor be a judge – then certainly not exercise dominion.[7]

Ambrosiaster states that woman 'has no kind of authority'. Why not? Because by civil law a woman could not hold any public function or exercise any authority. He goes on to say that she cannot be 'a witness in court, or exercise citizenship [i.e. take part in public meetings] or be a judge'. Why not? Because civil law forbade it. Now notice the argument. Woman does not bear the image of God *because* she is manifestly subject to man, as we can see from civil law! The real argument rests on Roman law, which is taken as right and just. And here the parent is revealed. The cuckoo raises its ugly head. The position of woman is not really decided by any Christian tradition or inspired text, but by the pagan Roman law which was believed to be normative.

Or take this example from the law book assembled by Gratian (1140):

> Wives are subject to their husbands by nature . . . As Augustine states: 'It is the natural order among people that women serve their husbands and children their parents, because the justice of this lies in (the principle that) the lesser serves the greater' . . . And Jerome states: 'God's word is blasphemed by either despising God's original sentence and reducing it to nothing, or by defaming the Gospel of Christ, when a woman, against the law and fidelity of nature, in spite of being a Christian and made subject by God's law, desires to dominate her husband, since even pagan wives serve their husbands by the common law of nature.'[8]

What is the subjection of women based upon? Nature. How do we know what is natural? Quoting Augustine and Jerome, the answer lies in law: 'the natural order of people', 'against the law and fidelity of nature', 'the common law of nature'. What they mean is: the law as they knew it, Roman civil law and family law. The pagan laws of ancient Rome thus became the basis for the Church's own legislation against women. The crass Latin bias against women is even expressed in these words which remained in the Church's Book of Law until 1917:

> You must know that Ambrose does not call the husband 'man' (Latin *vir*) on

account of his male sex, but by the strength (Latin *virtus*) of his soul; and you should realise that 'woman' (Latin *mulier*) is not called so because of the sex of her body but because of the weakness (Latin *mollicies*) of her mind.[9]

Since Church leaders took Roman law as the norm for what is right and just, the same negative rules regarding women found their way into Christian thought, practice and law. It is obvious that Christians who accepted the socially and culturally inferior status of women enshrined in civil law, could not envisage her in the leadership role demanded of bishops and priests. Here we find the true origin of the so-called 'christian' tradition of banning women from the ministry. But is this all?

Monthly periods

The Latin-speaking countries – more so it would seem than countries that had adopted Greek culture – abhorred menstruation. A taboo against women during their monthly periods was common. Not only were women considered to be 'impure' at such a time, but in danger of communicating their impurity to others. This is why Pliny the Elder said in a Latin classic that was quoted and requoted as an authority:

> Contact with the monthly flux of women turns new wine sour, makes crops wither, kills grafts, dries seeds in gardens, causes the fruit of trees to fall off, dims the bright surface of mirrors, dulls the edge of steel and the gleam of ivory, kills bees, rusts iron and bronze, and causes a horrible smell to fill the air. Dogs who taste the blood become mad, and their bite becomes poisonous as in rabies. The Dead Sea, thick with salt, cannot be drawn asunder except by a thread soaked in the poisonous fluid of the menstrual blood. A thread from an infected dress is sufficient. Linen, touched by the woman while boiling and washing it in water, turns black. So magical is the power of women during their monthly periods that they say that hailstorms and whirlwinds are driven away if menstrual fluid is exposed to the flashes of lightning.[10]

We can see this prejudice at work in the Fathers. 'For our salvation the Son of God was made the Son of Man. Nine months he awaited his birth in the womb, undergoing the most revolting conditions there, to come forth covered with blood.'[11] We see it at work in Church practice. 'Menstruous women ought not to come to the Holy Table, or touch the Holy of Holies, nor enter churches, but to pray elsewhere.'[12] 'While a priest is celebrating Mass, women should in no way approach the altar, but remain in their places, and there the priest should receive their offerings to God. Women should therefore remember their infirmity, and the inferiority of their sex: and therefore they should have fear of touching whatever sacred things there are in the ministry of the Church.'[13] The prejudice was repeated over and over again by medieval theologians.

Apart from preventing women from receiving communion during their monthly periods, it also became an obstacle to women's ordination. For who dared to imagine what could happen when a woman served at the altar?

The real culprit that stopped women from being received into the ministry was pagan bias. On the one hand, it consisted in the prejudice that considered women incapable of holding authority, a prejudice that lay enshrined in Roman civil law and that became part of Church law. On the other hand, there was the taboo that considered a woman's menstrual blood unclean and dangerous. How could such an inferior and unclean creature ever be a priest? And did Scripture not say the same thing?

READINGS FROM THE WOMEN PRIESTS WEBSITE

The Rabbinical tradition regarding women's monthly periods

http://www.womenpriests.org/traditio/uncl___jew.htm

Quotes from St Augustine that show his negative attitude towards women

http://www.womenpriests.org/traditio/august.htm

The law collection of Gratian

http://www.womenpriests.org/theology/gratian.htm

The taboo against menstruation

http://www.womenpriests.org/traditio/unclean.htm

Part III

CROSS-EXAMINING THE EVIDENCE

Rather than committing to memory who said what, remember the reasons people had for holding their views.

An assertion is as valid as the arguments on which it rests.

St Thomas Aquinas
De modo studendi (1265)

8

The Arguments Found in 'Tradition'

WHEN FLORENCE NIGHTINGALE arrived in the British military hospital at Scutari in 1854 during the Crimean War, she found that atrocious conditions prevailed. The barracks were overcrowded with the wounded and dying, and infested by fleas and rats. Furniture, clothing, bedding and medical supplies were deficient. Sanitary provisions were minimal. The water allowance per patient was one pint a day for all purposes. Florence took in hand a thorough reform of the local situation, but she did more: she began to campaign for the welfare of soldiers in the whole British army. And she invented a surprisingly effective tool – statistics.

To overcome the hostile reception by the army establishment, she started to compile lists of facts and to display them in simple diagrams. She would detail, month by month, how many soldiers had died in battle and how many had died of infectious diseases. She would make comparative tables of the costs of health prevention and of medical aftercare. She published these statistics in Britain and even presented them to Queen Victoria in October 1856. They achieved their purpose. A royal commission on the health of the army began work that same year.

In this chapter I will try to follow her approach. Leaving the detailed discussion of various arguments until later, I want to achieve clarity on some basic facts.

My main question is: what were the traditional arguments for refusing ordination to women? Now, during the first thousand years after Christ, the ordination of women to the priesthood was rarely discussed. In the few sporadic texts where it *was* mentioned we cannot discern any systematic reflection on the issue. Fathers of the Church, popes or local church councils responded to this or that event. These early testimonies are, of course, important and we will give due weight to them when tracing the origins of various arguments. It is more revealing to study the reasons given by the medieval theologians, because it was during this time that (a) the ban against women's ordination became part of church law, and (b) the reasons for it were methodically reflected on.

Rome quotes five medieval theologians in support of its arguments:

Aquinas, Bonaventure, Richard of Middleton, John Duns Scotus and Dur-andus à Saint-Pourçain. These will be my main source. I have carried out my own research on them. I obtained the original Latin texts, had them translated into English and analysed them in full.[1]

I have supplemented this list with eleven contemporary canon lawyers.[2] It should be noted that Church law and theology were closely related in those days. Commentators of Church law were theologians. Theologians used Church law as one of their principal sources.

My list therefore contains 16 medieval theologians who have expressed a theological judgement on women's ordination. This list seems to be complete as far as known written sources go. We can safely base a representative analysis on them. If we catalogue the reasons they gave for excluding women from ordination, we will have a fair idea of how the tradition of not ordaining women was justified.

- Gratian of Bologna (1140)
- Paucapalea (1148)
- Bandinelli (1148)
- Rufinus (1159)
- Sicardus of Cremona (1181)
- Huguccio (1188)
- Teutonicus (1215)
- **Thomas Aquinas** (1225–74)
- **Bonaventure** (1217–74)
- De Sergusio (1253)
- **Richard of Middleton** (13th century)
- **John Duns Scotus** (1266–1308)
- **Durandus à Saint-Pourçain** (1270–1334)
- De Baysio (1300)
- Joannes Andreae (1338)
- Antonius de Butrio (1408)

The arguments these theologians give can be grouped under two main headings: (a) women are inferior to men; and (b) women have been excluded from ordination by the Church.

Women are inferior to men

This is, without any doubt, the main argument presented. In short it comes to this: women lack the intelligence and leadership qualities that men possess. They obviously depend on men for guidance and need to be ruled by men. Women cannot hold any position of authority. Thus

Table 1: **Women's inferior status**

	Medieval theologians who held this view	Medieval theologians who presented this explicitly as an argument against the ordination of women	Total number of medieval theologians supporting this view
God made women subservient to men.	Gratian, Bandinelli, Sicardus, Huguccio, Teutonicus, **Aquinas**	Huguccio, **Bonaventure**, de Sergusio, **Middleton**, **Scotus**, **Durandus**, Andreae	12
Women are inferior to men by nature.	Gratian, Bandinelli, Sicardus, Huguccio, Teutonicus	**Aquinas**, **Bonaventure**, **Middleton**, **Scotus**, **Durandus**	10
Women are not created in the image of God, as men are.	Gratian, **Aquinas**, de Sergusio	Huguccio, **Bonaventure**, de Baysio, de Butrio	7
Women cannot hold public authority, as stated by law.	Sicardus, Teutonicus	Gratian, de Sergusio, Scotus	5
Women still carry the burden of Eve's sin.	Gratian, Sicardus, Teutonicus	Huguccio, de Baysio	5
Women cannot be ordained 'because of their sex', i.e. it is against their nature.		Bandinelli, Huguccio, Sicardus, Teutonicus	4
Women are not perfect human beings and thus cannot represent Christ.		**Aquinas**, **Bonaventure**, Andreae	3

women lack *that degree of pre-eminence* that is required in the spiritual leadership of the ordained ministers.

> In the female sex a pre-eminence of degree cannot be signified since she occupies a state of subjection.[3]

> Since it is not possible in the female sex to signify eminence of degree, for a woman is in the state of subjection, it follows that she cannot receive the sacrament of Order.[4]

> [Holy] Orders establish the ordained person in some degree of eminence, which has somehow to be signified in the eminence of nature of the person ordained. But woman possesses a state of subjection with regard to man, which also corresponds to her nature. For the female sex is naturally imperfect in comparison to the male sex.[5]

The inferior status of women is theologically justified in various ways. A woman is not created in God's image. God subjected women to men at creation, or God subjected women to men in punishment for Eve's sin. See Table 1 on page 61.

The Church excludes women

The second batch of arguments start from *the fact* of women's exclusion. This is most frequently attributed to Paul. Since he forbade women to speak in Church or to have authority over men, it is obvious that women cannot be ordained.

> Every Order is received towards the priesthood and teaching. But teaching belongs chiefly to priests, as it is held in *dist. 16. quaest. 1* [in church law]; and not to Deacons, unless by commission, when a sermon or an instruction is regarded as the reading of the Gospel, which it is fitting for deacons to read. But that deed is prohibited to women, 1. Timothy 2. '*Let the women learn in silence*', and '*I do not permit them [women] to speak or to teach*', where a gloss [reads], '*not only I but also the Lord does not permit it*'; and this is so because of the weakness of their intellect, and the mutability of their emotions, which they commonly suffer more than men. For a teacher ought to have a lively intellect in the recognition of truth, and stability of emotion in its confirmation.[6]

Some theologians – only four out of the sixteen – attribute the exclusion to Jesus Christ. They usually point to the fact that no women are mentioned in the Gospel as having been present at the Last Supper. The

Table 2: **The exclusion of women by the Church**

	Medieval theologians who held this view	Medieval theologians who presented this explicitly as an argument against the ordination of women	Total number of medieval theologians supporting this view
Paul forbids women to teach in Church or to have authority over men.	Gratian, de Sergusio	**Aquinas, Bonaventure, Middleton, Scotus, Durandus,** Andreae	8
Christ did not include a woman among the apostolic twelve. There were only men at the Last Supper.		de Sergusio, **Middleton, Scotus, Durandus**	4
Women cannot be ordained because it is forbidden by the Church.		Rufinus, Huguccio, Teutonicus, **Bonaventure**	4
Women may not touch sacred objects or wear sacred vestments.	Gratian, Rufinus	**Middleton, Scotus**	4
Women may not visit church during their monthly periods, etc.	Paucapalea, Rufinus, Sicardus		3
It is not proper for women to receive the tonsure.		**Middleton, Scotus**	2
Women are not perfect members of the Church.		de Baysio	1

words 'Do this is commemoration of me' can, in their opinion, apply only to men.

> The female sex is an impediment to the reception of [Holy] Orders because the male sex is required by necessity of the sacrament, whose principal cause is the institution of Christ, whose right it was to institute the sacraments, both regarding the administering of them as their reception. But Christ ordained only men in the supper when he bestowed upon them the power of consecrating, and after the resurrection when he gave them the holy Spirit saying: *whose sins you will remit, etc.*[7]

The theologians see the exclusion of women confirmed in other legislation. For women may not touch sacred objects, distribute communion, wear sacred vestments, or enter a church when having their periods. Some state that it is not proper for women to wear a tonsure – the distinguishing mark of a person entering the clerical state. In all these cases the argument is presented as a conclusion from less to more. If women may not even *touch a chalice*, how could they be allowed to be priests?

> Clerics need to be given the tonsure, as has been stated before. But 1 Cor. says it is a shame for a woman to shave her hair, and she should not. If she looks after her hair, it is her glory. Therefore, only clerics should be ordained, a woman ought not to be ordained.[8]

> The fact that the female sex impedes the taking of Orders, is clear in the Decrees [of church law], distinc. 23. *We do not permit women consecrated to God, or nuns, to touch the sacred vessels or the sacred palls, or to carry incense around the altar, etc., because – there is no doubt to any wise person – all such ministries [of women] are filled with reprehension and condemnation.* But what impedes the handling and touching of the sacred objects, impedes much more the reception of Orders. Therefore if sex impedes in the first [case], then also in the second.[9]

Table 2 (on page 63) sets out these views.

From what these theologians themselves say, it is clear that the weightiest argument is the inferior status of woman. That was the reason why Paul forbade women to teach, they say. Her lack of pre-eminence must also have been the reason why Jesus himself chose only men to continue his mission.

The legal position of women was well summarised by Henricus de Sergusio, who later became cardinal-bishop of Ostia and who is also known as Cardinal Hostiensis. He wrote the *Summa super Titulis*

Decretalium, also called the *Summa Aurea,* between 1250 and 1253, and the *Commentaria in Quinque Decretalium Libros* in 1268. He lists 'eighteen reasons why women are worse off than men'.

> *In many articles of our law, the situation of woman is worse than that of man.*[10]
> First, because a woman may not act as judge . . .
> Secondly, because she cannot undertake arbitration . . .
> Thirdly, because she may not teach, preach public sermons, hear confessions or exercise any other function belonging to the power of the keys . . .
> Fourthly, because she cannot receive holy orders . . .
> Fifthly, because she cannot start a court case . . .
> In the eighth place, because she cannot launch an accusation . . .
> In the ninth place, because she may not adopt a child . . .
> In the fourteenth place, because her condition is worse as a witness to a will . . .
> In the fifteenth place, because she cannot represent others in a court case . . .
> In the eighteenth place, in her subjection to man, and the need to veil her head, and her defective formation into the likeness of God.[11]

The key arguments

It is obvious that we do not need to discuss each and every single one of these medieval arguments against the ordination of women. The Roman authorities themselves concede the influence of bias. 'It is true that in the writings of the Fathers one will find the undeniable influence of prejudices unfavourable to women.'[12] We shall return to this Roman admission later. At this stage, everyone agrees that we need not waste time discussing the merits of reasoning involving the tonsure, women touching sacred objects or visiting church during their monthly periods and so on. Also, we may ignore the general statements of prejudice such as 'Women cannot hold public authority', or 'Women are not perfect members of the Church'. Everyone admits that such reasonings were invalid – even though the knock-on effect of these faulty reasonings may not be overlooked.

What, then, remains of arguments that deserve a fuller discussion? I have selected five, on one or more of the following criteria:

- they were the main theological reasons on which the tradition of non-ordaining women was explicitly based by medieval theologians;
- they rested on specific scriptural texts;
- they are still invoked by the Congregation for Doctrine as valid arguments today.

Table 3: **The five key arguments**

	Scriptural texts quoted in support of this argument	Number of medieval theologians who supported this argument	Status of this argument according to recent Vatican documents	Discussed in:
Women are not created in the image of God, as men are. Women are created subservient to men.	Gen. 1:26–27 Gen. 2:21–22 1 Cor. 11:7–9	13	*Not valid, according to Rome*	Chapter 9
Women are not allowed to teach in Church.	1 Tim. 2:11–15 1 Cor. 14:34–35	8	*Still valid today, according to Rome*	Chapter 10
Women still carry the burden of Eve's sin.	Gen. 3:16	5	*Not valid, according to Rome*	Chapter 11
Christ did not include a woman among the apostolic twelve.	Mark 3:13–19	4	*Main argument, according to Rome*	Chapter 12
Women are not perfect human beings and thus cannot represent Christ.		3	*Still valid today, according to Rome, with modification*	Chapters 13 and 14

In the following chapters we will look at these arguments in detail.

READINGS FROM THE WOMEN PRIESTS WEBSITE

Medieval Theology and 'Women Priests'
http://www.womenpriests.org/traditio/med___gen.htm
Overview of medieval theologians writing about
women
http://www.womenpriests.org/theology/overv___th.htm
Bonaventure (1217–74)
on women priests, general
http://www.womenpriests.org/theology/bona___gen.htm
Bonaventure's actual text on women priests
http://www.womenpriests.org/theology/bonav1.htm

9

Not Created in God's Image?

I WAS BORN IN INDONESIA during the final days of Dutch colonial rule. With considerable embarrassment I remember how, even as a small child, I became aware of my own status and rank as a white person, a *tuan blanda*, a *totok*. This distinguished me from the brown-coloured Indonesians and from the mixed race of so-called *indo-blandas*. Though in my family as Christians we believed that all human beings are equal – my parents taught in missionary schools! – I can recall the glow of social satisfaction inherent in belonging to a superior class of people. The tendency to ascribe higher and lower status to people seems ingrained in any human culture.

In the Middle Ages men considered themselves superior to women. It was a fact of life. Not only had the various European races brought their own patriarchal traditions with them. The almost universal adoption of ancient Roman law, with its institutionalisation of male dominance, made sure that men were the boss, whether at home, in politics, in the army, in business or in the pursuit of the arts and sciences. It truly was a man's world.

In such an environment, the question of the ordination of women was hardly discussed. In the few theological treatises where it was mentioned, as a curiosity, it was always dismissed on the basis of obvious male superiority. However, the argument was then often strengthened with a scriptural 'proof'. Men were superior because only the male had been created in God's image! St Bonaventure (1217–74), for instance, makes the following assertion:

> The male sex is required for the reception of Orders . . . for no one is capable of taking up Orders who does not bear the image of God, because in this sacrament a human being in a certain way becomes God, or divine, while he is made a participant in divine power. But it is the male who is, by reason of his sex 'Imago Dei', the image of God, just as it is said in the eleventh chapter of the first letter to the Corinthians. Therefore in no way can a woman be ordained.[1]

St Thomas Aquinas (1225–74) is a little more circumspect. Yes, women too are created in God's image, but only to some extent. The real image of God is the male.

> The image of God, in its principal signification, mainly the intellectual nature, is found both in man and woman. Hence after the word, 'to the image of God he created him', it is added, 'male and female he created them' (Gen. 1,27). Moreover it is said 'them' in the plural, as Augustine remarks, lest it should be thought that both sexes were united in one individual. However, in a secondary sense the image of God is found in the male, and not in woman: for the male is the beginning and end of woman; as God is the beginning and end of every creature. So when the apostle [Paul] had said that 'man is the image and glory of God, but woman is the glory of man', he adds his reason for saying this: 'for man is not of woman, but woman of man; and man was not created for woman, but woman for man'.[2]

Huguccio, from Bologna in Italy, wrote in 1188 that men, and not women, are the image of God for three reasons. The first is that God is the origin of everything, and the male is the origin of the whole human race. Secondly, that the Church arose from the side of Christ, just as the woman was taken from the side of Adam. And thirdly the male is the one who rules. 'Just as Christ is head of the Church and governs the Church so the husband is head of his wife and rules and governs her. And through these three causes the male is stated to be the image of God and not the woman, and therefore the male must not be like the woman a sign of subjection, but a sign of freedom and pre-eminence.'[3]

To the medieval mind, therefore, the picture was clear. Just observe the difference between men and women, they would say. A man automatically takes charge. He understands a situation. He is in control. The woman, on the other hand, is clearly his subordinate. She obeys her husband. She simply does what the man tells her to do. In this superior bearing of the male person, they would continue, we can see God himself in action. God is, after all, the omnipotent Lord who has charge of the whole world and rules everything by his powerful will. It is man, not woman, who reflects God in this manner. Therefore it is appropriate that it is only men, and not women, who are given the power to represent God through ordination.

The influential law book of Gratian on which future Church law was based (AD 1140), quotes Augustine and Scripture to prove that women are not made in the image of God.

> Women are in servile submission, on account of which they must be subject to men in everything. As Augustine says: 'This is the likeness of God in the

male that he is created as the only being from whom the others have come, and that he possesses, as it were, the dominion of God as his representative, since he bears in himself the image of the one God.' So woman is not created in the image of God; this is what (Scripture) says: 'and God created the male, according to the image of God he created him'. And therefore the apostle also says: 'a man certainly must not cover his head, because he is the image and reflection of God, but woman must cover her head because she is neither the reflection nor the image of God'.[4]

What about the Fathers of the Church?

Predictably, there is some difference here between the Greek and the Latin Fathers.

Epiphanius (315–403), a Greek-speaking bishop in Cyprus who was not particularly known for being friendly to women, stated quite clearly that both Adam and Eve were made in the image of God. God made Adam directly in his own image, he maintained, and Eve was, after all, made of one of Adam's ribs, so that the children they produced were also made in God's likeness and image.[5]

The Latin-speaking Tertullian in Carthage, North Africa (155–245), on the other hand, attributed likeness to God to men alone. Men are more intimate with God than women are, because they are 'God's image', he said. He accused women of trying to tempt men to sin, thereby destroying 'him who is God's image'.[6]

Pseudo-Ambrose from northern Italy (fourth century) anticipated the medieval position when he asserted: 'How can anyone maintain that woman is the likeness of God when she is demonstrably subject to the dominion of man and has no kind of authority? For she can neither teach nor be a witness in a court nor exercise citizenship nor be a judge – then certainly not exercise dominion.'[7]

It must be said in mitigation of what the Fathers thought that they based their arguments on scriptural texts which could be interpreted as ascribing male dominion, and being the image of God, only to men. It is this which we will now have to investigate.

Images of the Creator

The first creation account, Genesis 1:1–2:4, narrates the origin of the universe as a building process by God the architect. The world, as people knew it at the time – that is, in the fourth century BC, was thought of as a huge house. The floor of the house was made up of the flat earth. The sky was its ceiling. The sun, moon and stars were lights for day and night. The fish in the sea, the plants and animals on the land and the birds in the air were seen as furniture put in by God, and as sources of food.

The climax of God's building work was the creation of human beings. They were special because the world was built to be their home. They were also special because, like God, they could think logically and act with responsibility. They carried God's own image. Here follows the crucial text in a literal translation from the original Hebrew:

> God said: 'Let us make a human being (Adam) in our own image, in the likeness of ourselves, and let them rule over the fish of the sea, the birds of heaven, the cattle, all wild beasts and the reptiles that crawl upon the earth'. And God created the human being (Adam) in the image of himself. In the image of God, he created him. Male and female he created them.[8]

Now this passage can be understood in different ways. There was a strong rabbinical tradition that interpreted the text as stating that only the man was created in God's image. The word 'Adam' can be understood as 'man, male' or as 'human being', just like *homo* in Latin, *homme* in French or *man* in traditional English. Since the text says literally, 'In the image of God he created *him*', it *could* be interpreted as referring to the male person only. Many Rabbis favoured this interpretation because it agreed with the position of predominance which men enjoyed both in social and in religious life.[9] It was this rabbinical understanding of the inferior position of women that explains a very common prayer among male Jews until recently. In the so-called eighteen blessings they would thank God three times a day with these words: 'Blessed are you, Lord our God, king of the universe, for not having made me a Gentile, for not having made me a slave, for not having made me a woman.'

The original text should, however, for many reasons, be read in a different way.

(a) The word 'Adam' is obviously meant in its collective sense. This is clearly expressed by the following line: 'male and female he created them'.

(b) That both male and female are included is also clear from the fact that giving dominion over the other creatures is explicitly given to both men and women. 'God blessed them and said to them: "Be fruitful . . . and take charge of all living things . . . !" ' This is precisely the aspect in which human beings are reflecting God's image as creator.

(c) It can also be shown from this parallel passage in Genesis: 'When God created the human being [Adam], he made him in the likeness of God. Male and female he created them, and he blessed them and named them "human being" [*Adam*] when they were created.'[10]

(d) Two other Old Testament texts that comment on God creating human beings according to his image, apply this to both men and women.[11]

A helper or an equal?

The second creation story also influenced the thinking about man and woman. It describes how God drew the woman from the man, and is usually translated as follows:

> For the man there was not found a helper fit for him. So the Lord God caused a deep sleep to fall upon the man, and while he slept took one of his ribs and closed up its place with flesh. And the rib which the Lord God had taken from the man he made into a woman.[12]

In the rabbinical tradition which downgraded women, this text was explained as clearly demonstrating women's dependence on men. Man was created first. Woman came later, to be a helper to man. After all, woman was only a 'rib' of man's.[13] It would lead to many snide observations, as this one from the Middle Ages: 'A woman is more carnal than a man, as is clear from her many carnal abominations. It should be noted that there was a defect in the formation of the first woman, since she was formed from a bent rib, that is, a rib of the breast, which is bent as it were in a contrary direction to a man. And since through this defect she is an imperfect animal, she always deceives.'[14]

However, the original text is far more subtle and more just to women's status. The Hebrew word that was commonly translated as 'rib' (*tsela*) actually means 'side'. It stands for the side of a mountain, the side of the Tabernacle, the sides of the altar, the side wings of the Temple gates, and the sides or wings of the Temple building.[15] In fact, in no other verse of Scripture is the word *tsela* translated as 'rib'. The original text therefore says that God took one side – that is, one half – of the human being and formed it into Eve.[16]

This corresponds well to the ancient conception, according to which the original human being was male and female at the same time; this is technically known as him/her having been androgynous. From a description in Plato,[17] we know that the original human being was imagined to carry two faces, looking in opposite directions. It had four arms and walked on four legs. To make the two sexes, the creator God cut the human being into two halves, giving each half one face, two arms and two legs. We find a similar tradition among the rabbis.[18] So this is a better translation of the passage in Genesis:

> The Lord God made the human being (Adam) fall into a deep sleep. While he was sleeping, God took a 'side' from it and closed the gap with flesh. Then the Lord God built a 'wo-man' from the side he had taken from the human being. And he introduced her to the human being. The human being exclaimed: 'This at last is bones from my bones and flesh from my flesh! She will be called "wo-man" because she was split off from a man.' That is why a man leaves his father and mother and clings to his 'wo-man'. And so they become (again) one body.[19]

Whatever the details of this original concept, the scriptural text clearly states that woman is truly equal to man. She was not created separately, like the animals, after the human being had been created. She was truly 'the other half', 'flesh of my flesh and bones of my bones'. Rather than teaching the subjection of woman to man, this text proclaims their basic equality as human beings.[20]

What about Pauline texts?

Paul endorsed the new position of women as equal to men, a position which had come about through baptism in Christ. He states it explicitly: 'There is no longer man or woman . . . we are all one in Christ.'[21] However, at times, as a former rabbi, he could not help but fall back on some of the ancient reasoning. When he wrote to the new community in Corinth, he was upset about the fact that some women had stopped wearing a veil, as was the Jewish custom. Scholars do not agree about why Paul considered this such an important point. Could it be that by praying with their hair loosened, the Christian women of Corinth were giving the impression of imitating a Hellenistic cult?[22] Whatever his reason, Paul argues at length. Amongst his reasons, he refers to the old rabbinical interpretation of Genesis:

> For a man should not cover his head for he is the image of God and reflects God's glory. But a wife reflects her husband's glory. For man was not created from woman, but woman from man. Neither was man created for woman, but woman for man.[23]

These words of Paul were picked up in later tradition as a confirmation of the Genesis reading, according to which, it was thought, only a man is created in God's image, and not a woman. However, are we allowed to give such weight to these words of Paul?

To assess the doctrinal weight of this text we have to consider it in its context. Paul had heard from some Christians who visited him in Ephesus that there were uncontrolled scenes of trance and speaking in tongues during their prayer meetings.[24] It would seem that, as an expression of ecstatic frenzy, some women were tempted to take off their veils and loosen their hair. Perhaps they prayed with their arms raised high and their heads thrown back, as was the custom in certain oriental cults.[25] This must have upset other members of the community. Paul worried about it because it threatened to destroy order and peace. In a typically rabbinical fashion he begins to argue. He presents many reasons:[26]

- 'The head of every man is Christ, the head of every woman is her husband, etc.' (verse 3).
- 'A woman who prays with her head unveiled dishonours her head – it is as if she were shaven bald, etc.' (verses 4–6).
- 'For a man ought not to cover his head, since he is the image and glory of God; but woman is the glory of man' (verse 7).
- 'For man was not made from woman, but woman from man' (verse 8).
- 'Neither was man created for woman, but woman for man' (verse 9).
- 'That is why a woman ought to have a veil on her head, because of the angels' (verse 10).[27]
- [Pauline correction:] 'Nevertheless, in the Lord woman is not different from man, nor man from woman.[28] Woman may come from man, but man is born from woman. And all come from God' (verses 11–12).
- 'Judge for yourselves: is it proper for a woman to pray with her head unveiled? Does not nature itself teach you that for a man to wear long hair is degrading, but if a woman has long hair it is her pride . . . etc.' (verses 13–15).
- 'If anyone is disposed to be contentious, we recognise no other practice, nor do the churches of God!' (verse 16).

Remember, Paul's main point is that he wants women to cover their hair with a veil when they attend the Christian assembly. It is clear that he is just piling reasons on top of each other which he himself realises are 'rationalisations'; that is, they are not statements in their own right, but remarks that serve a limited purpose. He indicates this by correcting himself and by admitting that one could disagree with his arguments.

Rationalisations

We can compare this to some other passages in Paul:

It has been reported to me by Chloe's people that there is quarrelling among you. What I mean is that each one of you says, 'I belong to Paul', or 'I belong to Apollos', or 'I belong to Cephas', or 'I belong to Christ'.

- Is Christ divided?
- Was Paul crucified for you?
- Or were you baptised in the name of Paul?
- I am thankful that I baptised none of you except Crispus and Gaius; lest anyone should say that you were baptised in my name.
- I did baptise also the household of Stephanas.
- Beyond that, I do not remember whether I baptised anyone else. For Christ did not send me to baptise but to preach the gospel.[29]

Now if we analyse this passage we see that Paul is mainly concerned about stopping the Corinthians from forming parties within the community. He rationalises to argue his point, but in doing so he utters some absurd statements which would not make any sense in themselves. Is he really grateful for not having baptised anyone? He also corrects himself a couple of times – 'I baptised no one else . . . Of course, there was Stephanas . . . I remember no one else!' – even though he was speaking under inspiration! Finally, he says that he did not come to baptise, in spite of Jesus' command for his disciples to go out and baptise all nations! It is clear that this passage of Paul teems with rationalisations, which may not be interpreted as a list of dogmatic statements.

And what about this passage in the Letter to Titus?

There are many insubordinate men who must be silenced . . . One of them, a prophet among them, has witnessed: 'Cretans are always liars, beasts, and gluttons'. And this statement expresses the truth. So correct them with severity.[30]

The main purpose of the author is to make Titus, the Bishop of Crete, stand firm against some troublesome Jewish converts. However, what about the terrible condemnation of Cretans followed by the ominous words *and this statement expresses the truth*? Does this mean that, under inspiration, we are told that Cretans are always liars, beasts and gluttons? Cretans were considered cheats in the Greek world. To 'crete' about something (*krêtizein* in Greek) meant as much as 'to tell lies' about that subject. Plutarch mentions a saying 'to crete to the Cretan', meaning 'to cheat a cheat, to pay a charlatan with the same coin'.[31] Is it not clear that we are dealing here with a rationalisation, a thing said in the heat of an argument, which is not to be taken as a dogmatic statement?

The same applies to Paul's statement regarding the man being in the image of God and not the woman. He is falling back on rabbinical argumentation in the heat of the discussion. His true intention in this is

75

made clear when finally he says: 'Judge for yourselves; is it proper for a woman to pray to God with her head uncovered?' What Paul is saying about only man being in God's image is clearly a *rationalisation*, and not a formal theological assertion.

Moreover, Paul, who was more a true Christian rather than an Old Testament rabbi, immediately saw the weakness of his own argument. It needed correcting. In Paul's days it was not possible to erase text, as we do on the computer today, or even to scratch out passages, which could be read afterwards anyway. So after the offending passage he adds: 'but remember, in the Lord woman is not independent of man nor man of woman, for as woman was made from man, so man is born of woman. And all things are from God.'[32] In other words, as Paul so often does in his letters, he corrects himself and now states that 'in the Lord', (that is, in Christ) man and woman are truly equal. They depend on each other and each in his or her own way derives his or her existence from the other. Paul hereby amends the old rabbinical tradition – but, unfortunately, this correction was not picked up by tradition. People quoted the earlier lines, not the later ones!

No Catholic theologian today would support the belief that women are not created in God's image, or are created less in God's image than men are. With this admission, the whole medieval scheme of higher and lower status tumbles down. If women too carry God's image, women too are capable of leadership – and of exercising priestly authority. But had women not been forbidden to teach?

READINGS FROM THE WOMEN PRIESTS WEBSITE

John Wijngaards
The creation accounts in Genesis and women
            http://www.womenpriests.org/scriptur/genesis.htm
Discussion of 1 Corinthians 11:2–16
            http://www.womenpriests.org/scriptur/1cor11.htm
Explaining rationalisations
            http://www.womenpriests.org/scriptur/rational.htm
John Duns Scotus (1266–1308)
Actual text
            http://www.womenpriests.org/theology/scotus2.htm
Analysis of his arguments
            http://www.womenpriests.org/theology/scotus1.htm

10

Not Allowed to Teach?

Some years ago I gave a course for Christian writers in the district of Multan in Pakistan. The adult literacy rate among rural men, I was told, is 70 per cent, among women only 15 per cent. Until the advent of TV, the only instruction most people got was the Friday sermon by the *mullah* in the local mosque. It made me understand why the *mullahs* enjoy so much political power in Muslim countries. They have a captive audience. And the situation was not much different in the European Middle Ages. Most of the time only priests could read and write. They were the teachers who instructed the faithful through lengthy sermons at Sunday Mass. The priests controlled the sources of information for only they understood Latin, the language of Scripture, of liturgy, of Church law and theology.

Erasmus (1466–1536) has left us a satirical parody of how some preachers would flaunt their erudition. He describes an experience he had while visiting England.

> Preachers begin with a clever introduction. I have had the privilege of being among the audience of a preacher who was 80 years old and who had such a reputation as a theologian that one could imagine having met Scotus in the flesh. After declaring that he would explain to the common folk the mystery of Jesus' name, he stated with an amazing perspicacity of mind that all that can be said about Jesus' name is already contained in the letters of the word. It was surely an image of the Blessed Trinity, he said, that the word Jesus in Latin can only be inflected in three cases. Next, an unspeakable mystery lies in the fact that the nominative case 'Jesus' ends in 's', that the accusative case 'Jesum' ends in 'm' and the dative case 'Jesu' in 'u', because through these three letters it is indicated that he is *summus* (the highest), *medius* (the middle) and *ultimus* (the last). With a pair of compasses an even more profound mystery could be dug up in the word. He split the word 'Jesus' into two parts in such a way that the third letter remained as the pivot on its own. Then he proved that this letter 's' is called 'syn' in Hebrew. This word 'syn' means, if I am not mistaken, 'sin' in the English language from which, he said, it was as

clear as could be that Jesus takes away the sins of the world. This kind of nonsense preachers call the introduction . . .

In the next part of their speech – which is actually the sermon part itself – preachers explain a small passage from the Gospel, but they do this quickly and superficially, whereas in fact this should have been their main task. Then preachers assume a new character and introduce a theological question, normally one which floats between heaven and earth, obviously convinced that tackling such a question is also part of preaching. This is the moment when real theological pride manifests itself. Quoting each other, they throw about their splendid titles at this juncture, such as sublime teachers, profound and super-profound teachers, indisputable teachers, etc. Then they bamboozle the simple people with syllogisms, majors, minors, conclusions, corollaries, suppositions and more such scholastic nonsense.[1]

Since priests were preachers by definition, we need not be surprised that a presumed prohibition against female teaching in I Timothy was seen as a major obstacle to the ordination of women.

I permit no woman to teach or have authority over men. She is to keep silent. For Adam was formed first, then Eve. And Adam was not deceived, but the woman was deceived and became a transgressor.[2]

It became part of Church law:

Even if a woman is educated and saintly, she still should not presume to instruct men in an assembly. A lay man, however, should not presume to instruct in the presence of the clergy, unless he is asked by them to do so.[3]

From a study of medieval theologians we see that it became a standard argument which authors would copy one from the other. Compare these two texts:

[Women cannot receive holy orders] for it is said (1 Tim. 2:12): 'I suffer not a woman to teach in the Church, nor to use authority over the man.'[4]

Thomas Aquinas (1225–74)

'The office of teaching is conjoined to [holy] orders, but it is not fitting for women or children to teach, as to children because they lack reason and as to women because of the prohibition of the Apostle (Tim. 2). *I do not permit a woman to teach in the Church, nor to rule over her husband, etc.*'[5]

Durandus à Saint-Pourçain (1270–1334)

Now we know that Durandus is quoting Aquinas, or both a common source, for 1 Timothy 2:12 does not mention 'in the Church'. The text is a conflation with 1 Corinthians 14:34, which says: 'Let women keep silence in the churches'.

The mutual dependence is even clearer with other scholars, as we can see from the two extracts below.

> Every Order is received towards the priesthood and teaching. But teaching belongs chiefly to priests, as it is held in *dist. 16. quaest. 1.* We add: and not to Deacons, unless by commission, when a sermon or an instruction is regarded as the reading of the Gospel, which it is fitting for deacons to read. But that deed is prohibited to women, 1. Timoth. 2. *'Let the women learn in silence',* and *'I do not permit them [women] to speak or to teach',* where a gloss [reads], *'not only I but also the Lord does not permit it'*; and this is so because of the weakness of their intellect, and the mutability of their emotions, which they commonly suffer more than men. For a teacher ought to have a lively intellect in the recognition of truth, and stability of emotion in its confirmation.[6]

> *John Duns Scotus (1266–1308)*

> The office of teaching belongs to [Holy] Orders and every Order is arranged towards the priesthood, to whom this office properly belongs (*Dist 16, qu. 1*). We add that it also belongs to the diaconate (*Decret. Dist 25, 'perlectis' r. 92 at 'In facta'*), which should be interpreted thus: that the priest holds the principal office [of teaching] but the deacon by delegation, or that preaching for them means reading the Gospel. But teaching in public is not proper for a woman because of the weakness of her intellect and the instability of her emotions, of which defects women suffer more than men by a notable common law. But a teacher needs to have a vivid intellect to recognise the truth and stable emotions to persist in their expression . . .

> These two reasons we can also extract from the very apt statement in 1 Tim 2: *Let women keep silent in church in all submission – I do not permit a woman to teach nor to rule over a man.*[7]

> *Richard of Middleton (13th century)*

These two Franciscan authors obviously reflect the common thinking of the time: women cannot become priests because Paul has forbidden them to teach in church. And Paul's prohibition makes sense because women are emotionally unstable and intellectually not up to the demands of teaching.

The Congregation for Doctrine maintains that the Pauline prohibition still holds. Because women may not teach in the Christian community, they cannot be ordained priests.

The Apostle's forbidding of women 'to speak' in the assemblies (cf. 1 Cor.

14:34–35, 1 Tim. 2:12) is [not socially conditioned], and exegetes define its meaning in this way: Paul in no way opposes the right, which he elsewhere recognises as possessed by women, to prophesy in the assembly (cf. 1 Cor. 11:5); the prohibition solely concerns the official function of teaching in the Christian assembly. For Saint Paul this prescription is bound up with the divine plan of creation (cf. 1 Cor. 11:7; Gen. 2:18–24): it would be difficult to see in it the expression of a cultural fact. Nor should it be forgotten that we owe to Saint Paul one of the most vigorous texts in the New Testament on the fundamental equality of men and women, as children of God in Christ (cf. Gal. 3:28). Therefore there is no reason for accusing him of prejudices against women, when we note the trust that he shows towards them and the collaboration that he asks of them in his apostolate.[8]

So how to interpret 1 Timothy 2:12 and 1 Corinthians 14:34–35?

Anti-Gnostic measures against women

The prohibition for women to teach should be seen within its context. Like the other pastoral letters, 1 Timothy is now generally accepted by biblical scholarship as having been composed by a disciple of Paul who wrote in the apostle's name to indicate that he stood in the same tradition. It is dated to around AD 100 and was written possibly in Asia Minor or Greece. The main concern of 1 Timothy is to counteract the influence of Gnostic teachers.

The Gnostic teachings were of a mixed Hellenistic and Jewish origin. Gnostic doctrine included dualism, contempt for material things, dependence on *knowledge* (i.e. spiritual experience) rather than faith as a way to salvation, secret wisdom reserved for the elite few and restrictive teachings about sexual practice.

The accusations made by the author are mainly centred on 'speaking' and 'teaching'. He warns of:

- 'fruitless discussion';
- 'ignorant assertions about the law';
- 'wordly fables';
- 'godless philosophical discussions';[9]
- 'wrangling about words';
- 'talking nonsense';
- 'avoiding foolish speculations, the quibbles and disputes about the Law'.[10]

Gnostic teaching endangered men as well as women for we hear the biblical author complain about 'contention and grumbling among the men' and about 'backsliding and apostasy among the women'.[11] Yet, the author seems to be more concerned about women. In Gnostic circles women were upheld and glorified as 'favoured channels of revelation' and feminine imagery was freely applied to God and his/her emanations. The text about women's 'silence in the assembly' should be read in this context.[12] I will comment on the text in some detail.

'Let a woman learn in silence with all submissiveness.' (verse 11)

To whom should women be submissive? Since in our text the object is not specified, it is inappropriate to assume that universally man is the object. The Letter was written to deter women from submitting to false teachers, and so 'the admonition to learn with all submission seems to imply a learning from true teachers'.[13] 'Just as wives (Titus 2:5), children (1 Timothy 3:4), and slaves (Titus 2:9) must be submissive within their households, . . . so the community (especially women in our case), should not have contempt for their ministers.'[14]

'I permit no woman to teach or to have authority over men. She is to keep silent.' (verse 12)

There is no doubt about the fact that the author of 1 Timothy had imposed a prohibition on women that forbade them to teach or to have authority in his Christian assembly. However, the main question is: was this just a local and temporal prohibition, or a universal norm imposed under inspiration for all time to come? We can deduce that it was only a temporary and local prohibition from the following considerations:

1. When the verb 'to permit' (*epitrepsein*) is used in the New Testament, it refers to a specific permission in a specific context.[15] Moreover, the use of the indicative tense indicates an immediate context. The correct translation, therefore, is: 'I am not presently allowing';[16] 'I have decided that for the moment women are not to teach or have authority over men'.[17]
2. We know for a fact that Paul allowed women to speak prophetically in the assembly.[18] Women functioned in the Church as deaconesses.[19] We know, therefore, that women did speak in the assemblies. 1 Timothy 2:12 is an exception, a later ruling to counteract a specific threat.
3. The immediate context of the prohibition was the danger of Gnostic teaching that at the time affected mainly women. Enlarging its purpose to including a permanent norm for all time goes beyond the literal sense of the text and the intended scope of the biblical author.

The overall meaning of this verse is, therefore: 'Until women have learned what they need in order to get a full grasp of the true teaching, they are not to teach or have authority over men.'[20]

81

For Adam was formed first, then Eve. (verse 13)

And Adam was not deceived, but the woman was deceived and became a transgressor. (verse 14)

Yet woman will be saved through bearing children, if she continues in faith and love and holiness, with modesty. (verse 15)

It is clear that these verses are not carefully considered theological statements. This is because, strictly speaking, they do not make sense. If Eve is subject to Adam because she was created later, Adam and Eve are subject to the animals because they were created after the animals.[21] Then, according to the first creation story, Adam and Eve were created simultaneously: 'God created him, male and female he created them'.[22] Also, Adam was equally deceived and equally guilty as the story makes clear.[23] Pain in childbirth and being dominated by their husbands were seen as punishments for Eve, but the victory of woman over evil is ignored by our author. Are these heavy doctrinal pronouncements?

Why then did the biblical author of 1 Timothy quote the second creation story in Genesis so clumsily to back up his opinion? No doubt, the use of Genesis to teach women a lesson was common among Jewish expositors, as we saw in the previous chapter. But the Gnostics also used the creation story. These verses may well have been 'a polemic directed against several misconceptions concerning Adam and Eve'.[24] 'The gospel is struggling in Ephesus with Gnostic-influenced women trumpeting a feminist reinterpretation of Adam and Eve as a precedent for their own spiritual primacy and authority.'[25]

The polemic against Gnostic teachers may reveal the author's real point. In Genesis, Eve was deceived by the snake and transgressed; in Ephesus some women were deceived by false teachers, and for this reason they transgressed. Since, according to 1 Timothy 2:14, the emphasis is on the fact that Adam was not the one who was deceived, it reveals the context in which the letter was written, i.e. women are the ones who were causing the trouble. Therefore the author of 1 Timothy was addressing a specific situation.

It is possible that it was just the author's patriarchal prejudice against women, rather than the specific Gnostic context, that caused his rather anti-feminine outburst. If so, there is even more reason not to take this broken and clumsy interpretation of the creation story to be solemnly defined doctrine. These verses about Adam and Eve are typical rationalisations – that is, as we have seen, *ad hoc* reasonings to underscore something stated. They could only be fully understood by a specific audience within the context of the letter, and therefore had a limited scope.

The tragedy is that these verses were extensively used in later tradition to justify contemporary prejudices against women. They were supposed to prove from the inspired Scriptures that God subjected women to men and that women are more susceptible to temptation and deception.

A gloss in 1 Corinthians

The text of 1 Corinthians 14:33–34 is usually quoted in tandem with 1 Timothy. It states:

> As in all the churches of the saints, the women should keep silence in the churches. For they are not permitted to speak, but should be subordinate, as even the law says.

The passage has clearly been inserted into Paul's original letter at a later time The interpolation can be inferred from the following facts:

- Verses 34–35 appear *after* verse 40 in a number of important old manuscripts: the Claromontanus of Paris, the Boernerianus of Dresden, Minuscule nr 88, and versions of the Old Latin translation (the *Itala*, 2nd – 4th centuries). It shows that the verses were a gloss written in the margin of the original papyrus, which entered the body of the text in later copies.
- The rule that women should 'keep silence in the churches' (v. 34) flatly contradicts what Paul says about women prophesying in church in 1 Corinthians 11:5. See also: 'Whoever prophesies speaks to people for their upbuilding and encouragement and consolation'.[26]
- The phrase 'as even the Law says' (v. 34) contradicts Paul's teaching that we have been liberated from the Law.[27]

Although in 1 Timothy 2:12 the author used *didaskein* (teaching), while in 1 Corinthians 11:35 the word used is *lalein* (speaking), the parallelism of the two texts on women's/wives' restrictions is generally accepted by scholars. Probably 1 Corinthians 14:34–35 stems from a similar origin to 1 Timothy 2:11–14 – that is, an effort in Asia Minor of around AD 100 to counteract the Gnostic recruitment of women.

The limitation of biblical statements

The context of the passages restricting women from teaching in the assembly shows these texts not to have permanent validity for all time to come. They are passages with a limited scope. Is this rare in scripture? The answer is no: scripture abounds with statements, assertions, sayings, admonitions, prescriptions that had only a restricted reach.

- Remember Paul's advice to Timothy: 'Stop drinking just water. Drink a little wine. It will ease your indigestion and frequent illnesses.'[28] – Was this a revelation from God to teach us about the benefits of drinking wine?
- And Jesus said: 'Do not call yourself "teacher", for you have one Teacher and you are all brothers and sisters. Call no man "father" on earth, for you have one Father, who is in heaven.' – Did Jesus really forbid these titles for all time to come?
- 'I tell you, do not take any oaths . . . Let what you say be simply "Yes" or "No".' – Did Jesus ban the taking of sworn statements in court for all time to come? Was that his real intention?
- 'Do not offer resistance to violence. If someone strikes you on the right cheek, turn to him the other too.' – Did Jesus veto self-defence? Did he prohibit a state to have police or an army for all time to come?[29]

Why would a provisional and temporary prohibition have validity for all time to come? Can this really be considered a valid reason to exclude women from Holy Orders?

READINGS FROM THE WOMEN PRIESTS WEBSITE

Richard of Middleton (13th century)
on women priests, introduction
>   http://www.womenpriests.org/theology/middlto1.htm
on women priests, actual text
>   http://www.womenpriests.org/theology/middlton.htm
John Wijngaards
Discussion of 1 Timothy 2:11–15
>   http://www.womenpriests.org/scriptur/timothy.htm
Discussion of 1 Corinthians 14:33–34
>   http://www.womenpriests.org/scriptur/1cor14.htm
Explaining the principle of limited scope
>   http://www.womenpriests.org/scriptur/intscope.htm

11
Carrying the Burden of Eve's Sin?

It was only in the early Middle Ages that the ordination of women began to be discussed in theological treatises. It was always dismissed out of hand, usually with just a few lines of justification. The reasons given are instructive. Let us listen to Guido of Baysius's judgement in 1296:

> Women are unfit to receive ordination, for ordination is reserved for perfect members of the church, since it is given for the distribution of grace to other men. But women are not perfect members of the church, only men are.
>
> Moreover, woman was the effective cause of damnation since she was the origin of transgression and Adam was deceived through her, and thus she cannot be the effective cause of salvation, because holy orders cause grace in others and so salvation.[1]

For Guido, women are not perfect members of the Church because they do not reflect the glory of God.[2] Moreover, woman was the effective cause of damnation. This applies not only to Eve, but to all women. All women are defiled by sin and cannot administer grace. It is like saying that all women are carrying an incurable, infectious disease such as AIDS and can therefore not be doctors or nurses. Then what about Jesus' mother, Mary? Guido has his answer ready: 'A woman can be the cause of salvation *in a material way.* Indeed because woman was [after all] taken from man in a material way since she was made from Adam's rib. And in this way [that is, only materially] the Virgin Mary had to be the cause of salvation. And this is true that the female sex was the material cause of our salvation since Christ our salvation proceeded materially from the Blessed Virgin.'[3]

For medieval theologians, every woman carries the curse of sin. The consequences were that God punished her by subjecting her to man and this punishment was irreversible. She could not be ordained to any spiritual ministry. She always had to be treated with circumspection as a lasting source of temptation. On the question of why a mother remains unclean for forty days after giving birth to a son, but for eighty days after giving birth to a daughter, the Franciscan theologian Sicardus replies: 'Why was the time for a female child doubled? Solution: because a double curse lies on the feminine growth. For she carries the curse of Adam and also the [punishment] "you will give birth in pain".'[4]

And the law book of the Church made the curse official:

> Women must cover their heads because they are not the image of God. They must do this as a sign of their subjection to authority and because sin came into the world through them . . . Because of original sin, they must show themselves submissive.[5]

The opinion of the Fathers of the Church

The early Greek Fathers held no such idea as the curse of Eve lying on women. St Ignatius of Antioch (died AD 110) taught that the fall came through a woman, but so came redemption.[6] St Irenaeus (c.140–203) stated that, though the devil defeated the human race through a woman, he also lost through a woman, namely Mary, Jesus' mother.[7] He even maintained that Adam was more to blame than Eve.

> If you say that the devil attacked Eve as being the weaker of the two, [I reply that] on the contrary, she was the stronger, since she appears to have been the helper of the man in the transgression of the commandment. For she did all by herself resist the serpent, and it was after holding out for a while and after offering resistance that she ate of the tree, being tricked by deceit; whereas Adam, making no fight whatever, nor refusal, simply took the fruit handed to him by the woman, which is an indication of the utmost imbecility and effeminacy of mind. And the woman, indeed, deserves pardon since she was defeated in the contest by the devil; but Adam deserves none, for he gave in to the woman – although he had personally received the command from God.[8]

Such Greek voices were soon silenced by the Latin Fathers who began to explain women's subject state as a consequence of Eve's role in original sin. Tertullian (155–245) was one of the worst. Listen to this masterpiece of undiluted prejudice:

> Every woman should be walking about as Eve, mourning and repentant, in order that by every garb of penitence she might the more fully expiate that which she derives from Eve – the ignominy, I mean, of the first sin, and the odium [attaching to her as the cause] of human perdition. 'In pains and in anxiety you will bear children, woman; and you will desire your husband, but he will lord it over you.' And do you not know that you are [each] an Eve? *The*

sentence of God on this sex of yours lives on in this age: the guilt must of necessity live on too.

You are the devil's gateway!

You violated that [forbidden] tree!

You were the first to desert divine law!

You were she who persuaded him whom the devil was not valiant enough to attack (Adam)!

You destroyed so easily God's image, man!

On account of what you deserved – that is, death – even the Son of God had to die![9]

Now we should read Tertullian's words carefully. 'The sentence of God on this sex of yours lives on in this age.' What did he mean? What was the sentence of God? Being under the dominion of men. How do we know that it lives on in this age, in spite of Christ? Because women are still under the dominion of men! Remember Roman law?[10] Women were owned by their husbands and subject to their every command. Women could not hold any public responsibility or exercise any authority. They could not be witnesses in a court case or represent themselves. If so, Tertullian argues, God's punishment still lies on women! But God does not punish without guilt: 'The sentence of God on this sex of yours lives on in this age: [this means that] the guilt must of necessity live on too.' Therefore, every woman still carries the guilt of Eve's sin!

It becomes a theme repeated by many of the Fathers. St Chrysostom (344–407) reasoned like this: 'Does Eve's sin affect other women? Certainly; for the whole sex is weak and fickle, and scripture speaks of the sex collectively. For it says not Eve, but 'the woman ate', which is the common name of the whole sex, not her proper name. Was then the whole sex included in the transgression for her fault? . . . Yes, the whole female sex transgressed, and not the male.'[11]

St Jerome (347–419) repeatedly said that the punishment of Eve rests on every woman. But women can escape the punishment by bearing children, or even better by remaining virgins.[12] In a letter to Lucinus, a wealthy Spaniard who, together with his wife Theodora, had made a vow of sexual abstinence, Jerome stated that his wife had now 'become a man'. 'She was once your partner in the flesh but is now your partner in the spirit; once your wife but now your sister; once an inferior but now an equal; once a woman but now a man.'[13] The curious reasoning is, therefore, that *as a wife* Theodora carried God's curse of subjection. By abstaining from sexual intercourse she is free from the curse – and has become a man.

What do we find in Scripture?

Genesis 3:1–24 describes our human sinful condition in the myth of our two original ancestors, Adam and Eve. Both the man and the woman share in the rebellion against God. Both feel guilty and ashamed. On both, hardship is inflicted as punishment. The text then mentions examples of typical human hardship: a man's toil to produce a crop on hostile land, a woman's pain in childbirth and domination by the husband.

To the woman God says: 'I will multiply your pains in childbirth. You shall give birth to your children in pain. You will long for your husband, but he will lord it over you.' This is not to be understood as a licence to husbands to keep their wives in submission. It is a statement of fact. It notes the consequences of sin. In a perfect world men would not need to struggle to grow crops amidst drought, disease and locusts. In the same perfect world, women would not have pain in childbirth or face bullying by their husbands. This is now the accepted interpretation of Catholic scholarship.[14]

The rabbis interpreted this in terms of the guilt and punishment of women. This crops up in 1 Timothy 2:14 where the author adduces additional reasons for women to stick to a subservient role.

> For Adam was formed first, then Eve. And Adam was not deceived, but the woman was deceived and became a transgressor. Yet woman will be saved through bearing children, if she continues in faith and love and holiness, with modesty.

As I have shown in the previous chapter, these rationalisations were added in the context of pastoral concern that women could become entangled in Gnostic sects. It is clear that these verses are not carefully considered theological statements. And just think of the absurdity of imputing to later women guilt for Eve's transgression.

- Parents may not be put to death for their children, nor children for their parents. Each person should die for their own sin.[15]
- Even the Old Testament taught complete forgiveness: 'Though your sins are like scarlet, they shall be white as snow. Though they are red as crimson, they shall be like wool.'[16]
- If Eve's transgression was part of original sin, which it is not, it would still be wiped out by baptism. For baptism forgives all sins, including original sin.
- If some guilt would still cling to women, why would a similar guilt not cling to men? For God is not a respecter of persons and in Christ the distinction between men and women has vanished.[17]

In spite of all this, the official law of the Church maintained that women should be kept in submission also because of their responsibility for bringing sin into the world. I will set out here the official text from the *Corpus Iuris Canonici*, which I have provided with headings and comments to facilitate its reading.

[A legal question]

May a woman lay an accusation against a priest?

[The legal answer]

It seems not, because as Pope Fabian says, neither complaint nor testimony may be raised against the priests of the Lord by those who do not have, and cannot have, the same status with them.

Women cannot, however, be promoted to the priesthood or even the diaconate and for this reason they may not raise a complaint or give testimony against priests in court. This is shown both in the sacred canons [i.e. Church regulations] and the laws [i.e. Roman and civil laws].

[My comment]

Notice that the exclusion of women from ordination, cited as part of the argument, is based both on previous church laws and on civil law, which was the ancient Roman law! The law he refers to is mainly the principle that no woman can hold any authority.

[A legal objection]

However, it would seem that whoever can be a judge may not be prevented from being a plaintiff and women became judges in the Old Testament, as is clearly shown in the book of Judges [Deborah was a judge]. So those cannot be excluded from the role of plaintiff who have often fulfilled the role of judge and who are not forbidden by any word of Scripture to act as plaintiff. . . .

[The legal answer]

In the Old Testament much was permitted which today [i.e. in the New Testament] is abolished, through the perfection of grace. So if [in the Old Testament] women were permitted to judge the people, today because of sin, which woman brought into the world, women are admonished by the Apostle [Paul] to be careful to practise a modest restraint, to be subject to men and to veil themselves as a sign of subjugation.[18]

[My comment]

In other words, because of the enduring sin that rests on women – for they brought sin into the world – women are not allowed to hold authority in the New Testament, as they could in the Old. This shows that we live in a time of more perfect grace!

Rarely in my 45 years as a theologian have I come across such utterly ridiculous and twisted thinking. Yet the above text was part of the Church's official book of law, the *Corpus Iuris Canonici*, until 1918. This was the

kind of reasoning with which women were barred from priestly ordination.[19]

READINGS FROM THE WOMEN PRIESTS WEBSITE

Readings from 'tradition' on women carrying Eve's
guilt

> http://www.womenpriests.org/traditio/sinful.htm

Four articles on the psychological and social effects
of the negative Eve myth:

Anne Baring

'The Separation from Nature and the Loss of the
Feminine Aspect of Spirit'

> http://www.womenpriests.org/body/baring1.htm

'The Myth of the Fall and the Doctrine of Original
Sin'

> http://www.womenpriests.org/body/baring2.htm

Anne Baring and Jules Cashford

'Eve the Mother of all the Living'

> http://www.womenpriests.org/body/baring3.htm

'Eve in Christian Culture'

> http://www.womenpriests.org/body/baring4.htm

12

Deliberately Left Out by Jesus Christ?

In all its recent statements the Congregation for Doctrine has made clear that it considers Jesus Christ himself as the origin of the tradition of not ordaining women in the Catholic Church. By not making a woman a member of the apostolic team, it claims, Jesus set a permanent norm, which the Church will never be able to change.

> Jesus Christ did not call any woman to become part of the Twelve. If he acted in this way, it was not in order to conform to the customs of his time, for his attitude towards women was quite different from that of his milieu, and he deliberately and courageously broke with it . . . It must be recognised that we have here a number of convergent indications that make all the more remarkable the fact that Jesus did not entrust the apostolic charge to women.[1]

> The Church holds that it is not admissible to ordain women to the priesthood, for very fundamental reasons. These reasons include the example recorded in the Sacred Scriptures of Christ choosing his apostles only from among men; the constant practice of the Church which has imitated Christ in choosing only men; and her living teaching authority which has consistently held that the exclusion of women from the priesthood is in accordance with God's plan for his Church. The Gospels and the Acts of the Apostles attest that this calling (of men only) was made in accordance with God's eternal plan. Christ chose those whom he willed (cf. Mk 3:13–14; Jn 6:17), and he did so in union with the Father, 'through the Holy Spirit', after having spent the night in prayer (cf. Lk 6:12). Therefore, in granting admission to the ministerial priesthood to men alone, the Church has always acknowledged as a perennial norm her Lord's way of acting in choosing twelve men whom he made the foundation of His Church (cf. Rev. 21:14).[2]

The teaching authorities in Rome therefore declare that the omission of women from the apostolic team was a deliberate act on the part of Jesus, something he had decided upon in prayer after consulting the Father in the Holy Spirit. By not choosing women, he had, in fact, laid down a permanent norm, a rule the Church would never be able to change. They also say that this is the reason why, in tradition, women were not admitted to ordination.

What do we find in tradition itself?

It is not true that early tradition consciously based the exclusion of women on a decision taken by Jesus. The exclusion of women from ordination was simply a bare fact, hardly reflected upon. The real reasons, as we saw in the previous chapters, were the presumed inferior status of women and their womanly 'infirmity', referring to menstruation.

Early tradition has a few references to Jesus' omitting women from the apostolic twelve, but these bear clearly the hallmark of being rationalisations, i.e. external reasons given to cover up one's real reasons and motives. Let us examine them in a little more detail.

The earliest reference is found in the so-called '*Didascalia*', a fourth-century document from Syria containing admonitions for various groups in the Church, admonitions which were presented as spoken by the apostles. The instruction is particularly concerned about the influence of pastoral workers known as the 'widows'. Let me give some information about this first.

From the earliest apostolic times we see older women playing a pastoral role in the community: 'The aged women must conduct themselves as befits a holy calling; they must not be given to slander or drunken habits; they must teach what is good and train the young women to love their husbands and children.'[3] Here the widowed state seems to imply a demand for perfection and some kind of a mission directed to the young women of the community. 'Honour widows who are widows indeed . . . A widow indeed is one who has put her trust in God and perseveres day and night in the intercessions and the prayers. Before she can be inscribed on the role, a widow must be sixty years old at least, once married, one who has practised hospitality, washed the feet of the saints and been given to all good works.'[4] The interesting point is the enrolment on a register and the conditions it requires, for this makes it plain that we are concerned here not with all widows, but with some of their number who constitute a special category in the community. This is the first indication we have of an *order of widows*, parallel to the clerical orders in the Church.[5]

During the second and third centuries the order of 'widows' had acquired a clear position on the pastoral scene. The author of the *Didascalia* addressed a long chapter to widows. He was worried in particular about their presuming to instruct non-Christians without adequate knowledge. Here is the excerpt that refers to Christ's example:

> For the Lord God, Jesus Christ our teacher, sent us the twelve to instruct the people and the Gentiles; and there were with us women disciples, Mary Magdalene and Mary the daughter of James and the other Mary; but he did not send them to instruct the people with us. For if it were required that women should teach, our Master himself would have commanded these to give instruction with us.[6]

If we read this *by itself* – as it is quoted in Roman documents – we get the wrong impression. The reference to Jesus' example is only secondary. The real reason for worry is the danger of widows turning away prospective converts by an inapt presentation of Christian doctrine. Here is the text that immediately precedes the above quote, put within its structural framework:

[The central concern]

When a widow is asked a question by anyone, let her not straightaway give an answer, except only in general concerning salvation and faith in God; but let her send those that desire to be instructed to the leaders of the Church. And if people ask them questions, let the widows restrict themselves only to the refutation of idols and to the unity of God. But concerning punishment and reward, and the kingdom of the name of Christ, and his mysteries, neither a widow nor a layman ought to speak.

[Main reason: prospective converts may misunderstand Christian doctrine]

For when they [widows or lay people] speak without the knowledge of doctrine, they will bring blasphemy upon the word. For our Lord compared the word of his good news to mustard; but mustard, unless it be skilfully tempered, is bitter and sharp to those who use it. Therefore our Lord said in the Gospel, to widows and to all the laity: 'Cast not your pearls before swine, lest they trample upon them and turn against you and attack you.' For when the Gentiles who are being instructed hear the word of God not fittingly spoken, as it ought to be, unto edification of eternal life, how that our Lord clothed himself in a body, and concerning the passion of Christ: they will mock and scoff, instead of applauding the word of doctrine.

[Rationalization 1: Women are inferior]

This will happen all the more if the instruction is spoken to them by a woman – and she shall incur a heavy judgement for sin.

[Rationalization 2: Women should not teach (from 1 Tim. 2:11–15?)]

It is neither right nor necessary, therefore, that women should be teachers, and especially concerning the name of Christ and the redemption of his passion. For you have not been appointed to this, oh women, and especially

widows, that you should teach, but that you should pray and entreat the Lord
God.

[Rationalization 3: Jesus Christ did not send women to teach]

For the Lord God, Jesus Christ our teacher, sent us the twelve to instruct the
people and the Gentiles; and there were with us women disciples, Mary
Magdalene and Mary the daughter of James and the other Mary; but he did
not send them to instruct the people with us. For if it were required that
women should teach, our Master himself would have commanded these to
give instruction with us.[7]

The example of Jesus, seen in context, is no more than a rationalisation
to stop widows from making mistakes in the delicate area of instructing
converts. It follows on a clear expression of prejudice against women and
a misunderstood scripture text.[8] It has nothing to do with the ordination
of women. And, in spite of its wording, it is not the intention of the
author to exclude *other* women from teaching. For in the next chapter
the *Didascalia* tells women deacons to look after women converts, to

teach and instruct them how the seal of baptism ought to be kept unbroken
in purity and holiness. For this cause we say that the ministry of a woman
deacon is especially needful and important. For our Lord and Saviour also
was assisted in his ministry by women ministers, Mary Magdalene, and Mary
the daughter of James and mother of Jose, and the mother of the sons of
Zebedee, with other women beside. And there is a need of the ministry of a
deaconess for many things; for a deaconess is required to go into the houses
of the heathen where there are believing women, etc.[9]

In other words, the quote cannot be used to demonstrate that women
were not ordained priests because of the norm Jesus had set. Referring
to Jesus as an example in this was an aside.

Now the *Didascalia* was a treatise which was purported to have been
written by the apostles at the time of the Council of Jerusalem (AD 50).
Putting the instructions in the mouths of the apostles was probably just
a literary device, but how were later readers to know? So the text was
considered official teaching, carrying the authority of the apostles.[10]

And now what I call *the original sin effect* occurred. The initial misguided text assumed in later centuries the stature of an established truth.
Compare it to a fog in which drivers tend to focus on the tail lights of
cars in front of them. If the first one makes a false turn and drives into
a ditch, many others will follow his/her example. This is what happened
to the *Didascalia* passage.

The text was quoted by Epiphanius of Cyprus (315–403) in the context
of a diatribe against women who functioned as priests in the Collyrian

sect. Epiphanius was a misogynist who described women as 'feeble, untrustworthy and of mediocre intelligence'. He also says in the same passage: 'Of course, the devil knows how to make women spew forth ridiculous teachings', and, 'the Church has to fight such feminine madness'. The *Disdascalia* text also found its way into the *Statutua Ecclesiae Antiqua* (eighth-century France) and from there into the earliest law books of the Church (Gratian 1140).

It is instructive to read a reflection by Scotus (1266–1308) in his discussion on why women cannot be ordained priests. He says:

> I do not believe that by the institution of the Church or by the precept of the apostles there was removed any useful degree [ecclesiastical grade?] towards salvation from any person, and much less from a whole sex in life. Therefore if neither the apostles nor the Church are able to remove from any one person, and much less from the whole female sex, any useful degree towards salvation, unless Christ, who is their head, intended that it be removed, then it must be that Christ, who instituted this sacrament, laid it down by precept.[11]

In other words, the Church could not by itself leave women out. It *must* have been done on Jesus' explicit command! But that is precisely begging the question. There was no explicit command. So, let us go back to Jesus.

Non-decisions by Jesus

What can we prove from the non-fact of Jesus not choosing women among the twelve apostles? The answer is: nothing. There are so many significant elements in our Catholic faith and practice that Jesus did not decide, but which were later decided upon by the Church. Often it involved modifying what Jesus himself had done.

- Although Jesus followed a liberal interpretation of Jewish law, such as is clear from the way he looked on the Sabbath, he never abolished Mosaic Law as such.[12] At the Council of Jerusalem in AD 51, the leaders of the Early Church declared that Mosaic Law was no longer a matter of obligation to Christians except with regard to some practical pastoral measures.
- Jesus Christ formed various groups of disciples, such as the 12 apostles, the 72 disciples and the band of women disciples.[13] It was left to the Church gradually to give a more concrete expression to the sacrament of ordination. This resulted first in the establishment of deacons, then in appointing overseers (bishops) and elders (priests). It is only by the time of the Council of Trent that these three 'holy orders' were clearly

distinguished from the many minor ministries which had also arisen in the course of time.

- Jesus gave the power to bind and to loosen and to forgive sins.[14] However, it was only gradually that the sacrament of confession fully developed. This also applies to the legal conditions of 'jurisdiction' – that is, who has the sacramental power to forgive sins, as is now contained in Church law.

- Jesus did not specify anything regarding the sacraments of marriage, confirmation and anointing of the sick. Perhaps the beginning of these sacraments can be seen in some of Jesus' symbolic actions such as the miracle at the wedding of Cana, or his healing the sick. But Jesus did not in any way explicitly institute any of these sacraments. Does that mean, however, that they do not have a valid place in the practice of the Church, or that the Church had no right to institute them or regulate them as it does today?

- For Jesus, the inspired word lay in the Hebrew scriptures. He never left instructions about the writing of the four Gospels, or about the Letters which his apostles would write later. These things happened spontaneously under the prompting of the Holy Spirit. Does Jesus' silence about the inspiration of these New Testament texts mean that they were not inspired? Or does it mean that the Church did not have the authority and competence to determine which of the books were genuine, which not?

- Jesus Christ did not found religious orders and congregations. He did not establish the present structures in the Church – the Roman curia, ecumenical councils, bishops' conferences and so on. Did he not leave all these things to his Church? Does his silence on these matters mean disapproval?

- Jesus Christ did not establish Church law, or define its provisions. He did not envision the beatification and canonisation of saints, the consecration of churches and cathedrals, priestly training to be given in seminaries, and so on. Can his silence on all these topics be construed as his having laid down a perpetual norm against them?

It is utterly ridiculous to read into a thing Jesus did *not* do, his laying down a permanent norm that would need to be followed for all time by the future Church. This is all the more so when we understand the background of Jesus' actions: the reason why he did certain things and why he omitted others.

Jesus' vision

In practically all matters of faith and practice, Jesus did not determine any of the details. What he did – and this was his crucial contribution – was to present ideals. In what he did and said, he laid down *principles* that were to form the foundation for the Church's future faith and life. For instance, Jesus never established religious orders or congregations. On the other hand, by his sketching the counsels of perfection, Jesus outlined the principles on which later religious life could be based. It was up to the community of future believers, under the inspiration of the Holy Spirit, to give various colourful forms to his vision in this regard.

The same applies to Jesus' involvement with women. It is clear that in his kingdom women would take the same place as men. This has been explained at greater length in Chapter 5. Whereas in the old dispensation women took second place to men, since only men were full members of the covenant, in his kingdom women were baptised and became disciples on a precisely equal footing. Though Jesus himself did not express this specifically, it is clear that this principle about women – which St Paul expressed explicitly: 'No longer male or female, but all are one in Christ' (Gal. 3:28) – implicitly requires an inclusion of women in the ministerial priesthood as it was going to be developed by the Church.

However, why then did Jesus not include women among the apostolic twelve?

Limitations

What Jesus himself could implement of his vision was clearly limited by the conditions of his time and his own specific circumstances. We should not forget that Jesus had to present his message to a society that was completely patriarchal from both a religious and a socio-cultural point of view. The roles which Jesus' contemporaries attributed to men and women were totally different from those of today. Though Jesus had close women disciples, he could not, without complicating his message enormously, have women in leadership roles that would be totally misunderstood at the time.

Remember that his public ministry lasted for only three years, most of which were spent in preparing his Galilean compatriots for the totally new religious vision that he preached. He had to travel from village to village on foot. There were no newspapers, radio or TV bulletins. There are only fifty-two weeks in a year and he could only address one crowd at a time. Expecting Jesus to solve and put into practice every implication of his world-changing vision is totally unrealistic.

We can see the same restriction at work regarding the abolition of slavery. Though Jesus' vision implied a total equality for all – and again it is Paul who saw this clearly – Jesus himself did not make an explicit plea for the abolition of slavery. The question is simply: what could he do within the short time available to him? On the other hand, when he was nailed on the cross he drew to himself the injustices of all time, including slavery and the oppression of women. And by rising from the tomb he won, in principle, freedom from every form of unjust domination.

Understanding symbolism

For the apostolic team Jesus chose the number twelve, to symbolise the twelve tribes of Israel, the twelve sons of Jacob. It was natural for him to choose twelve *men* to express this symbol, but what was significant was not their manhood but their starting a new Israel. Maleness was not the point of the symbolism.

On the other hand, Jesus' actions were inclusive. He was as sensitive to women as to men. He responded with love to the repentant prostitute who poured ointment on his feet, the widow of Naim who walked behind the bier of her dead son, the woman who was bent double with arthritis, the widow in the Temple who put two small coins in the offering box, and the women of Jerusalem who wept as they saw Jesus carrying his cross.[15]

Jesus learnt from women and drew them into his ministry: the woman suffering from a flow of blood; the Syro-Phoenician mother, whose faith he praised; Martha's sister Mary, whose discipleship he upheld although she upset the conventional expectations of a woman's role; the Samaritan woman, who became the apostle to her own village; and Mary of Magdala, Joanna and Suzanna, who were part of the apostolic band. Do these symbolic actions of Jesus not cry out for the inclusion of women in the ministerial priesthood?[16]

Recent research has again highlighted that community meals played an important part in Jesus' ministry. At all these events, as far as we can find out from the Gospels, women were present. So we can presume the same was true about the Last Supper. Moreover, the Last Supper was specifically the Passover meal, at which, according to Jewish law, the women of the family were also to be present.[17] We can presume therefore with full confidence that women were there when Jesus said, 'Do this in commemoration of me'. These words were also spoken to women.[18] Who is therefore to say that women were excluded by Jesus himself from participation in the future ministry?

The claim that Jesus barred women from the ministry cannot be substantiated, either from scripture or from tradition.

READINGS FROM THE WOMEN PRIESTS WEBSITE

Selections from the 'Didascalia Apostolorum'
> http://www.womenpriests.org/traditio/didasc.htm

Selections from the 'Apostolic Constitutions'
> http://www.womenpriests.org/traditio/aposcons.htm
> http://www.womenpriests.org/traditio/aposcon2.htm

Jesus Christ:
* chose twelve apostles
> http://www.womenpriests.org/scriptur/mark3.htm
* did not directly fight male dominance
> http://www.womenpriests.org/scriptur/myth1.htm
* was truly human
> http://www.womenpriests.org/scriptur/christlm.htm
* grew in wisdom
> http://www.womenpriests.org/scriptur/christgr.htm
* did not know everything
> http://www.womenpriests.org/scriptur/christig.htm
* left decisions to the later Church
> http://www.womenpriests.org/scriptur/norm.htm
* was open to women
> http://www.womenpriests.org/scriptur/christop.htm
* established a radically new baptism and priesthood
> http://www.womenpriests.org/scriptur/baptism.htm

Suzanne Tunc
'The meals of Jesus' community'
> http://www.womenpriests.org/scriptur/tunc.htm

Marjorie Reiley Maguire
'Bible, liturgy concur: women were there'
> http://www.womenpriests.org/scriptur/maguire.htm

13

Not Human Enough to Represent Christ?

THE FINAL TRADITIONAL ARGUMENT we need to consider is the representation of Christ. In our own time, the Congregation for Doctrine has revived this argument. It concedes that it does not have conclusive force, but it feels that this argument shows the 'profound fittingness that theological reflection discovers between the proper nature of the sacrament of Order, with its specific reference to the mystery of Christ, and the fact that only men have been called to receive priestly ordination'. In other words, once we understand this point we will sit up and exclaim: 'Aha, that's why! Now it all makes sense!'

The Congregation develops this argument by stating that the priest does not act in his own name, but in the person of Christ. The supreme expression of this representation, it argues, is found in the altogether special form it assumes in the celebration of the Eucharist, which is the source and centre of the Church's unity, the sacrificial meal in which the People of God are associated in the sacrifice of Christ. The priest, who alone has the power to perform it, then acts not only through the effective power conferred on him by Christ, but acts *in persona Christi*, taking the role of Christ, to the point of being his very image, when he pronounces the words of consecration. The question therefore arises: can a woman act in the person of Christ? The Congregation thinks not.

> The Christian priesthood is of a sacramental nature: the priest is a sign, the supernatural effectiveness of which comes from the ordination received, but a sign that must be perceptible and which the faithful must be able to recognize with ease. The whole sacramental economy is in fact based upon natural signs, on symbols imprinted upon the human psychology: 'Sacramental signs,' says Saint Thomas, 'represent what they signify by natural resemblance'. The same natural resemblance is required for persons as for things: when Christ's role in the Eucharist is to be expressed sacramentally, there would not be this 'natural resemblance' which must exist between Christ and his minister if the

role of Christ were not taken by a man: in such a case it would be difficult to see in the minister the image of Christ. For Christ himself was and remains a man.

Christ is of course the firstborn of all humanity, of women as well as men: the unity which he re-established after sin is such that there are no more distinctions between Jew and Greek, slave and free, male and female, but all are one in Christ Jesus (cf. Gal. 3:28). Nevertheless, the incarnation of the Word took place according to the male sex: this is indeed a question of fact, and this fact, while not implying an alleged natural superiority of man over woman, cannot be disassociated from the economy of salvation.[1]

When I began to teach in India, in 1965, I was surprised to find that in seminary plays women's roles were acted by men. The reason was simple: there were only men around. I found it quite unnatural for a man to present himself as a woman, in spite of the make-up and the woman's saree. Later things changed, and it was agreed that men should act men's roles and women play women's roles. The Congregation takes up a parallel position with regard to the drama of the Eucharist. Jesus Christ was a man, it states. Only a man can properly represent him to the community.

Since the Congregation quotes St Thomas Aquinas in this context, let us first examine the origin of the argument.

Women are imperfect human beings

Thomas Aquinas did, indeed, believe that a woman could not be a sacramental sign representing Christ. We should read his words carefully.

Certain things are required in the recipient of a sacrament as being requisite for the validity of the sacrament, and if such things be lacking, one can receive neither the sacrament nor the reality of the sacrament. Other things, however, are required, not for the validity of the sacrament, but for its lawfulness, as being congruous to the sacrament; and without these one receives the sacrament, but not the reality of the sacrament. Accordingly we must say that the male sex is required for receiving Orders not only in the second, but also in the first way. Wherefore even though a woman were made the object of all that is done in conferring Orders, she would not receive Orders, for since a sacrament is a sign, not only the thing, but the signification of the thing is required in all sacramental actions; thus it was stated above that in Extreme Unction it is necessary to have a sick man, in order to signify the need of healing. *Accordingly, since it is not possible in the female sex to signify eminence of degree, for a woman is in the state of subjection,* it follows that she cannot receive the sacrament of Order.[2]

Aquinas states that a woman cannot receive ordination validly. The reason he gives, however, is significant. It is not, as the Congregation seems to say, that a woman does not look like a man, but that a woman 'cannot signify eminence of degree'. It sounds ominous – and it is!

Aquinas explains himself further in another text. Some people have wondered why God would make imperfect human beings such as women. Aquinas replies that women, though deficient as human beings, have a purpose in God's overall scheme of things.

> It can be argued that woman should not have formed part of the world as it was initially created. For Aristotle says that a female is a misbegotten male. But it would be wrong for something misbegotten and [hence] deficient to be part of the initial creation. Therefore woman should not have been a part of that world.
>
> Yes, with regard to its particular nature [i.e., the action of the male semen], a female is deficient and misbegotten. For the active power of the semen always seeks to produce a thing completely like itself, something male. So if a female is produced, this must be because the semen is weak or because the material [provided by the female parent] is unsuitable, or because of the action of some external factor such as the winds from the south which make the atmosphere humid. But with regard to *universal nature* the female is not misbegotten but is intended by Nature for the work of generation. Now the intentions of Nature come from God, who is its author. This is why, when he created Nature, he made not only the male but also the female.[3]

What did he mean? Women do play a useful role in the overall scheme of things, but considered in themselves they are unfinished. Only men are complete human beings. Females become females because something has gone wrong in the process of their conception and birth.

Aquinas and his contemporaries still followed ancient Greek and Roman notions. They considered the semen to be the active principle in conception. Only men produced seed and therefore only men were responsible for procreation. They taught that semen was cast into the womb as seed into the soil. The process of embryonic development was activated by the semen and nourished by the blood of the mother.

> When thirsting for children a man falls into a kind of trance, softened and subdued by the pleasures of procreation as by sleep, so that again something is drawn from his flesh and from his bones and is . . . fashioned into another man. For the harmony of bodies being disturbed in the embrace of love, as those tell us who have experienced the marriage state, all the marrow and generative part of the blood, like a kind of liquid bone, coming together from

all the members worked into foam and curdled, is projected through the organs of generation into the living body of the female.[4]

We see here how the heat of passion serves to create the semen, and so passion and its concomitant pleasure for both men and women were considered essential to procreation. Foetuses developed their full potential, their maleness, if they amassed a decisive surplus of 'heat' and 'vital spirit' in the early stages in the womb. Females were the result of insufficient heat being absorbed by the foetus. This belief is the medical basis of Aristotle's contention that women were 'misbegotten males'. Women's softer, moister and colder bodies meant they were less formed and ordered by nature than men. Proof of this is women's inability to 'concoct' semen from blood, as it was thought that men did. Therefore, any excess nourishment over what was needed for sustenance had to be secreted from the body so that women would not be 'water-logged'. This quotation from Aretaeus the physician demonstrates the interconnections between heat, semen, maleness and superior formation: 'The semen, when possessed of vitality, makes us men hot, well braced in limbs, heavy, well-voiced, spirited, strong to think and act.'

But it is not semen per se that created new life. The semen was the vehicle for the spiritual principle, the 'vital heat' which was the first and efficient cause of life. Aristotle taught that the cause of life is not fire or any such force, but the *spirit* included in the semen and the accompanying foam. The proof of the spiritual nature of semen was that it is white, as opposed to menstrual blood which is red. Sexed bodies become symbolic of aspects of the cosmos: woman's nature is analogous to earth, and man's to the heavens. Hence male superiority was based on an understanding of men's optimal formation in the womb, from which flowed superior personal characteristics, and their power to procreate.[5]

So now we understand what Aquinas means: a woman is misbegotten because 'if a female is produced, this must be because the semen is weak or because the material [provided by the female parent] is unsuitable, or because of the action of some external factor such as the winds from the south which make the atmosphere humid'. Women are therefore not perfect human beings. For women are, after all, not fully created in God's image. It can be seen in the fact that women have inferior intellects and are emotionally unstable. That is why they are subject to men. It also explains why Paul forbade them to teach. Women thus occupy an inferior status. And that is the reason why they cannot represent Christ, '*since it is not possible in the female sex to signify eminence of degree*'.

The Congregation for Doctrine quoted Thomas Aquinas in the matter of representing Christ, without telling us about the background of Aquinas' opinions. Do they seriously want to claim validity for the traditional argument? But if they do not, then what remains of the argument in our better understanding of human biology and the equality between the sexes?

Can a woman not represent Christ?

Women carry the image of Christ

The Congregation for Doctrine maintains that a woman cannot preside over the Eucharist because Christ was a man, and only a man can symbolise him properly. The Eucharist is a sacrament which essentially depends on its sign value. The water poured in baptism signifies the cleansing action of God. We may not substitute petrol or milk, for these do not have the same symbolic meaning. The oil used at the anointing of the sick expresses healing. We could not legitimately apply water or vinegar in its stead. In the same way, it is argued, Christ's maleness requires maleness in the priest who represents him at the Eucharist. For the priest is Christ's image.

But what makes the priest an image of Christ? If the natural resemblance between the minister of the Eucharist and Christ formally concerned the maleness of Christ, then strictly speaking everything would have to be done to make the priest today resemble as closely as possible what we gather a Jew of the first century looked like. This is not being flippant; it is the logical corollary of the Congregation's argument. If natural resemblance means physical likeness, then for the sake of making the image more perfect the priest ought to dress at Mass as a first-century Jew dressed. As it is, the priest at Mass dons vestments which serve to hide his very maleness and to highlight his ministry as *representative image*, not as physical likeness of Christ the mediator.[6]

It is crucial to understand the difference between a 'photocopy' and an 'image'. To be a symbol does not require that the symbolic person or function or object be a *literal copy* of the person, function or object symbolised. On the contrary, a symbolic manifestation or expression loses both vigour and viability, meaning and vitality if it becomes a stereotype. A bank note, for example, represents the State, which promises the owner to repay its nominal value in gold. The note will carry a symbolic image: a ruling monarch or a founding father. It does not need to carry a picture of the gold coins it takes the place of. Again, the queen of England need not be represented by a woman, and the president of the United States, if he is a man, by another man. Ambassadors represent the authority, the power, the function, not sex or gender. A woman may not be a photo likeness of Christ, but she can be, and is, Christ's image. This is, after all, exactly what Paul is teaching:

> In Christ Jesus you are all children of God, through faith. For all of you who were baptised into Christ, *have put on Christ*. There is neither Jew nor Greek, there is neither slave nor free, there is neither male nor female. For you all are one in Christ Jesus.[7]

> And we all, with unveiled faces, reflecting the glory of the Lord, are being changed into his likeness from one degree of glory to another.[8]

> We know that God co-operates with all those who love him . . . They are the ones he chose especially long ago who he intended to become true images of his Son.[9]

In other words, every baptised person, including every baptised woman, carries the image of Christ.

> Is *Inter insigniores* saying that having women at the altar would be the equivalent of using pizza instead of bread, or Coke instead of wine? Are we being told that the sign-value would be defective because women are of a fundamentally different nature than men, and therefore of Christ? Are we to understand that a woman cannot resemble Christ sufficiently for the faithful to see Christ in her, for her to become a sacrament of Christ? . . . What would be the reaction if one said that a particular race or nationality could not adequately image Christ? And yet in another age and among certain groups, this too would have been acceptable. The sacramentality of the priesthood cannot demand a male presence in the same way that the celebration of the Eucharist requires the elements of bread and wine. Christ is the destination and ultimate identity of each human being, and all are called to be remade in his image. Thus women are not called to be lesser images of Christ than are men.[10]

Women act in the person of Christ

The Congregation for Doctrine says that a woman cannot act in the person of Christ at the Eucharist. But women are already acting in the person of Christ. It is common sacramental doctrine that the minister of every sacrament acts as a vicar of Christ. With regard to baptism, it is the explicit teaching of the Church that anyone with the use of reason, having the right intention and employing due matter and form, may be the minister of this sacrament. The minister, male or female, acts *in persona Christi*. 'By his power Christ is present in the sacraments, so that when a person baptizes it is really Christ himself who baptizes.'[11]

The ministers of the sacrament of matrimony are the partners themselves. As Pius XII succinctly expressed it in *Mystici Corporis*: 'The spouses are ministers of grace to each other.'[12] The sacrament of matrimony is a permanent sacrament. Consequently, as long as the marriage lasts husband and wife remain ministers of Christ's love and grace to each other. In the words of St Augustine: 'When a man marries, it is Christ who marries her; when a woman marries, it is Christ who marries him.'[13]

Women also act in the person of Christ as Christians in their daily lives, and they do so *as women*. The Early Church honoured a rule of faith: '*What is not assumed [into Christ's humanity] is not saved*.' This defined the proper understanding of the human *persona* in the fourth-century controversy on the humanity of Christ. Any notion of the humanity of Christ that excluded anything essentially human from his existence was judged an inadequate notion according to this rule, since the excluded human dimension would not share in the hypostatic union and so not enjoy the union's saving effects. But the Congregation for Doctrine comes very close to making Christ's maleness an essential part of his incarnation.

> Christ is of course the firstborn of all humanity, of women as well as men: the unity which he re-established after sin is such that there are no more distinctions between Jew and Greek, slave and free, male and female, but all are one in Christ Jesus (cf. Gal. 3:28). Nevertheless, the incarnation of the Word took place according to the male sex: this is indeed a question of fact, and this fact, while not implying an alleged natural superiority of man over woman, cannot be disassociated from the economy of salvation: it is, indeed, in harmony with the entirety of God's plan as God himself has revealed it, and of which the mystery of the Covenant is the nucleus.[14]

'*What is not assumed [into Christ's humanity] is not saved*. If maleness is constitutive for the incarnation and redemption, female humanity is not assumed and therefore not saved.'[15] Giving Jesus' maleness a privileged status, as the Congregation for Doctrine does, particularises the human notion of *persona* in a way that puts it at odds with the ancient rule of faith, thus destroying the Christian notion of human person implicit in our Christian awareness. Christ's being a male cannot exclude women from any part of the salvation he brought, sacraments and all. Since woman too is a person in Christ, she can act in his *persona*.

A man is, first and foremost, a male *person* and a woman is a female *person*. This means that *both* men and women have always in common that capacity for full humanness and for the full range of symbolic action and function that the primacy of personhood involves. There are differences between male and female, but they both are totally subservient to being a person. Any added symbolic meaning in gender may never lose sight of the primacy and meaning of personhood in both men and women. To cherish that value and to respect that validity require, therefore, that the symbolism of sexuality be subservient to ministerial status. It functions within the larger and more adequate context of the *personal*, and not within a limited sexual-anatomical perspective.[16]

It is interesting to reflect on discussions among moralists as to what kind of water is required for the symbolism of baptism. Would dirty water, for instance, not invalidate the baptism – since the sacrament signifies cleansing? The Church has rejected such subtle distinctions. *Any water* is valid for baptism: ditch water as much as rain water, salt water as much as spring water, chlorinated water and carbonated water as much as filtered water; in short, anything that is water. The analogy to Holy Orders is clear. Any person who is in Christ can represent him at the Eucharist.

At the Eucharist the priest also acts in the person of the Church

The Congregation for Doctrine puts the main emphasis on the priest's task at the moment of consecration. In its view the priest is then fully identified with Christ.

> The supreme expression of this representation is found in the altogether special form it assumes in the celebration of the Eucharist, which is the source and centre of the Church's unity, the sacrificial meal in which the People of God are associated in the sacrifice of Christ. The priest, who alone has the power to perform it, then acts not only through the effective power conferred on him by Christ, but *in persona Christi*, taking the role of Christ, to the point of being his very image, when he pronounces the words of consecration.[17]

> Saying 'in the name and place of Christ' is not however enough to express completely the nature of the bond between the minister and Christ as understood by tradition. The formula *in persona Christi* in fact suggests a meaning that brings it close to the Greek expression *mimema Christou* [i.e. doing an impression of Christ]. The word *persona* means a part played in the ancient theatre, a part identified by a particular mask. The priest takes the part of Christ, lending him his voice and gestures.[18]

But is this really true? We obtain a different picture from studying the liturgy itself. Throughout the eucharistic prayer the priest speaks *in name of the community*. It is enough to read the words themselves, as we find them, for instance, in the traditional 'Roman' eucharistic prayer. The priest always speaks of 'we', 'us', 'all of us', etc. I will just indicate here the beginning of sentences (italics are mine):

- '*We* come to you, Father, with praise and thanksgiving through Jesus Christ your Son. Through him *we* ask you to accept and bless these gifts *we* offer you in sacrifice . . .'
- '*We* offer them for your holy catholic Church . . .'
- 'Remember, Lord, those for whom *we* now pray . . .'
- 'Remember *all of us* gathered here before you. You know how firmly *we* believe in you and dedicate ourselves to you . . .'
- 'In union with the whole Church *we* honour Mary . . .'
- 'Father accept this offering from your whole family. Grant *us* your peace in this life and save *us* from final damnation . . .'
- 'Bless and approve *our* offering . . .'

The priests says 'we', 'us'. He speaks as representative of the community. And the words of consecration fit into the same pattern.

Following Thomas Aquinas and other medieval theologians, Rome gives the impression that the words of consecration stand apart; that while the priest speaks these words, he steps outside his role as leader of the community and suddenly speaks only in the name of Christ. 'The priest, who alone has the power to perform it, then acts not only through the effective power conferred on him by Christ, but *in persona Christi*, taking the role of Christ, to the point of being his very image, when he pronounces the words of consecration.' This is not the case. Let us look at the text itself, as we find it in the first eucharistic prayer (the so-called Roman Canon). I will give a literal translation from the Latin text, which is at least ten centuries old.

[Invocation prayer]

Bless and approve our offering, make it acceptable to you, an offering in spirit and in truth. Let it become for us the body and blood of Jesus Christ, your only Son, our Lord

[Institution narrative]

who on the day before he suffered took bread in his sacred hands and looking up to heaven, to you, his almighty Father, gave you thanks and praise. He broke the bread, gave it to his disciples, and said: 'Take this, all of you, and eat it: this is my body which will be given up for you'. When supper was ended, he took the cup. Again he gave you thanks and praise, gave the cup to his disciples, and said: 'Take this, all of you, and drink from it: this is the cup of my blood, the blood of the new and everlasting covenant. It will be shed for you and for all so that sins may be forgiven. Do this in memory of me'.

It is clear that the words of consecration are part of the whole euchar-istic prayer. Textually, the institution narrative depends upon the invocation which precedes it, and the narrative is unintelligible except as a continuation of the invocation. The narrative does not stand alone or in disjuncture from the rest of the eucharistic prayer. Moreover, the institution narrative, which quotes the *verba Christi*, is spoken in the third person: it is a quotation within a narrative recital addressed as part of a prayer to God the Father, and it is encompassed within a prayer spoken in the name of the whole Church.

An examination of all eucharistic prayers shows that even at the moment of consecration the priest does not really step into the character of Christ or play his part, even though he uses certain words and ges-tures of Christ. The form of this part of the Mass is not drama; it is narrative, in which the priest speaks throughout of Christ in the third person, clearly as someone other than himself, even in the pronunciation of the words of consecration. He unmistakably maintains his direct rep-resentation of the Church and his identity as its minister right through the sacred action.

Christian antiquity, at least until the fourth century, universally viewed the entire prayer as consecratory. Western theological reflection, for a variety of reasons, had by the high Middle Ages singled out the institution narrative as 'words of consecration'. More recent theological reflection, attentive to the nature and structure of the eucharistic prayer, has returned to the older view. Isolating the 'words of consecration' ignores the structure of the eucharistic prayers, which are composed of a number of elements, of which the institution narrative is certainly one, but, equally important, the *epiclesis* [calling down of the Spirit] is another. It is the *epiclesis* that is considered consecratory in the Byzantine tradition.

The well-known liturgist, Ralph A. Keifer, who was general editor for the International Committee for English in the Liturgy (ICEL), comes to this conclusion:

> At no point in the eucharistic prayer does the priest speak directly in the name of Christ. He continually speaks in the name of the church. Even the institution narrative, which quotes the *verba Christi*, is spoken in the third person: it is a quotation within a narrative recital addressed as part of a prayer to God the Father, and it is encompassed within a prayer spoken in the name of the whole church. The Congregation contends that the priest represents the church because he first represents Christ himself as head and shepherd of the church . . . On the level of *sign*, in what is said and done at the act of Eucharist, the exact opposite is the case. It is only by praying in the name of the church that the priest enacts his role as consecratory representative of Christ.

109

Thus in the articulation of the eucharistic prayer in the Roman rite no clearcut distinction is made between the priest's representing the praying church and his representing Christ the head and shepherd of the church. The two roles are enacted simultaneously. Even on a view which insists on pinpointing a temporal moment of consecration with the recitation of the *verba Christi*, there is still no disjunctive representation of Christ as the head and shepherd of the church apart from the priest's representation of the church as the body and bride of Christ. In reciting the institution narrative, the priest continues to speak on behalf of the praying church. And since, on the level of sign, the representation of Christ is grounded in representation of the Church, it would seem that a woman could perform the priestly role of representing Christ as well as a man.[19]

The sign of Christ's priesthood is love

One problem with the Congregation for Doctrine's approach is that it is excessively cultic. But Christ's priesthood is about much more than presiding at the Eucharist. It implies a service of the Christian community in many pastoral fields: instructing and affirming people in faith; absolving and healing; encouraging and empowering; guiding people to God in prayer and leading them in action.[20]

What does it mean to be such a spiritual leader representing Christ? Listening to Christ himself, we hear him stress *love* as the sign he requires.

- Christ proved his love by laying down his life for his friends. That is the leadership he expects.
- It is by such love that the true shepherd is distinguished from the hireling.
- Readiness to serve, not the power to dominate, enables one to be like Christ.
- Not in presiding at table alone but in washing people's feet is the Master recognised.[21]

One should note that we are not dealing here with love as a mere moral requirement but with an element that has *sign value*. 'By this love you have for one another, everyone will know that you are my disciples.' Although elsewhere Christ spoke of love as a commandment, he is here addressing the apostles on the very occasion when he is ordaining them as his priests. His 'Do this in memory of me' presupposes pastoral love as the special sign by which his disciples should be recognised. It is such love he demands from Peter before entrusting him with the apostolic commission.[22]

Such considerations do not directly prove that women could be ordained priests. They demonstrate, however, that Scripture itself lays stress on values such as sympathy, service and love on the level of the sacramental sign, rather than on accidentals like being a man. Are we not nearer to Christ's mind when we stipulate that a woman filled with the spirit of Christ's pastoral love is a more 'fitting' image of his presence than a man who were to lack such love? And will women, with their special charisms of healing and insight, of sensitivity and care, of attention and self-effacing generosity, not represent Christ's priestly love in ways that men cannot? Does the Catholic Church at present not lack the priestly service that women could give 'in the person of Christ'?

It is clear from the above considerations that women can represent Christ, and could also do so in the administration of the sacraments and in the Eucharist.

READINGS FROM THE WOMEN PRIESTS WEBSITE

Thomas Aquinas:
* on women's lower status
> http://www.womenpriests.org/theology/aqui___inf.htm
* on how women are born
> http://www.womenpriests.org/theology/aqui___wom.htm
* on women's ordination
> http://www.womenpriests.org/theology/aqui___ord.htm

Kim Powers
'Of godly men and medicine: ancient biology and
the Christian Fathers on the nature of woman'
> http://www.womenpriests.org/theology/power1.htm

Anne Jensen
'The Representation of Christ, Ecclesiastical Office,
and Presiding at the Eucharist'
> http://www.womenpriests.org/related/jensen1.htm

John Wijngaards
Women can represent Jesus Christ at the Eucharist:
* because women are equal in Christ
> http://www.womenpriests.org/theology/pers___equ.htm
* women too bear Christ's image
> http://www.womenpriests.org/theology/pers___ima.htm
* women already act as other Christs
> http://www.womenpriests.org/theology/pers___chr.htm
* women reflect better Christ's feminine traits
> http://www.womenpriests.org/theology/pers___fem.htm
* women too can represent Christ's love, which is the
essence of his priesthood
> http://www.womenpriests.org/theology/pers___lov.htm

14

Not Man Enough to Represent the 'Groom'?

In recent years the authorities in Rome have produced a new argument for the non-ordination of women, one that was unknown to antiquity. It is based on the symbolic relationship between Christ and the Church as the bridegroom and his bride. The imagery was commented on in tradition, of course, but never in the context of excluding women from ordination. Also, Rome admits that this is not an argument based on facts, but an argument of 'congruence', an 'analogy of faith'.[1] Let me explain what this means.

We believe in the Blessed Trinity: Father, Son and Holy Spirit. The theological rationale for this can be found in Scripture and tradition. But theologians add their arguments of congruence: reasons why it is 'fitting' that there should be three Persons in God. One of them was the popular notion that the Father by *knowing* himself generates the Son, and that Father and Son generate the Spirit by their mutual *love*. Such reasoning is no more than a pious reflection, or a useful image from our own limited human experience. Arguments of congruence will never *prove* that there should be three Persons in God.

Such, by Rome's own admission, is the novel argument based on symbolism. It aims to show that 'it makes good sense' for women to be excluded from the priestly ministry. So what do the Roman documents say? In brief, the 'argument' comes to this:

- At creation God gave men and women a distinct dignity and vocation.
- When God concluded the covenant, he (!) was the bridegroom and Israel his bride. In the same way Christ is the bridegroom and the Church his bride.
- This symbolism is so important that Jesus Christ *had* to become human *as a man*.
- Jesus wanted this symbolism to continue by insisting that *only male priests* represent him at the Eucharist.

Let us examine this in more detail.

What makes a woman a woman?

Pope John Paul II, while repeatedly stressing that he recognises the equality of women and men, states that women are 'different' because of the 'femininity' they received at creation.

> The personal resources of feminity are certainly no less than the resources of masculinity: they are merely different. Hence a woman, as well as a man, must understand her 'fulfilment' as a person, her dignity and vocation, on the basis of these resources, according to the riches of the femininity which she received on the day of creation.[2]

The Pope then continues to fill in the specific nature of femininity. Woman is first and foremost 'mother', a person dedicated to be open to new life. 'Motherhood is linked to the personal structure of the woman and to the personal structure of the gift [of life].' 'The biblical exemplar of "the woman" [Eve] finds its culmination in the motherhood of the Mother of God.' This puts women in a special category.

> Motherhood has been introduced into the order of the Covenant that God made with humanity in Jesus Christ. Each and every time that motherhood is repeated in human history, it is always related to the Covenant which God established to the human race through the motherhood of the Mother of God.[3]

After talking about virginity as the other major vocation of woman, the Pope identifies 'love' in the sense of 'self-giving' as the characteristic feature of womanhood.

> [Love is] decisive for the dignity of women both in the eyes of God – the Creator and Redeemer – and in the eyes of human beings – men and women. In God's eternal plan, woman is the one in whom the order of love in the created world of persons takes first root. The order of love belongs to the intimate life of God himself, the life of the Trinity . . . It enables us to grasp in an essential manner the question of women's dignity and vocation: the dignity of women is measured by the order of love . . . Unless we refer to this order, we cannot give a complete and adequate answer to the question about women's dignity and vocation . . . This concerns each and every woman, independently of the cultural context in which she lives, and independently of her spiritual, psychological and physical characteristics, as for example, age, education, health, work, and whether she is married or single.[4]

Now such spiritual philosophising turns out to be highly dangerous.

For it imposes a particular understanding as absolutely normative, since it is supposed to derive from woman's created nature. But can we truly say what constitutes a woman's identity? Studies in the fields of anthropology, psychology, biology, history and sociology show that 'far from being fixed and immutable from conception onward, gender identity is in fact variable and diverse and arises over a long period of time as a result of the interplay of complex cultural and other forces.'[5] The Pope's definition excludes women from large realms of human experience. 'In our ecclesiastical jargon we run the risk of confining the feminine to an essentialist cage. Woman is presented first as mother, then as virgin. Nothing is said about woman as partner. The "essential" difference between man and woman is highlighted, and the nature and task of woman is seen as care and concern for others. A professional life is not envisaged for her, for that would involve concern about herself.'[6] It is the first step to banning women from the priestly ministry.

The ideal of 'selfless love' which the Pope proclaims to be woman's vocation sounds like another attempt by men to curtail women's full human growth. 'The characteristics of the eternal woman are opposed to a developing, authentic person, who will be unique, self-critical, self-creative, active and searching. By contrast to these authentic personal qualities, the eternal woman is said to have a vocation to surrender and hiddenness; hence the symbolism of the veil. Selfless, she achieves not individualization but merely generic fulfilment in motherhood, physical or spiritual.'[7] It is time for women 'to wake up, to bid farewell to passivity, to kiss Sleeping Beauty goodbye and take responsibility for their lives'.[8]

The symbolism of bridegroom and bride

The Pope now turns to scriptural imagery which, in his view, expresses a key truth about the nature of God's relationship to humanity, and the specific roles God gave to men and women. Already in Old Testament times God is presented as the husband, Israel as his wife. This symbolism reaches its climax in Christ.

> Christ is the Bridegroom; the Church is his bride, whom he loves because he has gained her by his blood and made her glorious, holy and without blemish, and henceforth he is inseparable from her. This nuptial theme, which is developed from the Letters of Saint Paul onwards (cf. 2 Cor. 11:2, Eph. 5:22–23) to the writings of Saint John (cf. especially Jn 3:29, Rev. 19:7, 9), is present also in the Synoptic Gospels: the Bridegroom's friends must not fast as long as he is with them (cf. Mk 2:19); the Kingdom of Heaven is like a king who gave a feast for his son's wedding (cf. Mt. 22:1–14). It is through this Scriptural

language, all interwoven with symbols, and which expresses and affects man and woman in their profound identity, that there is revealed to us the mystery of God and Christ, a mystery which of itself is unfathomable.[9]

The main source for this nuptial theme is found in Ephesians. It requires further discussion. The 'church' in this text, as everywhere else in the New Testament, stands for 'the community of believers'.

> Be subject to one another out of reverence for Christ. Wives, be subject to your husbands, as to the Lord. For the husband is the head of the wife, as Christ is the head of the church, his body, and is himself its Saviour. Husbands, love your wives as Christ loved the church and gave himself up for her, that he might sanctify her, having cleansed her by the washing of water with the word, that he might present the church to himself in splendour, without spot or wrinkle or any such thing, that she might be holy and without blemish. In the same way husbands should love their wives as their own bodies. He who loves his wife, loves himself. For no man ever hates his own flesh, but nourishes and cherishes it, as Christ does the church, because we are members of his body. 'For this reason a man shall leave his father and be joined to his wife, and the two shall become one.' *This is a great mystery, and I mean in reference to Christ and the church*; however, let each one of you love his wife as himself, and let the wife see that she respects her husband.[10]

The text is part of the so-called 'household codes' that contain practical instructions for masters and slaves, parents and children, husbands and wives.[11] This means that the example of Christ's wedding serves the purpose of inculcating the right attitudes between husband and wife. A metaphor has here grown into an allegory. Like a groom Christ loves his church. He cleansed her from sin through baptism – reference to the bridal bath before the wedding. He nourished her through the Eucharist – reference to the wedding meal. He became one flesh with her – reference to intercourse during the wedding night. The quotation from Genesis 'the two shall become one flesh' gives the author an opportunity to remark: 'This is a great mystery, and I mean in reference to Christ and the Church'.

The symbol of Christ's 'marriage' to the community of believers should be seen in the context of rabbinical imagery that described the coming of the Messiah as a wedding feast.[12] Perhaps there is an allusion to the 'sacred marriage' – *hieros gamos* – the marriage of a god with a human being, that was found among Hellenistic writers and that would become a major theme in second and third century Gnostic sects.[13] The image of marriage, of 'becoming one body', comes naturally to the author of Ephesians because he is concerned about the building up of the body of the Church in Christ, who is its head.[14]

Why does he call the union of Christ and his Church a 'great mystery'? Ephesians makes this abundantly clear. The mystery is God's purpose with the whole of humankind which has now been revealed, namely 'to unite all things in Christ'.[15] The stress here is on *all*. In the past the Gentiles had been excluded from the Covenant. God's great mystery now revealed is that the Gentiles too can be members of Christ's body. 'You can perceive my insight into the mystery of Christ, which was not made known to people of other generations as it has now been revealed to his holy apostles and prophets through the Spirit, that is, how the Gentiles are co-heirs, members of the same body and partakers of the promise in Christ Jesus.'[16] This explains the remark in the text on husbands and wives. As the author speaks about Christ loving his body, the Church, he sees 'the great mystery' already foreshadowed in the creation passage. 'A man [= Christ, the Son of Man] leaves his father and mother [= incarnation] and clings to his wife [= the whole of humankind]. The two become one flesh [= one Church].'[17]

So far, so good. Rome, however, sees the 'great mystery' in another light. It seems to think that the 'mystery' reveals something about sex and gender, about God being somehow male and humankind female, about the created difference between men and women. Rome sees a cosmic nuptial symbol that transcends imagery because it is *real*. The bridegroom passage in Ephesians describes reality rather than speaking only in metaphors. And this reality has enormous consequences for the incarnation. For Christ, as the divine bridegroom, had to be *a man* and *only men* can represent him at the Eucharist.

> It is through this Scriptural language, all interwoven with symbols, and *which expresses and affects man and woman in their profound identity*, that there is revealed to us the mystery of God and Christ, a mystery which of itself is unfathomable.[18]

> The fact that Christ is a man and not a woman is neither incidental nor unimportant in relation to the economy of salvation . . . God's covenant with men is presented in the Old Testament as a nuptial mystery, the definitive reality of which is Christ's sacrifice on the cross . . . Christ is the bridegroom of the Church, whom he won for himself with his blood, and the salvation brought by him is the new covenant. By using this language, revelation shows *why the incarnation took place according to the male gender*, and makes it impossible to ignore this historical reality. For this reason, *only a man can take the part of Christ*, be a sign of his presence, in a word 'represent' him (that is, be an effective sign of his presence) in the essential acts of the covenant.[19]

117

The Bridegroom – the Son consubstantial with the Father as God – became the Son of Mary. He became the 'son of man', *true man, a male*. The symbol of the Bridegroom is masculine ... The Eucharist is the sacrament of the Bridegroom and the Bride ... Since Christ, in instituting the Eucharist, linked it in such an explicit way to the priestly service of the Apostles [who were all men], it is legitimate to conclude that he thereby *wished to express the relationship between man and woman, between what is 'feminine' and what is 'masculine'.* It is a relationship willed by God both in the mystery of creation and in the mystery of redemption. It is the Eucharist that expresses the redemptive act of Christ the Bridegroom towards the Church the Bride. This is clear and unambiguous when the sacramental ministry of the Eucharist, in which the priest acts *in persona Christi*, is performed by *a man*.[20]

In other words, the image of the bridegroom, Rome says, is so important that the Son of God had to become human as a man. When the 'Word became flesh', the Word could not have lived among us as a woman. This symbolism may not be lost in the Eucharist which re-enacts creation and redemption. A male groom, Christ, presides at his wedding feast. Therefore he excluded women and chose only men to represent him as his priests.

Symbolism run amok?

We may begin by observing that the conclusions drawn from Ephesians 5:21–33 regarding the nuptial mystery go beyond the meaning of the inspired text. In no way does the 'mystery' consist in God revealing that he wants to save people as a male. The masculinity of the bridegroom may be part of the image; it is not part of the contents. When Jahweh calls Israel his 'wayward wife', does it follow that God is truly male or God's people truly female? The image speaks about relationship, not sex and gender.

Images can be instructive, of course, but they remain no more than images. They are metaphors. Christ is compared to a bridegroom in three Gospel passages, but he is also compared to a shepherd, a judge, a rabbi, a light, a door, a vine, a loaf of bread, a path, a servant, a mother hen and a thief who comes in the night. Some of these images could be construed as at least equally important as the bridegroom image. The Old Testament often sees God as the owner of a vineyard.[21] This is a rich symbol involving owner, workers, vines, wine. Jesus frequently refers to the image.[22] That Jesus supplied the wine at Cana is highly significant from the perspective of creation, redemption and the outpouring of the Spirit.[23] Moreover, the sign is directly eucharistic. By applying the symbol of 'the vine nurturing the branches' to Jesus, the Gospel of John adopts female imagery, as elsewhere in the Gospel.[24] The nurturing with 'flesh and blood', which is more truly eucharistic than 'presiding as the bridegroom', could much better be represented by a woman than by a man. Why should one symbol prevail over the other?

But if we take the Pope's eucharistic imagery seriously, the symbolic significance of the phallus is now emphasised as it has never been in Christian tradition. 'To argue that Christ's eucharistic gift of self is the action of the bridegroom in such a way that it requires a male body, is to make it an act of coitus and not of self giving in death. The symbolic function of the priesthood is therefore no longer primarily concerned with death but with sex, since male and female bodies both die and therefore either sex could represent the death of Christ.'[25] With the masculinity of the bridegroom taking central stage, Christ's *kenosis* (self-emptying) at Mass assumes the overtones of a male orgasm. Hans Urs von Balthasar, one of Rome's theological advisers, has made the image quite explicit. Von Balthasar was a member of the Papal Theological Commission since 1967 and became one of Pope John Paul II's favourite theologians. The Pope named him a Cardinal in 1988, a few days before he died. Von Balthasar does not mince his words:

> The priestly ministry and the sacrament are means of passing on seed. They are a male preserve. They aim at inducing in the Bride her function as a woman.[26]

> What else is his Eucharist but, at a higher level, an endless act of fruitful outpouring of his whole flesh, such as a man can only achieve for a moment with a limited organ of his body?[27]

Tina Beattie adds this comment:

> The 'what else ... but' implies that it is nothing else. This is the Eucharist understood not primarily as Christ's identification with the universal human tragedy of death, but rather as the identification of Christ's death with the uniquely male experience of penile ejaculation ... The justification given for the essentialisation of the male priesthood has reduced the symbolic richness of the Mass so that it is indeed nothing but a cosmic male orgasm, as von Balthasar suggests. The female body, lacking the 'limited organ' which allows for this experience, cannot represent Christ in the Eucharist. Ultimately this means that women have become bystanders in the metaphysical consummation of homosexual love, a marriage between men and God in which the male body is both the masculine bridegroom and the feminine bride, the masculine God and the feminine creature, the masculine Christ and the

feminine church. This makes Catholic theology more explicitly phallocentric than has been the case in the past, since the phallus has become the defining symbol of Christ's giving of self in the Mass.[28]

Beattie calls it *homosexual* love, because whereas the Pope excludes women from representing the bridegroom, he explicitly includes men when talking of 'the bride'. 'All human beings – both women and men – are called through the Church to be the "Bride" of Christ, the Redeemer of the world. In this way, "being the bride" and thus the "feminine" element, becomes a symbol of all that is "human".'[29] Men have it all, women have nothing.[30]

Making sense of it all?

There is much more that would need to be said about the symbolism proposed by Rome. For one thing, insisting that only a male priest can represent Christ as the masculine bridegroom, effectively cuts off women from the symbolic support they need in their own journey of faith.

> The woman at the altar enlarges people's understandings and imaginings about God. In prayers and in celebration, the ordained person is representative of the people to God and of God to the people. If the image is always male, God is represented only as male. As women are included symbolically as representative people, the image of God is larger. The feminine becomes more than the Spirit dimension. Sonship begins to include daughters.[31]

Analysing the experience of women priests in other Christian denominations and probing the Catholic search, Kelley Raab has convincingly demonstrated the absolute need of female identity persons in the Catholic Church of our time. Women priests are now psychologically required for a healthy spirituality and a truly Catholic liturgy. It is a dimension I am not able to do justice to in this book, but it exposes the male-only symbolism still defended by Rome to be injurious to the Church.[32]

By Rome's own admission, the symbolism of the bridegroom and the bride is no more than an 'argument of congruence'. And, as Thomas Aquinas (1225–74) pointed out, 'a theology based on symbols does not *prove* anything'.[33] Moreover, our reflections have shown that the symbolism, in its sexual application, does not have a valid scriptural basis and does not make sense.

Rome often mentions the bridegroom 'argument' in one breath with the argument based on acting *in persona Christi*, which we discussed in the previous chapter. It clearly attempts to present the traditional argument in a new garb. But even with this facelift the argument fails. Women can represent Christ, as validly and as fully as men can.

READINGS FROM THE WOMEN PRIESTS WEBSITE

John Wijngaards
'Nuptial Imagery and the Sacramental Priesthood'
http://www.womenpriests.org/theology/nupt__gen.htm
Tina Beattie
'The Female Body and the Sacramental Priesthood
in neo-orthodox Catholic Theology'
http://www.womenpriests.org/body/beattie3.htm
Elizabeth A. Johnson
'Basic Linguistic Options: God, Women, Equivalence',
from *She Who Is. The Mystery of God in Feminist Theological Discourse*, Crossroad, 1997, pp. 42–57.
http://www.womenpriests.org/theology/johnson2.htm

15

Verdict on the Presumed 'Tradition'

THE SECOND VATICAN COUNCIL stated that Scripture and tradition are not two separate sources of revelation. They belong together.

> Sacred tradition and sacred Scripture, then, are bound closely together, and communicate one with the other. For both of them, flowing out from the same divine well-spring, come together in some fashion to form one thing, and move towards the same goal. Sacred Scripture is the speech of God as it is put down in writing under the breath of the Holy Spirit. And tradition transmits in its entirety the Word of God which has been entrusted to the apostles by Christ the Lord and the Holy Spirit ... Sacred tradition and sacred Scripture make up a single sacred deposit of the Word of God, which is entrusted to the Church.[1]

The implication is that, in order to be valid, tradition must be scriptural. And a tradition does not become scriptural just because Fathers of the Church, theologians or the *magisterium* of the Church quote some scriptural texts. *In order to be validly scriptural, the use made of Scripture must be legitimate.* This means that the only valid sources of tradition are those written sources which employ Scripture according to the intended meaning of the inspired authors. In this respect the presumed 'tradition' banning women from ordination has been proved to be a fake, for its scriptural basis is inadequate.

When we go to a museum and we see an ancient human skull, we accept the information presented by the museum on its antiquity, origin and significance. We rely on the museum having a scientific basis for such claims. But what if the scientific basis is flawed? For 41 years, from 1912 to 1953, the British Museum in London exhibited the cranium and jawbone of the so-called 'Piltdown Man', a supposedly ancient human from the Pleistocene period. The presumed scientific basis turned out to be a mixture of deliberate fraud and archaeological incompetence – the jawbone belonged to an orang utang! The same applies to 'traditions' in the Church. Their value does not depend on how long they have been exhibited, but on their basis.

But has the Church had its own 'Piltdown Man' embarrassments?

Unscriptural traditions

In Chapter 2, I outlined the presumed 'tradition' that defended slavery. It was based on misunderstood texts in the Old Testament, in the Gospels and in St Paul's Letters. Remember, as late as 1866 the Congregation for Doctrine taught that it was 'not against Divine Law [i.e. Scripture] for a slave to be sold, bought, exchanged or given'. The fact that slavery was upheld for nineteen centuries by Fathers of the Church, medieval theologians and popes did not give the tradition any greater validity. For it rested on a flawed scriptural basis.

Another infamous example has been the so-called 'tradition' that excluded non-Catholics from salvation. Until at least 1854, the official teaching emanating from Rome was that there was no salvation outside the Church. Here are some statements by the *magisterium*:

- In a profession of faith prescribed by Pope Innocentius III in 1208 we read: 'We believe that outside the one, holy, Roman, Catholic Church no one will be saved.'
- In the IVth Lateran Council of 1215: 'There is one universal Church of the faithful outside which no one at all is saved.'
- Boniface VIII solemnly defined in his Bull *Unam Sanctam* of 1302: 'We declare, we proclaim, we define that it is absolutely necessary for salvation that every human creature be subject to the Roman Pontiff.'
- The Council of Florence in 1442, under Pope Eugene IV: '[The Holy Roman Church] firmly believes, professes and preaches that no-one remaining outside the Catholic Church, not only pagans, but also Jews, heretics or schismatics, can become partakers of eternal life; but they will go to the "eternal fire prepared for the Devil and his angels" (Mt. 25:41), unless before the end of their life they are received into it. For union with the body of the Church is of so great importance that the sacraments of the Church are helpful only for those remaining in it; and fasts, almsgiving, and other works of piety, and exercises of a militant Christian life bear eternal rewards for them alone. And no one can be saved, even if he sheds his blood for the name of Christ, unless he remains in the bosom and unity of the Catholic Church.'[2]

We find the 'tradition' already with the Fathers: Origen, Cyprian, Jerome, Augustine and Fulgentius. The 'tradition' was mainly based on two Scripture texts: 'I give you the keys of the Kingdom of Heaven. Whatever you bind on earth shall be bound in heaven. Whatever you loose on earth shall be loosed in heaven.' And: 'Whoever believes and is baptised will be saved. Who does not believe will be condemned.'[3] Through the centuries it was argued that these texts are exclusive in what they state. They attribute universal power to the hierarchy and make baptism the only means of salvation. However, Jesus' absolute way of speaking is a specific literary form, the *hyperbole*, a characteristic Jewish idiom to make a point.[4] Jesus stressed the importance of baptism without entering into the wider question of how virtuous people are saved in and through their own religions. The exclusive interpretation went beyond his intention.

In the nineteenth century the Roman authorities began to modify their teaching, stating that one could belong to the Church also 'in desire' and that this sufficed for salvation. Vatican II completed this process by clearly stating that there is salvation for those outside the Church.

> Those also can attain to everlasting salvation who through no fault of their own do not know the Gospel of Christ or his Church, yet sincerely seek God and, moved by grace, strive by their deeds to do his will as it is known to them through the dictates of conscience.[5]

This recognition has the following implications. The presumed 'tradition' that was thought to limit salvation to Catholics and on which the *magisterum* based its doctrinal justification was, in fact, not part of the real tradition handed down from Christ. The so-called 'tradition', which was claimed to be *scriptural* has been proved to be not scriptural. The biblical texts were quoted illegitimately. Their interpretation went beyond the inspired and intended sense. The real tradition that came down from Christ and the apostles was contained in other Scripture texts, such as Christ's respect for the religious sincerity of Romans, Samaritans and Syro-Phoenicians; and Paul's teaching that God judges everyone, Jews or non-Jews, according to the dictates of their own conscience.[6] Only this tradition was valid because its basis was biblical.

The biblical basis for not ordaining women

In the presumed 'tradition' for not admitting women to ordination four scriptural reasons were given. None of these holds up to scrutiny, as we saw in the preceeding chapters.

Women were believed *not to have been created in God's image*, at least not to the full extent that men were. We could find no satisfactory scriptural basis for this assertion. The first creation story in Genesis was misunderstood, through dependence on rabbinical interpretations. Similar rabbinical remarks in Paul's Letters can be shown to be typical

Pauline rationalisations, not doctrinal statements. The real source was cultural prejudice: 'How can anyone maintain that woman is in the image of God when she is demonstrably subject to the dominion of man and has no authority?'[7] (Chapter 9).

It was said that *no woman was ever allowed to teach in Church*. The prohibition was derived from 1 Timothy 2:12 and 1 Corinthians 14:34–35. These texts do not, however, imply a permanent exclusion of women from teaching in Church. They reflect a specific measure taken by local church leaders, which are not applicable to later times. The justification for accepting the ban on women's teaching had a cultural origin. 'This is so because teaching in public is not proper for a woman because of the weakness of her intellect and the instability of her emotions, of which defects women suffer more than men by a notable common law. But a teacher needs to have a vivid intellect to recognise the truth and be emotionally stable . . .'[8] (Chapter 10).

Women were believed *to carry the punishment for Eve's sin*. The references in 'tradition' to Genesis incorrectly put most of the blame on Eve. Moreover, any guilt incurred by the Fall was wiped out by Christ, and men and women share equally in Christ's redemption. Prejudice was again at the root of this incredible distortion of Scripture. 'Women are unfit to receive ordination, for ordination is reserved for perfect members of the church, since it is given for the distribution of grace to other men. But women are not perfect members of the church, only men are. Moreover, woman was the effective cause of damnation since she was the origin of transgression and Adam was deceived through her, and thus she cannot be the effective cause of salvation, because holy orders cause grace in others and so salvation.'[9] (Chapter 11).

Jesus Christ had deliberately left women out of the apostolic team, it was said. He wanted to exclude women from the priesthood for all time to come. A study of the Gospels proved this to be an insupportable conclusion. Jesus left women out of his team for practical reasons, as an *ad hoc* measure. So many non-decisions by Jesus were later on filled in by the Church. Jesus' vision clearly included women as equal in every respect and this logically requires their inclusion in the full priestly ministry.[10] Blaming Jesus for excluding women is mentioned first in the *Didascalia* (fourth century) in the context of stopping widows from instructing converts.[11] Unfortunately, this text, and the social bias it contained, snowballed into becoming some kind of surrogate scriptural argument. 'When the Gentiles who are being instructed hear the word of God not fittingly spoken, as it ought to be, unto edification of eternal life, how that our Lord clothed himself in a body, and concerning the passion of Christ: they will mock and scoff, instead of applauding the word of doctrine. This will happen all the more if the instruction is spoken to them by a woman – and she shall incur a heavy judgement for sin . . . If it were required that women should teach, our Master himself would have commanded these to give instruction with us.'[12] (Chapter 12).

The final reason against the ordination of women, which is still favoured by the Congregation for Doctrine, is not scriptural at all. *Jesus Christ was a man, so he can only be represented at the Eucharist by a man.* The argument contradicts everything else we know from Scripture: women's equal share in baptism, women's equally reflecting Christ's image, women's already acting in the person of Christ, the priority of love rather than gender in Christ's priesthood. It also has an abysmal origin. It springs from a mistaken biological interpretation. St Thomas Aquinas, who is quoted by the Congregation in support of its position, held that women cannot represent Christ because they cannot signify eminence of degree. 'The active power of the semen always seeks to produce a thing completely like itself, something male. So if a female is produced, this must be because the semen is weak or because the material [provided by the female parent] is unsuitable, or because of the action of some external factor such as the winds from the south which make the atmosphere humid . . . A female is a deficient and misbegotten male.'[13] (Chapter 13).

The imagery of the bridegroom and bride may not be legitimately interpreted as confirmation of the representational argument, as Rome interprets it. It is just one image among many. The 'great mystery' alluded to in Ephesians 5:32 does not refer to *masculine* incarnation, but to the inclusion of the Gentiles. There is no scriptural basis for contending that Christ had to become human as a man. Insisting on Christ's maleness as a predominant eucharistic symbol distorts the true meaning of the sacrament (Chapter 14).

What more needs to be said? The presumed 'tradition' had no authentic scriptural basis. Perhaps there were mitigating circumstances for the medieval theologians, such as their inadequate rules of scriptural interpretation, defective knowledge of biology, insufficient access to reliable historical data, and the overwhelming and seductive power of Roman law. Such excuses do not hold good today. The practice of not ordaining women can clearly be seen to have sprung from social and cultural prejudice. And as St Cyprian aptly remarks: 'A practice without truth is merely an ancient error.'[14]

Where will we find traces of the real tradition, genuinely scriptural and Catholic?

READINGS FROM THE WOMEN PRIESTS WEBSITE

John E. Thiel
'Tradition and reasoning: a nonfoundationalist perspective'

http://www.womenpriests.org/traditio/thiel.htm

Ida Raming
'The twelve apostles were men – '

http://www.womenpriests.org/theology/raming4.htm

Janet Cranshaw
'Pondering the Issue of Women's Ordination in the Roman Catholic Church'

http://www.womenpriests.org/theology/cranshaw.htm

John Wijngaards
Genuine tradition
* agrees with Scripture

http://www.womenpriests.org/traditio/biblical.htm

* draws on proper knowledge

http://www.womenpriests.org/traditio/informed.htm

* grows in time

http://www.womenpriests.org/traditio/dynamic.htm

Part IV

PICKING UP THE PIECES

It can happen, and it has happened, that what was at first dissent from common teaching, has subsequently been accepted as the doctrine of the Church. One could name several other issues, such as the Church's judgment on the absolute necessity of explicit Christian faith for salvation, on the morality of owning and using human persons as slaves, on the taking of interest on loans, on religious liberty, and on non-Christian religions, where what was at first a dissenting opinion has become the doctrine of the Church.

Francis A. Sullivan
Theological Studies 58 (1997), pp. 509–15

Part IV
SIGNIFICANCE IN THE PROCESS

16

Genuine Tradition

As CATHOLICS WE BELIEVE THAT Jesus Christ entrusted the 'deposit of faith' to his apostles. They in turn passed this on to the young churches they founded and these have, through one century after the next, handed it on to us. This is the tradition. Now the tradition was not, and is not, a collection of clearly defined truths. It is a complex, dynamic persuasion, a living practice whose contents are only gradually fully discovered and more clearly defined. Jesus' words apply here about the householder who brings out of his storeroom 'things new and old'.[1]

It has always been recognised in the history of the Church that the real Gospel was not a written text. Paul said: 'You are a letter from Christ, written not with ink but with the Spirit of the living God, not on tablets of stone but on tablets of human hearts.'[2] In terms of the tradition of faith, this came to mean that Christ had entrusted to his community of believers an internal awareness of his revelation that exceeded everything written in either the New Testament, or in later Church documents. It was the reality in the consciousness of the believing community, the 'Gospel in the heart'. Clement of Alexandria expressed it in this way: 'By the Saviour's teaching, given to the apostles, the unwritten tradition of written tradition has been handed down to us, written by the power of God in new hearts, which correspond to the newness in the book of Isaiah.'[3] Nicephorus of Constantinople stated: 'Everything done in the Church is tradition, including the Gospel, since Jesus Christ wrote nothing but put his word into the souls of people.'[4]

St Thomas Aquinas says, with St Augustine, that all Scripture, including the New Testament, when considered as *written* and therefore external to the heart of people, is a mere letter that kills. External means of communication continue to be used under the New Dispensation but these are only secondary realities. Their role is merely to support the interior fruit, the primary reality. They are only a help. The central reality is *the grace of the Holy Spirit*, i.e. the grace in which the new law properly consists, the law of the Spirit written not in ink, but by the Spirit of the living God, not on tablets of stone but on tablets of human hearts.[5]

The concept of the 'Gospel in the heart' was taken up strongly by Catholic theologians in their defence of traditional doctrine against the Reformers who narrowed revelation to only those truths explicitly stated in Sacred Scripture.[6] Joseph Ratzinger, the present Cardinal Prefect of the Congregation for Doctrine, has shown that the 'Gospel in the heart' was very much discussed at the Council of Trent (1601–12). Cardinal Cervini proposed to the Council three principles and foundations of our faith:

1. The sacred books which were written under the inspiration of the Holy Spirit.
2. The gospel which our Lord did not write, but taught by word of mouth and implanted in people's hearts, and part of which the evangelists later wrote down, while much was simply entrusted to the hearts of the faithful.
3. Guidance of the Spirit: since the Son of God was not going to physically abide with us for ever, he sent the Holy Spirit, who was to reveal the mysteries of God in the hearts of the faithful and teach the Church all truth until the end of time.[7]

When it comes to specific questions, such as 'Can women too be ordained priests?', we have to be extremely careful. For such truths may be contained in the internal core tradition without the carriers of that tradition even being aware of it. Cardinal Newman has written extensively on such pregnant, latent tradition.

> Naturally as the inward idea of divine truth, such as has been described, passes into explicit form by the activity of our reflective powers, still such an actual delineation is not essential to its genuineness and perfection. A peasant may have such a true impression, yet be unable to give any intelligible account of it, as will easily be understood. But what is remarkable at first sight is this, that *there is good reason for saying that the impression made upon the mind need not even be recognized by the parties possessing it. It is no proof that persons are not possessed, because they are not conscious, of an idea.* Nothing is of more frequent occurrence, whether in things sensible or intellectual, than the existence of such unperceived impressions . . . Consider, when persons would trace the history of their own opinions in past years, how baffled they are in the attempt to fix the date of this or that conviction, their system of thought having been all the while in continual, gradual, tranquil expansion; so that it were as easy to follow the growth of the fruit of the earth, 'first the blade, then the ear, after that the full corn in the ear', as to chronicle changes, which involved no abrupt revolution, or reaction, or fickleness of mind, but have been the birth of an idea, the development, in explicit form, of what was already latent within it . . . Now, it is important to insist on this circumstance,

because it suggests the reality and permanence of inward knowledge, as distinct from explicit confession. *The absence, or partial absence, or incompleteness of dogmatic statements is no proof of the absence of impressions or implicit judgments, in the mind of the Church. Even centuries might pass without the formal expression of a truth, which had been all along the secret life of millions of faithful souls.*[8]

Unpacking the true tradition

We can now tackle the question: 'Is the priestly ordination of women contained in the Church's tradition?' Twenty centuries of experience as Jesus' community has taught us to distinguish different areas within tradition: root convictions, explicit testimonies and implied beliefs. Some examples may clarify what I mean.

Catholics have grown used to accepting the Immaculate Conception of Mary and her Bodily Assumption into heaven as doctrines of faith. These truths are not found in Scripture and they were not taught by the apostles. They were contained in a deep conviction that the redemption Jesus Christ had brought us was fully implemented in his mother. The faithful carried this conviction from the earliest times. This was the *root tradition*, which remained latent for a long time. Then we find some Fathers of the Church expressing their belief in the Immaculate Conception and the Assumption explicitly. The beliefs of the faithful were also implied in what they did, such as feasts and devotions to Mary, which revealed the depth of the latent tradition. Now these various aspects of tradition were not separate. Together they formed part of the one living tradition.

Or consider the doctrines of the primacy and infallibility of the Pope. Jesus gave authority to the apostles which was the *root tradition*, but explicit testimonies to the role of the 'bishop of Rome' only emerged in later centuries. The Church's persuasion that the Pope has special authority was implicitly, and thus latently, contained in the acceptance of papal supremacy. But St Peter himself would not have been able to formulate the extent and limits of the Pope's infallibility in *ex cathedra* pronouncements as declared by Vatican I. And, in spite of his respect for Mary, he might well have rejected as esoteric gobbledegook the phrase that 'the blessed Virgin Mary was preserved from all stain of original sin in the first instant of her conception, in view of the merits of Christ'.[9]

That women can be ordained priests is contained in the root conviction that men and women are baptised equally in Christ, which implies openness to all the sacraments, including priestly ordination. This root conviction was carried by the *sensus fidelium*, as explained in Chapter 6.

Women's openness to Holy Orders was given explicit recognition in the ministries entrusted to women, especially in their sacramental ordination to the diaconate. It was also implied in the devotion to Mary as priest. It manifests itself today in the fact that many Catholic women feel called to be priests. In fact, the implicit belief erupted in many forms throughout the centuries.

Women in priestly ministry?

New historical evidence confirms that in some parts of the Church women have functioned as priests. For instance, in the south of Italy tombstones attest to the presence of women priests. In the catacomb of Tropea, a fifth-century inscription reads: 'Sacred to her good memory. Leta the *presbytera* lived 40 years, 8 months, 9 days, for whom her husband set up this tomb. She preceded him in peace on the day before the Ides of May.' A sarcophagus in Salona mentions: 'I, Theodosius, bought for three golden solids a plot in the cemetery of Salona from the *presbytera* Flavia Vitalia.' The term '*presbytera*' is sometimes used in ancient sources as 'the wife of a priest', but not here. In 494 Pope Gelasius wrote a letter to the southern provinces of Italy, condemning the ministry of women. 'We have heard to our annoyance that divine affairs have come to such a low state that women are encouraged to officiate at the sacred altars, and to take part in all matters imputed to the offices of the male sex, to which they do not belong.'

An analysis of the available facts makes Professor Giorgio Otranto conclude that the ministry of women priests was a fact in the three provinces of Lucania, Bruttium and Sicily. It is confirmed by the testimony of Bishop Atto of Vercelli (ninth century). Atto stressed that in the ancient Church not only men but also women were ordained and officiated as the leaders of communities; they were called *presbyterae* and they assumed the duty of preaching, directing and teaching.[10]

In a separate study, historical inscriptions about 'women bishops' have been analysed, including Theodora Episcopa, the mother of Pope Paschal I (817–24). The previous interpretation of these having been the wives of bishops is rejected, after careful analysis. A basis in pastoral practice is no longer ruled out. 'The women bishops mentioned in inscriptions have in research always been interpreted as having been the wives of bishops, in harmony with the Catholic paradigm that denied any plausibility to female bishops. However, on the ground of tombstone evidence it seems likely that some women in Rome itself and in the Roman provinces actually functioned as bishops.'[11]

134

It would also seem that some regions of the 'Celtic Church' were more open to women in the ministry. The Celtic Church, mainly present in Ireland and Britain, manifested divergent practices in the fifth to the ninth centuries, such as the 84-year Easter cycle, the Celtic tonsure, variations in liturgy, baptismal rites and monastic rule. There were also differences regarding episcopal consecration and jurisdiction. Cogitosus tells us that St Brigid of Kildare (died 528) was ordained bishop by Bishop Mel. Brigid had jurisdiction over the double monastery of nuns and monks. She invited her friend St Conleth to function as the local bishop for the people, under her jurisdiction.[12] St Hilda of Whitby in England (614–80) held similar jurisdictional powers.

Another glimpse of Celtic practice can be seen in the Breton region of Gaul at the beginning of the sixth century, where two Celtic priests were reported to be assisted at Mass by women. 'While the priests distributed the Eucharist, the women held the chalices and administered the blood of Christ to the people.'[13] Much of what really happened has been obliterated by the imposition of Roman discipline on Celtic communities in later centuries.

Women priests may have existed in the Saxon dioceses of Germany, the Netherlands and England. The tenth-century Chronicle of Widukind mentions 'priests of either sex'.[14] The historian George Fabricius, who drew from the annals at Quedlinburg, mentions eleven abbesses who were ordained as *sacerdos maxima*, among them Ebba, abbess of the monastery at Coldingham, and Etheldreda of Ely. Three of the abbesses of Quedlinburg were ordained as *sacerdos maxima*. In the eleventh century the ordination of Mechtild took place in the cathedral of Halberstadt in the presence of twelve archbishops and bishops.[15] Croziers and other episcopal insignia have been found in the tombs of early medieval abbesses.[16]

These examples do not prove that ordaining women was a common practice. On the contrary, they may have been exceptions that were later rigorously suppressed by the dominating Latin culture. What they do show, though, is that Christian awareness, left to itself, would admit women to the priesthood. They reveal a natural openness in Christian consciousness.

During the Middle Ages, when the whole weight of Latin anti-feminine culture was brought to bear on women in the Church, we find the surprising devotion to Mary of Magdala. And Mary, it should be remembered, was seen to have done in her life what no other woman could ever dream of doing. According to ancient tradition, the apostles did not believe in the resurrection of Christ. It was Mary of Magdala who preached the Gospel to them and brought them back to accepting Christ. Peter had

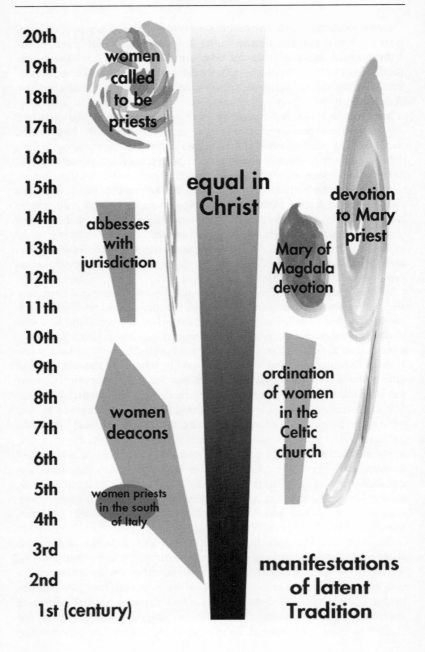

20th
19th — women called to be priests
18th
17th
16th
15th
14th — equal in Christ — devotion to Mary priest
13th — abbesses with jurisdiction
12th — Mary of Magdala devotion
11th
10th
9th
8th — ordination of women in the Celtic church
7th — women deacons
6th
5th — women priests in the south of Italy
4th
3rd
2nd — manifestations of latent Tradition
1st (century)

objected to Mary's role because she was only a woman. Then Levi rebuked him: 'I see that you are contending against women like adversaries. But if the Saviour made her worthy, who are you to reject her? Surely the Saviour knows her very well. That is why he loved her more than us.'[17] Tradition had it that Mary later travelled to France and preached the Gospel there.[18]

Preaching was the preserve of priests. Women could not be ordained priests because they were forbidden to preach.[19] But Mary of Magdala *had* preached. And devotion to her soared. We find her on statues, paintings, friezes, altar panels and manuscript illustrations. Usually she is presented as either receiving her commission from Christ, reading Scripture or preaching to townsfolk. A twelfth-century Psalter of St Albans in England shows her addressing the assembled apostles, who respectfully listen to her, their heads bowed. She obviously functioned as a counter-heroine.[20] And Mary of Magdala was not alone.

The Middle Ages knew legends of many women saints who had disguised themselves as men to become monks – Saints Pelagia, Marina, Apollinaria, Euphrysinia, Reparata, Theodora and Hilaria, to mention just a few.[21] In a twelfth-century church at Vézelay in the South of France, we find on the capital of one of the columns a depiction of St Eugenia, who wears a tonsure and habit, but who also exposes her breasts. The scene of the capital recounts the fact that Eugenia had to reveal herself as a woman before court when she had been falsely accused of having committed adultery. This happened after she had ruled the monastery for some years as its abbot.[22] Catholics of the day obviously knew that women were capable of more than the passive roles ascribed to them by men.

St Catherine of Siena (1347–80), Doctor of the Church, wanted to disguise herself and so become a Dominican priest. The plan did not work. Later she expressed her frustration to God in prayer. 'My sex, as you know, is against me in many ways, both because it is not highly considered by men, and also because it is not good, for decency's sake, for a woman to mix with men.' But God reassured her: 'Am I not He who created the human race, and divided it into male and female? I spread abroad the grace of my Spirit where I will. In my eyes there is neither male nor female, rich nor poor, but all are equal, for I can do all things with equal ease.'[23] It resonated with St Catherine's conviction that she could be a priest. The God of her visions did not tell her to submit to her subordinate position as a woman. Many other women stood up against their patriarchal environment, such as Hildegard of Bingen, Mechtild of Magdeburg, Mechtild of Hackeborn, Catherine of Genoa and Julian of Norwich. Their significance is only now coming to light.[24]

In recent days this deeply Catholic conviction was shown again when

Bishop Felix Davidek ordained women as deacons and priests in the Czech Republic during the days of communist persecution. At a diocesan synod he stated: 'Today humankind needs and is literally awaiting the ordination of women. The Church should not oppose it. This is the reason why we have gathered here. This fact leads us to the need for prayer and the need for sacrament. Nothing else. Society needs the service of women. It needs the service of women as a special instrument for the sanctification of the second half of humankind.'[25]

READINGS FROM THE WOMEN PRIESTS WEBSITE

Giorgio Otranto
'Notes on the Female Priesthood in Antiquity'
 http://www.womenpriests.org/traditio/otran___1.htm
'The Problem of the Ordination of Women in the
Early Christian Priesthood'
 http://www.womenpriests.org/traditio/otran___2.htm
Letter by **Bishop Atto of Vercelli**
 http://www.womenpriests.org/traditio/atto.htm
Letter by Bishops Licinius, Melanius and Eustochius
on Celtic women in the ministry
 http://www.womenpriests.org/traditio/kelts.htm
Excerpts from biography of **Catherine of Siena**
 http://www.womenpriests.org/called/siena.htm
The veneration of **Mary of Magdala**
 http://www.womenpriests.org/magdala/intro.htm
Interview with **Ludmila Javorová**, first Czech Catholic woman priest
 http://www.womenpriests.org/called/javo___int.htm

17

Nine Centuries of Women Deacons

THE CONGREGATION FOR DOCTRINE BASES its opposition to women priests also on what it believes to be an indisputable fact. The Church has never ordained women as priests. This has been the unchanging and constant practice throughout the past 2000 years.

> The Catholic Church has never felt that priestly or episcopal ordination can be validly conferred on women . . . Since that period [of the Middle Ages] and up to our own time, it can be said that the question has not been raised again, for the practice has enjoyed peaceful and universal acceptance . . . The Church's tradition in the matter has thus been so firm in the course of the centuries that the magisterium has not felt the need to intervene in order to formulate a principle which was not attacked, or to defend a law which was not challenged.[1]

The Congregation thus claims that the practice of not ordaining women proves by its own fact that it is part of sacred tradition. But does it? It would not be difficult to expose the fallacy of such a claim. A practice by itself, however long, proves nothing. For nineteen centuries the Church practised slavery. Did that prove it belonged to tradition? But with regard to ordaining women, the Congregation even got its facts wrong. For women *did* receive the sacrament of ordination during the first millennium of the Church. Tens of thousands were ordained as deacons and thus participated in the first level of the sacramental ministry of the priesthood.

In the Early Church a plethora of ministries had arisen that all seemed more or less related to the priesthood. They included acolytes, readers, catechists, doorkeepers and subdeacons. When, during the time of the Reformation, many of the sacraments came under attack, including that of the priesthood, the Council of Trent declared in 1563 that three ministries had from the earliest times formed part of the sacrament of Holy Orders: the episcopate, the priesthood and the diaconate.

> Whereas the ministry of so holy a priesthood is a divine thing; to the end that

it might be exercised in a more worthy manner, and with greater veneration, it was suitable that, in the most well-ordered settlement of the Church, there should be several and diverse orders of ministers, to minister in the [one] priesthood, by virtue of their office; orders so distributed as that those already marked with the clerical tonsure should ascend through the lesser to the greater orders. For the sacred Scriptures make open mention not only of priests, but also of deacons; and teach, in most weighty words, what things are especially to be attended to in their ordination . . . If anyone says, that, in the Catholic Church there is not a hierarchy by divine ordination instituted, consisting of bishops, priests and deacons; let him be anathema.[2]

The Congregation for Doctrine acknowledges that there were women deacons in the Early Church, but it denies that they received a sacramental ordination. The diaconate for women was only a minor ministry, it says, a blessing, a commission to perform some practical tasks, not a sacrament. But are they right?

We know that women deacons were ordained in the Early Church through precisely the same ordination rite as male deacons. This fact is so crucial that I will move step by step through the ancient rite, proving that the diaconate given to women was as much a sacrament as the diaconate given to men. In this chapter I will base my text on the rituals in an ancient Greek manuscript discovered in the library of Cardinal Francis Barberini. It had come from the monastery of St Mark in Florence, which in turn had received it from the inheritance of Nicolai de Nicolis. That is why I call the manuscript the Nicolai manuscript. An analysis of the *uncial script* used by the copyist would indicate that the copy was transcribed between the ninth and the twelfth centuries at the latest. The contents are much older and reflect Byzantine practice in the sixth to eighth centuries AD. Remember that at that time East and West had not yet split in the Church.[3]

The manuscript is a *rituale*,[4] i.e. it contains detailed instructions on the ceremonies and prayers to be used at the ordination of bishops, priests, deacons, subdeacons, readers, acolytes and doorkeepers. It has separate ordination rites for male deacons and female deacons. For easy comparison these rites are set out side by side in this chapter. I reproduce the complete text, interrupted only by an unavoidable word of comment.

Opening ceremony

'The Ordination of Deacons'	*'Ordination prayer for Deaconesses'*
After the sacred offertory, the doors [of the sanctuary] are opened and before the Deacon starts the litany 'All Saints',	After the sacred offertory, the doors [of the sanctuary] are opened and, before the Deacon starts the litany 'All Saints',

the man who is to be ordained Deacon is brought before the Archbishop. And when the 'Divine Grace' statement has been said, the ordinand kneels down.	the woman who is to be ordained Deacon is brought before the Bishop.[5] And after the Bishop has said the 'Divine Grace' with a loud voice, the woman to be ordained bows her head.

As the Orthodox theologian Evangelos Theodorou points out, the setting for both ordinations indicates that we are dealing with a major order. To begin with, the ordination is called *cheirotonia*, which is Greek for the 'imposition of hands'. Then, the ordination takes place in the sanctuary before the altar. Remember how even today in the oriental rites the sanctuary that encloses the altar is hidden from the people through a sacred screen. Now the doors of the screen are opened to admit the candidates into the sanctuary itself. Moreover, the ordination of both male and female deacons takes place during the liturgy of the Eucharist and at a very solemn moment, namely after the sacred Anaphora (offertory). So-called minor orders, such as the lectorate and subdiaconate, are imparted by a simple imposition of hands (*cheirothesia*) outside the sanctuary and not during the Eucharist.

When the candidate stands before him, the bishop makes a public proclamation designating the candidate by name for the diaconate. The text reads as follows: 'Divine Grace, which always heals what is infirm and makes up for what is lacking, promotes [so-and-so] to be a Deacon. Let us therefore pray that the grace of the Holy Spirit may descend on him/her.'[6]

The time, the place, the solemn declaration in the presence of the people and the clergy – all this imparts a public character to the ordination. The intention is obviously for all to know that 'so-and-so' will from now on be a deacon.[7]

First laying on of hands

Male ordinand	*Female ordinand*
The Archbishop puts the sign of the cross on his forehead three times, imposes his hand and prays:	The Bishop imposes his hand on her forehead, makes the sign of the cross on it three times, and prays:
'Lord our God, in your providence you send the working and abundance of your Holy Spirit on those who through your inscrutable power are constituted liturgical ministers to serve your immaculate mysteries, please,	'Holy and Omnipotent Lord, through the birth of your Only Son our God from a Virgin according to the flesh, you have sanctified the female sex. You grant not only to men, but also to women the grace and blessing of the Holy Spirit.

preserve, Lord, this man whom you want me to promote to the ministry [*leitourgia*] of the diaconate in all seriousness and strictness of good behaviour, that he may guard the mystery of faith with a pure conscience. And give him the grace, which you have given to Stephen your first martyr.

And after having called him to the work of your ministry, in your good pleasure make him worthy to perform the degree [of responsibility] you entrust to him. For those who perform it well, will acquire for themselves a high degree [of reward]. Make your servant perfect, for yours are the kingdom and the power.'

Please, Lord, look on this your maid-servant and dedicate her to the ministry [*leitourgia*] of your diaconate, and pour out into her the rich and abundant giving of your Holy Spirit.

Preserve her so that she may always perform her ministry [*leitourgia*] with orthodox faith and irreproachable conduct, according to what is pleasing to you. For to you is due all glory and honour.'

To appreciate the importance of this section, we need to go back to basics. Sacraments are, by definition, sacred signs. In its long history the Church has come to accept two aspects of the 'sign' in each sacrament: the *matter* (an object or an action) and the *form* (the words that are spoken). In baptism, the washing with water is the matter, the words 'I baptise you in the name of the Father, the Son and the Holy Spirit' are the form. These two elements make up the substance of the sacramental sign. Where we find them present, we know that the sacrament has been validly administered. And being precise in details here is no luxury, as the Catholic Church has always insisted.

In the case of Holy Orders, from time immemorial the imposition of hands has been considered as the *matter* of the sacrament, the invoking of the Spirit on the ordinand as the *form*. These constitute the essence of the sacramental sign, by which everyone knows that this person has been truly ordained. By laying his hands on the head of the ordinand and by invocatory prayer, the bishop imparts the sacrament.

In the ceremony we are studying here we find that the Holy Spirit is called down on both the man and the woman for the ministry of the diaconate. Both are therefore *sacramentally* ordained. Note also that the prayer is said aloud for the whole congregation to hear.

The Intercessions

Male ordinand	Female ordinand
One of the other Deacons now starts a litany of intercessions: for the salvation of our souls, for peace in the world, for our Archbishop, for our Emperor, etc.	One of the other Deacons now starts a litany of intercessions: for the salvation of our souls, for peace in the world, for our Archbishop, for our Emperor, etc.

We know from parallel rituals in other manuscripts that special prayers for the ordinands were included. One of the prayers we find was: 'For [so-and-so] the Deaconess, who has just been ordained, and for her salvation, let us pray the Lord. That the most merciful Lord may give her a sincere and faultless diaconate, let us pray the Lord.'[8]

Second imposition of hands

Male ordinand	Female ordinand
While the officiating Deacon makes these intercessions, the Archbishop, still imposing his hand on the head of the ordinand, prays as follows:	While the Deacon makes these intercessions, the Archbishop, still imposing his hand on the head of the ordinand, prays as follows:
'God, our Saviour, with incorruptible voice you have foretold it, you announced that he would be first who would perform the ministry of the diaconate, as it is written in your holy Gospel: "Whoever wants to be first among you, must be your servant [diakonos]", please, Lord of all, fill this servant of yours whom you have made worthy to enter the ministry [leitourgia] of the diaconate, through the life-giving coming of your Holy Spirit, with all faith, charity, power and holiness.	'Lord, Master, you do not reject women who dedicate themselves to you and who are willing, in a becoming way, to serve your Holy House, but admit them to the order of your ministers [leitourgōn]. Grant the gift of your Holy Spirit also to this your maidservant who wants to dedicate herself to you, and fulfil in her the grace of the ministry of the diaconate, as you have granted to Phoebe the grace of your diaconate, Phoebe whom you had called to the work of the ministry [leitourgia]. Give her, Lord, that she may persevere without guilt in your Holy Temple, that she may carefully guard her behaviour, especially her modesty and temperance.
For grace is given to those you deem worthy, not by the imposition of my hands, but by the visitation of your rich mercy, so that, purified from sin, he may on that fearful day of your judgement be presented to you without guilt, and receive the reward of your unfailing promise. For you are our God, God of	Moreover, make your maidservant perfect, so that, when she will stand before the judgement seat of your

mercy and salvation, etc. etc. [sic!]'

Christ, she may obtain the worthy fruit of her excellent conduct, through the mercy and humanity of your Only Son.'

Again the bishop performs the laying on of hands and invokes the Holy Spirit. Just like the first imposition, this action by itself would suffice to impart the sacrament. Only candidates for the three major orders: bishops, priests and deacons receive a double imposition of hands. Perhaps the second imposition arose from a felt need to make absolutely sure that the candidate was validly ordained. Notice also that this second invocation of the Holy Spirit is spoken softly by the bishop. It seems to reinforce the intercessions spoken aloud by the officiating deacon.

Investiture

Male ordinand

The Archbishop takes away the [man's] scarf from the ordinand and lays a stole [on his shoulders]. He kisses him and hands him the holy thurible and makes him incense the holy gifts when they are exposed on the [altar] table.

Female ordinand

The Archbishop puts the stole of the diaconate round her neck, under her [woman's] scarf, arranging the two extremities of the stole towards the front.

Both the male and the female deacon receive the stole as their official vestment. The male deacon, one of whose future tasks it will be to assist at the altar during the Eucharist, is handed the thurible and made to incense the gifts for the first time.

Distributing communion

Male ordinand

When [at the time of communion] the newly ordained has taken part of the sacred body and precious blood, the Archbishop hands him the chalice. He in turn makes all those who approach him take part in the sacred blood.

Female ordinand

When [at the time of communion] the newly ordained has taken part of the sacred body and precious blood, the Archbishop hands her the chalice. She accepts it and puts it on the holy table [the altar].

Both the male and the female deacon are handed the chalice by the bishop. According to Byzantine practice, this chalice contains parts of the consecrated bread immersed in the consecrated blood. By holding the chalice in their hands, both the male and female deacon accept the task of distributing communion. Since male deacons assisted at the Eucharist in church, the male deacon starts to distribute at his ordination. Female deacons took communion to the sick. We will return to the tasks allocated to male and female deacons in the next chapter. Suffice it here to note that there is no difference in the ministry to which both were ordained. Also women deacons were ordained 'to serve your Holy House', 'to the work of the ministry [*leitourgia*] . . . in your Holy Temple'.

Each sacrament is by definition a visible sign, something people can see and distinguish from something else. Male and female deacons were ordained to the same diaconate, through identical rituals, under parallel invocations of the Holy Spirit. If a man was sacramentally ordained and a woman not, how were people to know? The truth is simple. Women deacons were admitted to Holy Orders. Otherwise we make a mockery of the intention of the ordaining bishops and the rite of ordination itself.

> If anyone says that, through sacred ordination, the Holy Spirit is not given, and that therefore the Bishop says in vain: 'Receive the Holy Spirit', or that through this ordination the character [of Holy Orders] is not imprinted . . . *Let him be anathema.*[9]

The sacramental character, which the Council of Trent described as 'a spiritual and indelible seal', is also received by deacons. Theologians do not agree on how the 'character' imprinted through the diaconate relates to the 'character' of the priesthood and the 'character' of the episcopacy. Many think the diaconate 'character' predisposes to the reception of the other 'characters'. In this context many point to the old rule which prescribed that no one should be ordained a priest without first being ordained a deacon.[10] The women who received the 'character' of the diaconate truly shared in the sacrament of ordination and could have been ordained priests.

READINGS FROM THE WOMEN PRIESTS WEBSITE

Texts of ordination rites from:
* the Apostolic Constitutions
                    http://www.womenpriests.org/traditio/deac___con.htm
* the Nicolai manuscript
                    http://www.womenpriests.org/traditio/deac___gr1.htm
* the George Varus manuscript
                    http://www.womenpriests.org/traditio/deac___gr2.htm
* Vatican manuscript no. 1872
                    http://www.womenpriests.org/traditio/deac-___gr3.htm
* reconstructed from 7 manuscripts
                    http://www.womenpriests.org/traditio/deac-___gr4.htm
* Syriac manuscript
                    http://www.womenpriests.org/traditio/deac___syr.htm

18

The Reality of Women Deacons

TRADITIONAL THEOLOGIANS WHO REJECT the ordination of women dismiss the phenomenon of the 'deaconesses' as irrelevant for a number of reasons:

- 'Church Councils forbade the ordination of women as deacons.'
- 'Women deacons did not assist at the Eucharist as male deacons did.'
- 'The ordination of deaconesses was only a blessing, not a real sacrament.'
- 'Women deacons were only a fringe phenomenon of local and temporary significance.'

It is these objections that we will now inspect.

Church Councils forbade it . . .?

The Council of Nicea (AD 325) is often quoted to prove that the ordination of women was not considered sacramental by the Early Church: 'With regard to the deaconesses who hold this position we remind [church leaders] that they possess no ordination [*cheirotonia*], but are to be reckoned among the laity in every respect' (canon 19). But what does the passage really mean?

The decree in question deals with the followers of Paul of Samosata, a heresy which the First Council of Nicea sought to counter. The Council lays down rules on how they should be received back into the Church.

> With regard to Paulicians who take refuge in the Catholic Church, it has been decided that they definitely need to be [re]baptized. If, however, some of them have previously functioned as priests, if they seem to be immaculate and irreprehensible, they need to be baptized and ordained by a bishop of the Catholic Church. In this way one must also deal with the deaconesses or with anyone in an ecclesiastical office. With regard to the deaconesses who hold this position we remind [church leaders] that they possess no ordination [*cheirotonia*], but are to be reckoned among the laity in every respect.[1]

The Council basically declared all the Paulician sacraments invalid: baptism, priesthood and diaconate. The reason was Paul of Samosata's refusal to accept Jesus as the Incarnate Son of God, and all sacraments are imparted in Jesus' name. The Council particularly rejected the Paulician women's diaconate since it was not given through ordination [*cheirotonia*] as the Catholic diaconate was. However, the Council did not reject women deacons as such.[2]

Another favourite quote is canon 26 of the 'Council of Orange' (AD 441): 'Altogether no women deacons are to be ordained. If some already exist, let them bend their heads to the blessing given to the [lay] people.'[3] This, however, was not a universal council of the Church, but a local synod in Gaul, involving only a few dioceses. The prohibition demonstrates opposition to the women's diaconate in parts of the Western Church. At the same time it attests to the fact that women deacons were ordained elsewhere.

In fact, two general Councils of the Church explicitly acknowledge the existence of women deacons. They lay down a minimum age in the same breath as they lay down minimum ages for priests and male deacons.

- **Chalcedon** (AD **451**): 'A woman shall not receive the laying on of hands as a deaconess under forty years of age, and then only after searching examination. And if, after she has had hands laid on her and has continued for a time to minister, she shall despise the grace of God and give herself in marriage, she and the man united to her shall be anathematized.'[4]
- **Trullo** (AD **692**): 'Let the canon of our holy God-fearing Fathers be confirmed in this particular also; that a priest be not ordained before he is thirty years of age, even if he be a very worthy man, but let him be kept back. For our Lord Jesus Christ was baptized and began to teach when he was thirty. In like manner let no deacon be ordained before he is twenty-five, nor a deaconess before she is forty.'[5]

A different ministry . . .?

Male deacons were ordained to serve at the altar, we are told. Their ministry was *eucharistic* and therefore male deacons were ordained sacramentally. Women deacons, however, only performed subsidiary tasks. The ordaining bishop did not intend to ordain them to a sacramental ministry.[6]

Differences in the day-to-day division of work do not prove there was a separate diaconate, however. Many officials in the Curia in Rome, for example, have been ordained as bishops and archbishops for diplomatic reasons. They work mostly in administration. Though the use of ordination for organisational purposes is ethically questionable, it does not make such an ordination to the episcopate less valid than that of pastoral bishops. The diaconal/priestly/episcopal status is determined by the ordination rite, not by subsequent work. It was pastoral prudence that inspired Church leaders to employ women deacons differently. Women serving the bishop in the sanctuary, which was screened off from the people during the holiest of moments, might invite the suspicion of impropriety. Moreover, women also had to battle with the prejudice of presumed ritual uncleanness during their monthly periods. But it is wrong to infer from this that, therefore, a woman deacon was ordained to a lower form of diaconate than a man.

The ordination rite of the woman deacon itself contradicts this since she was handed a chalice, as the man was. The ordination prayers dedicated women deacons, as much as their male colleagues, to the 'ministry' (the Greek word is *leitourgia*) in God's Holy Temple. Moreover, we know from ancient Church laws in Syria that women deacons assisted at the altar when there were no male deacons, and that they took communion to the sick.[7] 'With permission of the bishop, the deaconess may pour wine and water into the chalice.'[8]

One of the main tasks of the woman deacon was to assist at the baptism of women catechumens. It was the woman deacon who instructed them before baptism, 'teaching unskilled and rural women with clear and sound words, both as to how to respond to the questions put by the baptizer at the moment of baptism and how to live after the reception of baptism'.[9] The woman deacon also assisted at the baptism itself.

At the entrance to the baptistry, the officiating bishop or priest would anoint the catechumens with a sign of the cross on the forehead, saying a prayer such as: 'I anoint you with the oil of gladness which overcomes all violence of the enemy and by which you will be protected in the name of the Father, the Son and the Holy Spirit.' Then the woman deacon would take the catechumens into the baptistry itself. There she would strip them of all their clothes and ornaments. The woman deacon would then anoint them with the oil of catechumens over every part of their body.

It is clear that both the stripping and anointing were total. 'The person to be baptised is stripped naked . . . All silver and gold ornaments, and clothes, are taken off . . . Anoint that person on his breast, his arms, his stomach, his back, in the middle of both hands, etc.' 'The deacon removes from the catechumen all clothes, ornaments, earrings and whatever they wear . . . He pours the oil for anointing into the cup of his hands and rubs it on the whole body of the catechumen, also in between the fingers of his hands and the toes of his feet, and his limbs, and his front and his back.'[10]

It is obvious that the anointing of women demanded the service of women deacons. 'Ordain a deaconess who is faithful and holy for the ministrations towards women. For sometimes he [the bishop] cannot send a deacon, who is a man, to the women, on account of unbelievers. You must therefore send a woman, a deaconess, on account of the imaginations of the bad. For we stand in need of a woman, a deaconess, for many necessities; and first in the baptism of women, the deacon shall anoint only their forehead with the holy oil, and after him the deaconess shall anoint them: for there is no necessity that the women should be seen by the men.'[11]

Ancient baptistry viewed from top

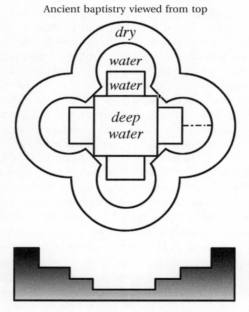

Cut-away viewed from the side

From the ancient rituals we can more or less reconstruct what happened next. Ancient baptistries were like small ponds, with steps leading into the water. The deaconess led the (female) catechumen down the steps, from the west to the east, so that the catechumen faced east. In the middle the font was about 3 feet deep. According to some sources, the bishop or priest (the baptiser) had also descended into the font. This

150

person then immersed the catechumen three times, saying a formula such as: 'I baptise you in the name of the Father, the Son and the Holy Spirit.' The baptiser then handed the newly baptised person to the deacon or deaconess, who brought them up the steps, dried them with a towel and helped them put on a white dress. This is a possible interpretation of the ancient instruction:

> After that, either thou, o bishop, or a presbyter that is under you, shall in the solemn form name over them the Father, and Son, and Holy Spirit, and shall dip them in the water; and let a deacon receive the man, and a deaconess the woman, that so the conferring of this inviolable seal may take place with a becoming decency. And after that, let the bishop anoint those that are baptised with ointment.[12]

It is also possible, and even likely, that the immersion itself was done by the deacon or the deaconess while the baptismal formula was spoken either by them or by the bishop or priest who stood outside the baptistry. The immersion of a female catechumen by the deaconess seems to follow from a number of indications. The expression 'to receive' in 'the deacon shall *receive* a man', 'the deaconess shall *receive* a woman' may originally have meant 'immerse'. We find the expression in some baptismal rituals. The anxiety that 'no man should see' a female catechumen naked and that the conferring of baptism be done 'with becoming decency' required that the deaconess did both the anointing and the immersion. Also, the opposition to women 'baptising' among some Latin Fathers in the West, obviously reflected a full involvement of female deacons in other regions of the Church.

In any case, it is clear that women deacons carried a distinct and equivalent ministry to male deacons.

Only a blessing . . .?

In the early Middle Ages theologians were aware of the fact that the Council of Chalcedon (AD 451) had fixed a minimum age of 40 years for 'deaconesses'. Since the institution of women deacons had ceased to exist in the West for some centuries, they were puzzled as to what this diaconate had meant. Their ignorance of the historical facts is clear in what they write.

> There is no doubt that formerly there existed the custom of ordaining deaconesses, that is: readers of the gospels. Because no deaconess was allowed to be ordained before the age of forty and after ordination they were forbidden to

marry. But women have no part in the order of the priesthood, nor can they have any. (Rolandus Bandinelli, 1148)[13]

In the past some nuns were ordained to be deaconesses, not to holy orders but to some ministry such as to proclaim the Gospel during matins or something similar. At present this does not happen, but without any specific institutions there are still some nuns in some places who read the Gospel . . . Deaconesses were ordained, that is: they were elected and established with some solemnity in one or other ministry, which agrees with deacons. Perhaps they sang or read out the Gospel during matins as well as prayer. This ministry and dignity was called the diaconate. (Hugucchio, 1188)[14]

Some people have asserted that the male sex is necessary for the lawfulness and not for the validity of the sacrament [of ordination], because even in the *Decretals* (cap. Mulieres dist. 32; cap. Diaconissam, 27, qu. i) mention is made of deaconesses and priestesses. But deaconess there denotes a woman who shares in some act of a deacon, namely who reads the homilies in the Church; and priestess [*presbytera*] means a widow, for the word 'presbyter' means elder. (Thomas Aquinas, 1225–74).[15]

Clearly it was the opinion of certain people that women of old had received Orders. For it states [in the twenty-seventh Cause Question 1 = canon 23 of the Decree of Gratian]: 'We have decided that a deaconess should not be ordained before the age of forty'. And in the same Question, 'If anyone ravishes or disturbs a deaconess', and similarly in Distinction thirty-two [of the Decree of Gratian], mention is clearly made of a *presbytera* [which could mean 'female priest' in Latin]. But surely if we pay attention to what is said in Distinction thirty-two, *Presbyteram*, etc., it is shown there that widows and older women, and matrons were called *presbyteras*; and from this it is gathered that the women who shared with the deacons in reading the homily were called deaconesses. They received some kind of blessing. Therefore in no way should it be believed that there were ever women promoted to sacred orders according to the canons [laws of the Church].' (Bonaventure, 1217–74)[16]

It is obvious that the medieval theologians in the West were simply ignorant of the facts surrounding women deacons. Their assessment of the women's diaconate carries no value. If they had known the ordination rite, they would have changed their mind.

A fringe phenomenon?

Literary sources have left us ample records of deaconesses in different parts of the Byzantine Empire. We know quite a few deaconesses by name, often because of their connections with Church leaders. They represent thousands whose names remain hidden, like those of male priests and deacons.

Olympias in Constantinople had been ordained by Bishop Nektarios. She was a friend of St Gregory of Nazianzus and later of St John Chrysostom, whom she greatly helped during his conflict with the emperor and his exile. At her time, Constantinople's main cathedral, the Hagia Sophia, counted among its clergy 60 priests, 100 male deacons and 40 women deacons. She died in AD 418.

Theodoret of Cyrus (AD 466) tells the story of a deaconess in Antioch who instructed and converted the son of a pagan priest in the Christian faith. Out of propriety, or perhaps for safety reasons, she is known as '*Anonyma*'. This was the period of the persecutions under Emperor Julian (361–63). After fully preparing the young man for baptism, she helped him escape from his father's house so that he could join the Christian community in a safer locality.

Radegunde, a Thuringian princess from southern Gaul and wife of the Frankish king Clothaire I, fled from her palace in AD 550 and was ordained a deacon by Bishop Medardus of Noyon. She founded a 'free' convent in Poitiers – free, that is, from episcopal or political interference – and evangelised the surrounding area.

From the correspondence of the Fathers of the Church we know *Procula* and *Pentadia*, to whom St Chrysostom wrote letters. *Salvina* who later became a deaconess in Constantinople, wrote letters to St Jerome. Severus, Bishop of Antioch, mentions the deaconess *Anastasia* in his letters. The deaconess *Macrina* was the sister of St Basil the Great. She had a close friend who was also a deaconess: *Lampadia*. The deaconess *Theosebia* was the wife of the Doctor of the Church, St Gregory of Nyssa. The Orthodox calendar of saints includes 22 women deacons who are mentioned by name, as well as the seven women deacons who were martyred with Bishop Abdjesus in fifth-century Persia.[17]

The names of deaconesses have also been preserved on tombstones. At least 28 have been identified. Here are some typical examples:

- *Sophia of Jerusalem* (fourth century AD?). The Greek inscription reads: 'Here lies the servant and virgin of Christ, the deacon, the second Phoebe [Rom. 16:1], who passed away in peace on the 21st day of March . . . May the Lord God . . .'

153

- *Theodora* of Gaul carried this Latin inscription on her tomb: 'Here rests in peace and of good remembrance Theodora the deaconess who lived about 48 years and died on 22 July 539.'

Tombstone of Athanasia

- *Athanasia* of Delphi in Greece (fifth century): 'The most devout deaconess Athanasia, established deaconess by his holiness bishop Pantamianos after she had lived a blameless life. He erected this tomb on the place where her honoured [body?] lies. If someone else dares to open this tomb in which the deaconess has been buried, may he receive the fate of Judas, who betrayed our Lord Jesus Christ . . . Nothing less the clerics who were found gathered . . .'
- The deaconess *Eneon* at Jerusalem had ministered to the sick: 'Tomb of Eneon, daughter of Neoiketis, deaconess in this hospital.'[18]

Not scriptural?

The Church has known deaconesses right from the apostolic age. Paul mentions 'Phoebe, our sister, who is a servant (*diakonos*) of the Church at Cenchreae. She has often been a helper both to myself and to many others'.[19] Did the word *diakonos* applied to Phoebe carry with it the sense of a precise ministerial function which it would have later where women were concerned? We do not know for certain, even though *diakonos* did soon become a well-circumscribed function in the Church.[20] Also, Clement of Alexandria (AD 150–215) puts the women's ministry right back to apostolic times. 'The apostles, giving themselves without respite to the work of evangelism as befitted their ministry, took with them women, not as wives but as sisters to share in their ministry to women living at home: by their agency the teaching of the Lord reached the women's quarters without arousing suspicion.'[21]

This early diaconate of women is confirmed by a classical passage in 1 Timothy that is often overlooked:

> Deacons must be men of grave behaviour; they must be examined and if found blameless may afterwards serve as deacons. The women must be of grave behaviour, not slanderers, temperate, in every respect faithful. Deacons must be married only once.[22]

The whole passage is about those serving in the diaconate, both men and women. Cardinal Daniélou, who defended the sacramental nature of the women's diaconate, writes as follows: 'The word "deacon" is here [in 1 Timothy 3:8–12] used in its technical sense. It also seems clear that by "the women" in question, who are clearly distinguished from the wives of the deacons while the description of them is parallel to that of the deacons, we must understand *women deacons*. It indicates a ministry which formed part of the ordained ministry itself.'[23] This is confirmed by the fact that Pliny the Younger in AD 112 reports on the presence of two *women deacons* in a Christian community in Asia Minor.[24]

READINGS FROM THE WOMEN PRIESTS WEBSITE

Texts from Church Councils:
* the Council of Nicea
> http://www.womenpriests.org/traditio/can__nic1.htm
* the Council of Chalcedon
> http://www.womenpriests.org/traditio/can__chal.htm
* the Council of Trullo
> http://www.womenpriests.org/traditio/can__trul.htm

Tasks of women deacons:
* role at baptism
> http://www.womenpriests.org/traditio/deac__bap.htm
* apostolate in the parish
> http://www.womenpriests.org/traditio/deac__apo.htm
* service at the altar
> http://www.womenpriests.org/traditio/deac__alt.htm
* supervisory roles
> http://www.womenpriests.org/traditio/deac__dis.htm

19

The Devotion to Mary as Priest

In THIS CHAPTER WE WILL study another manifestation of latent Catholic tradition which shows that the faithful, in their hearts of hearts, knew that women too could be ordained priests. It follows from the fact that love for Mary has included down the centuries, among popes, theologians and people, a conviction that she is a model priest. In our time we have come to be more circumspect about Marian devotions, aware as we are that misunderstandings and excesses in previous centuries offended the sensitivity of many Christians in other denominations.

I want to make my purpose crystal clear. I am not advocating a return to the devotion to Mary Priest, however excellent its pedigree. I am simply pointing out its significance as a spontaneous witness to Catholic conviction that Mary was 'as much a priest as any ordained man'. And if Mary is a priest, then any woman can be priest, since the priesthood is denied to women on the grounds of their being women. It reminds me of that famous court case in England involving a black slave.

In 1767 Granville Sharp, a pioneer campaigner for the abolition of slavery, tried to free a slave called Jonathan Strong, arguing in court that in England no human being can be held in slavery. The owner of the slave, however, won the court case as it was decided that a black person is not a full human being. Slaves, therefore, remain the property of their master, even in England. Sharp did not give up. In 1772 he initiated another court case in Liverpool to free the black slave James Somersett. He won the case only after producing the expert witness of scientists who examined James and declared him a human being like everyone else. The court then decided that a slave, even a black person, gains freedom the moment he/she sets foot on English territory. For what applied to one black person, applied to all. The same is true in the case of Our Lady. In spite of all her privileges, she was, and remains, a woman.

The belief that Mary is a priest

With our short ecclesiastical memories we have almost forgotten that in the run-up to its dogmatic definition in 1854, Mary's Immaculate Conception was often justified on the grounds of her being a priest. Tradition frequently applied Hebrews 7:26 to her: 'It is fitting that we should have such a high priest, holy, blameless, unstained, separated from sinners, exalted above the heavens.' The Benedictine prior Jacques Biroat wrote in 1666 that 'Paul's reasoning [in Hebrews 7:26] is relevant to Christ's mother. She shares in the priesthood of her son and is the origin of our reconciliation to God. Therefore, she had to be entirely innocent and separated from sinners. She had to be preserved from original sin.' Mary was immaculately conceived because she had to be a priest without stain.

Mary has captured the Catholic imagination more than any other person except Jesus Christ. Generation after generation has seen in her the highest reflection of saintliness and love. Catholics have been fond of Mary because she is Jesus' own mother. They also respected her as his closest associate in redemption, as his first 'priest'.

A pastoral worker in Holland recently drew my attention to a sixth-century mosaic depicting Mary wearing a chasuble and stole. She had come across its description while researching on the theme of Mary visiting Elizabeth. During the summer she and her husband planned their holiday around it. It took them to the ancient parish church of Parenzo in Croatia and, indeed, the coloured mosaic behind the altar showed Mary in priestly garments blessing a pregnant Elizabeth. For reasons that will become clear later on in this article, she, as most Catholics today, had not been aware of the link between Mary and the priesthood. Jean-Jacques Olier (1608–57), the founder of the famous seminary of St Sulpice in Paris, could have told her differently:

> The Blessed Virgin's greeting had the effect, on St John in Elizabeth's womb, of the sacramental words of baptism, sanctifying him and imparting the fullness of the gifts of the Holy Spirit . . . Thus the Blessed Virgin, as bishop in the Church, confirmed the son of the high priest Zechariah, making him holy and, through the imposition of her power, imprinting the Holy Spirit on him.[1]

All Christian believers share in Christ's priesthood, but the priestly role ascribed to Mary went well beyond the common priesthood of the faithful. Ferdinand Chirino de Salazar SJ (1575–1646) echoed century after century of tradition when he wrote:

> Christ, 'the anointed', poured out the abundance of his anointing on Mary, making her a saint, a queen and a priest forever. Mary obtained a priesthood

more eminent and excelling than that possessed by anyone else. For in unison with priests who are performing the sacred mysteries and together with Christ and in the same mystical way as he does, she always offers the Eucharistic sacrifice, just as, at one with him, she offered the sacrifice on Calvary.[2]

Tradition focused on Mary also as *a sacrificial priest*, a belief that had started in the Early Church and one that I want to emphasise, since this is the aspect of the priesthood of which Rome declares all women incapable.

Mary's exclusion from ministry?

In the context of the bridegroom and bride argument, Rome has recently held out Mary as the model of woman's true vocation as mother and virgin.[3] It presents this as a continuation of the ancient theme of Mary as mother and model of the Church. It has begun to speak of two dimensions in the Church: the *marian* one and the *apostolic-petrine* one.[4]

The *apostolic-petrine* dimension exists in the hierarchy. In this dimension bishops, priests and deacons represent Christ, the bridegroom. The function can only be fulfilled by men, since Christ is male. Though Rome calls this a service, the priestly dimension holds the real power in the body of the Church: of teaching, governing and, most important to Rome, performing sacred rites such as the eucharistic sacrifice. The *marian* dimension consists in the response of love: presenting one's body as a living sacrifice, giving witness to Christ and living a good Christian life. It corresponds to a woman's double vocation of motherhood (giving life) and virginity (gift of self in celibacy). It corresponds to the Church's role as the bride. In short it means the call to sanctity.

Whereas men can partake of both the marian and the petrine dimensions, women share only in the marian one. This should not distress them, according to Rome, for the marian dimension is higher, is more sublime, than the petrine one.

> The Marian dimension of the Church is antecedent to that of the Petrine, without being in any way divided from it or being less complementary. Mary Immaculate precedes all others, including obviously Peter himself and the Apostles. This is so, not only because Peter and the Apostles, being born of the human race under the burden of sin, form part of the Church which is 'holy from out of sinners' [*sic!*], but also because their triple function [of teaching, governing and sanctifying] has no other purpose except to form the Church in line with the ideal of sanctity already programmed and prefigured in Mary. A comtemporary theologian has rightly stated that Mary is 'Queen of

the Apostles without any pretensions to apostolic powers: she has other and greater powers' (H. U. von Balthasar, *Neue Klarstellungen*).[5]

The picture is clear. The two key words are sanctity and power. Women should not have any pretensions to apostolic power, i.e. ordination, because their call to holiness is of a higher order. 'A woman who desires priesthood is thus said to choose the "lesser part", and to deny and betray the "more" she is. In the past women were kept out of the priestly ministry on the pretext of their "inferior status"; now a "state of eminence" is ascribed to them with non-ordination as the same result.'[6]

Much could be said at this point. Rome's paternalistic attitude to women reminds me of an acquaintance of mine whose mother-in-law took up residence with the family for a long time. When she expressed a wish to drive the family car, he was at his wit's end as to how to disssuade her. In the end he hit upon this ploy. He told her that it would be below her dignity to drive the car, since important people left the driving to their 'chauffeur'. I doubt whether it convinced her. Women are taken in by double-speak as little as men are.

> Mary is metaphorically relegated to hearth and home. There is not even speculation that Mary was present at the Last Supper. Her role on Calvary, at the resurrection, and at Pentecost is a private one, always secondary to the public role of the male apostles. The exaltation of this domesticated Mary as a model for women devalues actual women in practice . . . It promotes obedience, passivity, and subordination as key religious values for good women, the very values that were thrown out of the window by the women who announced the resurrection of Jesus to the apostles.[7]

I do not intend to explore all aspects of the Pope's Marian symbolism here.[8] In the context of our search for latent tradition, I will restrict myself to pointing out that, in the age-old Mary Priest devotion, all those priestly, apostolic, petrine functions which are now being denied to women, were ascribed to Mary. In spite of her being a woman, real priestly powers were attributed to her.

Mary was a sacrificial priest

The Fathers of the Church pointed out that Mary belonged to a priestly family, as her relationship to Elizabeth shows. She was 'Aaron's staff which has budded forth as a guarantee of the eternal priesthood' (St Methodius). According to legends, Mary had spent her childhood in the Holy of Holies, where only the High Priests could enter and then once a year. 'Who has ever seen or heard anything the like, that a woman was introduced into the intimacy of the Holy of Holies, a place inaccessible even to men?' (St Germanus of Constantinople). The Fathers loved calling Mary 'the sanctuary', 'the ark of the covenant', 'the golden thurible' and 'the altar of incense', implying her priestly dignity. 'Hail young woman, sacrificial priest, world-wide propitiation for mortals, by whom from the East to the West the name of God is glorified among all nations and who in every place offers a sacrifice of incense to his name, as the holy Malachi says' (Theodore the Studite).[9]

Mary's priesthood was worked out in much more detail during the Middle Ages. Points of departure were the scriptural texts in which Mary was seen to have performed sacrificial functions. At the presentation in the Temple, for instance, Mary functioned as 'an ordained virgin who offered Jesus for our reconciliation as a victim agreeable to God', in the words of St Bernard of Clairvaux (1090–1153). Ubertino of Casale (1259–1330) added that there was no other priest. Only she could offer Jesus, and she was, after Jesus himself, the greatest of all priests. It became a common theme.

> When the sacred Virgin arrived at the altar, she knelt down, inflamed by the Holy Spirit more than the seraphim are, and holding her son in her arms, she offered him as a gift and acceptable sacrifice to God, praying in this way: 'Accept, almighty Father, the oblation which I offer for the whole world. Accept now from the arms of your handmaid this holy morning sacrifice which will be offered to you again, later, from the arms of the cross as the evening sacrifice'.[10]

Many theologians commented on the fact that Mary stood under the cross, in the posture of a sacrificing priest. Among them we find St Antoninus of Florence, a Doctor of the Church (1389–1459).

> Mary is the 'queen who stands at God's right hand in golden apparel' (Ps. 45:14). She is also the righteous priestess because she did not spare her own son, but stood by the cross, not as blessed Ambrose says, to just witness the sufferings and death of her son, but to further the salvation of the human race, committed as she was to offering the Son of God for the salvation of the world.[11]

As Fr F. W. Faber put it in 1857: 'Mary was the minister of the Incarnation. She had as little the right to come down from Calvary as a priest would have to leave the altar while the sacrifice of Mass is going on.'[12]

Was Mary's being a woman not a problem?

As we have seen, in the Roman culture that dominated the thinking of the Latin Fathers no less than that of medieval theologians, it was inconceivable for a woman to be entrusted with the leadership roles implied in the priesthood. Women were considered inferior to men both intellectually and emotionally. As 'incomplete human beings' they could not hold any public office. Consequently they were deemed incapable of wielding sacred power or of representing Christ who, as a man, had been a complete human being. Because of their monthly periods women were also 'a ritual risk', best kept out of the sanctuary for fear of defilement. Theological rationalisations were added for good measure: Christ had not chosen a woman among the apostolic team; God kept women in submission as punishment for their share in original sin; Paul had forbidden women to teach, and so on. How did this apply to Mary?

During the first ten centuries, the tradition of Mary's priestly status grew without being explicitly confronted with the ban against women, though the tension was there. In the fourth century, Epiphanius of Salamis had pointed out that if Mary had been a priest, Jesus would have been baptised by her and not by John the Baptist. It did not stop tradition extolling Mary's priestly dignity. But the contradiction was tackled head on only by legal-minded medieval scholars.

It was St Albert the Great, Doctor of the Church (1200–1280), who formulated the classic solution. Mary has not received the sacramental character of Holy Orders, he tells us, but she possesses the substance of the sacrament in abundance. In any hierarchy, superiors possess all powers and dignities of their inferiors. Since Mary occupies the highest level in the Church, she possesses eminently whatever dignities and powers priests, bishops and even popes possess.

> Although the most blessed Virgin did not receive the sacrament of [Holy] Orders, she possessed in full whatever dignity and grace is conferred by them. And a sevenfold grace is conferred in Holy Orders; but she was full of grace in every way.
>
> • Also, there are in the sacrament of orders: spiritual power, ministerial dignity, and executive power. But the most blessed Virgin possessed these three [powers] within herself excellently and equivalently. Ministers of the Church possess a beneficial dignity through their [sacramental] character of excellence, but the most blessed Virgin possessed the crown of the triumphant kingdom as well as of the Church militant. Whence the greatest of ministers is called the Pope, and he is the servant of the servants of God;

> she is the Queen and Mistress of Angels; he is the servant of the servants of God; she is the Empress of the whole world.
>
> - Also, in ministers resides a spiritual and temporal power from God, either delegated or vicarious; in her resides a perpetual plenitude of celestial power from ordinary authority.
> - Also, in ministers resides the power of binding or dissolving by the use of keys; in her there is the legitimate power of dominating by binding or dissolving through imperial rule.
>
> And thus it is clear that the blessed Virgin does not lack to any degree whatever there is of grace and dignity in [Holy] Orders.[13]

Did St Albert the Great not realise that this has consequences for an exclusion of women from ordination merely based on their sex? I believe he did. It is significant that he carefully listed the standard objections against the ordination of women, but then, in deviation from his practice regarding all other questions, omits to pronounce his own judgement on them. Entrapped though he was in the cultural and theological prejudices of his time, did he grasp that in Mary the ban against women might have been decisively broken?

Other theologians followed St Albert's thinking in a number of ways:

- In ordinary priests the sacramental character is external, in Mary it lies inherent.[14]
- It was the Holy Spirit himself who anointed her at the moment of her conception.[15]
- Mary shared in the priestly anointing Jesus had received, who was, after all, the 'anointed' *par excellence.*[16]
- Just as Jesus was never formally ordained, although he is the high priest for ever, so Mary is the greatest priest after him without sacramental ordination.[17]

The devotion to Mary Priest obviously struggled to make a point sometimes stated explicitly: 'In Mary the obstacle of her sex has been overcome by the authority of the saints, by the example of scripture and the power of reason.'[18] Do we not have here the voice of latent tradition: an awareness in the heart of Christian belief, strong in spite of surrounding prejudices, that the priesthood cannot be refused to women because of their sex, since, if anyone is a priest, Mary is?

Why did it stop?

Discussion of Mary's priesthood came to an abrupt end at the beginning of this century. While Leo XIII in 1903 had still accepted, with approval, a painting of Mary in priestly vestments, the Holy Office forbade in 1913 the practice of portraying Mary as a priest.[19] In 1907 St Pius X had still attached a 300-day indulgence to the prayer: 'Mary, Virgin Priest, pray for us',[20] but in 1926 the Holy Office declared that the devotion to Mary Priest 'is not approved and may not be promoted'.[21] Is it a coincidence that just at that time the campaign for women's ordination began to stir in other Christian Churches?

READINGS FROM THE WOMEN PRIESTS WEBSITE

Texts of St Albert the Great:
* Mary possessed the priesthood equivalently
                    http://www.womenpriests.org/mrpriest/albert3.htm
* Mary can rightly be called an apostle, evangelist and pastor
                    http://www.womenpriests.org/mrpriest/albert5.htm
* Mary acted as a sacrificial priest
                    http://www.womenpriests.org/mrpriest/albert2.htm
Texts of more than 90 **theologians and writers** who wrote on Mary's priesthood
                http://www.womenpriests.org/mrpriest/mpr__list.htm
Aspects of Mary Priest devotion:
* Mary as sacrificial priest
                    http://www.womenpriests.org/mrpriest/m__sacrif.htm
* Mary as model priest
                    http://www.womenpriests.org/mrpriest/m__priest.htm
* Mary and holy orders
                    http://www.womenpriests.org/mrpriest/m__orders.htm
Galleries of Mary Priest illustrations:
* Mary wearing an episcopal pallium
                    http://www.womenpriests.org/mrpriest/gallery1.htm
* Mary in priestly vestments
                    http://www.womenpriests.org/mrpriest/gallery2.htm

20

Women with a Priestly Vocation

O<small>N</small> 19 O<small>CTOBER</small> 1997, St Thérèse of Lisieux was officially declared a Doctor of the Church. Although the Roman authorities may not have realised this, their recognition of Thérèse's orthodox faith and soundness of teaching has consequences for the ordination of women. For St Thérèse had a profound longing to be a priest and so, implicitly, gave testimony to her deep 'Catholic sense' that women can and should be ordained.

> If I were a priest, how lovingly I would carry you in my hands when you came down from heaven at my call; how lovingly I would bestow you upon people's souls. I want to enlighten people's minds as the prophets and the doctors did. I feel the call of an Apostle. I would love to travel all over the world, making your name known and planting your cross on a heathen soil.[1]

Céline, Thérèse's sister who was closer to her than anyone else, tells us:

> The sacrifice of not being able to be a priest was something Thérèse always felt deeply. During her illness, whenever we were cutting her hair she would ask for a tonsure, and then joyfully feel it with her hand. But her regret did not find its expression merely in such trifles; it was caused by a real love of God, and inspired high hopes in her. The thought that St Barbara had brought communion to St Stanislaus Kostka thrilled her. 'Why must I be a nun, and not an angel or a priest?' she said. 'Oh! What wonders we shall see in heaven! I have a feeling that those who desired to be priests on earth will be able to share in their honour of the priesthood in heaven'.[2]

Priestly vocations among women

In the past, calls to the priesthood among women were simply squashed by the weight of official prejudice. The issue has become more visible in our own day with thousands of Catholic women expressing the call to the priesthood. Every vocation needs to be tested, of course. But if a Catholic woman, after a process of prayer and discernment, shows all such signs of a genuine vocation as are generally accepted for men, may we say that her vocation cannot be from God just because she belongs to the female sex?

Over the past few years I have collected the testimonies and life stories of more than eighty Roman Catholic women who feel called to the priestly ministry. Some I know personally. Some have corresponded with me. Some have left the record of their inner searchings and their pastoral involvements in magazine articles and books. They hail from many parts of the globe: Australia, Canada, the USA, England, Ireland, Scotland, Italy, Spain, Germany, France, Austria, Switzerland, Belgium and the Netherlands.

What will strike any unbiased observer is that the women speaking in these testimonies are balanced, dedicated, spiritual and competent people. Almost all possess theological qualifications. Many have proved their mettle in prolonged and demanding pastoral ministries. We are not dealing here with fanatics or with women who want to be ordained to redress a psychological hurt. We are listening to women who care and who know they cannot give others the spiritual and sacramental support they should be able to, as priests.

Claire Daurelle, who died in October 1998, ministered in la Duchère, a run-down parish of Lyons, for 25 years. 'I discovered my vocation gradually and reluctantly', she told *La Croix* in an interview. 'I have been commissioned to preach, baptise, wed and bury. I keep saying to my bishop: "Complete the job and impose your hands on me!" He answers that he may not.'[3]

A lay missionary who prefers to remain anonymous, serves rural communities in a remote corner of Africa. She does everything for her people: conducts Sunday service with sermons and communion, teaches the catechism, baptises and blesses marriages. What she cannot do is hear confession, preside at the Eucharist and anoint the sick. For this she relies on the occasional priest who visits every two or three months. 'I *am* the priest for these people day in day out', she tells me. 'Can this really be God's will that an outsider, who doesn't even speak the people's language, represents Christ better only because he is a man? What message does this give to my people about the dignity of women in the Church? Or about Christ's priority of love?'

Thirty-year-old Ulrike Murr from the archdiocese of Munich in Germany has studied both theology and chemistry. She earns her living as a college lecturer, but spends most of her free time serving in the parish. 'I have known myself called since I was young', she says. 'I have wrestled with my priestly vocation. I have tried to run away from God, but I cannot. My spiritual director and many of the people entrusted to my care affirm that I would make a good priest. I cannot understand the hierarchy. Here I stand offering a precious gift: the total dedication of my whole life to be another Christ. But the door is slammed in my face. At the same time we are urged to pray for vocations.'

On Maunday Thursday every year Catholic women hold prayer vigils in front of key cathedrals all over Britain. They wear something purple to symbolise their mourning for women's lost and rejected gifts. 'We sing, we pray, we keep silent and we think of our foremothers who have been such an inspiration to us', says Helen Blackburn, who feels a personal call to the priesthood. Born in Lancashire, she now represents the Catholic Women's Ordination in Scotland. 'For some reason, those opposed to women's ordination often seem to think it is perfectly acceptable to be rude to people like myself', Helen continues.

> I have had people who barely know me demand to know what kind of books I read and whether I go to Mass. Even priests have made unpleasant jokes at my expense. One or two have even asked me why I don't just become an Anglican. At the Chrism Mass last year, a woman to whom I was handing out a leaflet at the cathedral door, took it, ripped it in half and almost flung it back at me. She was so angry, but the incident made me feel sad. I put the torn pieces into my pocket and kept them for several days. I just couldn't stop wondering what it is about the issue of women's ordination that brings out so much emotion in people. Does ripping a leaflet in half make someone feel better? Is it fear of change, fear of the unknown, fear of what the hierarchy might think? I don't have any answers but I do think the ban on discussion contributes significantly to the problem.

No isolated phenomenon

Formerly any potential vocations to the priesthood among women were quickly nipped in the bud or side-tracked into religious life, and their historical record wiped out. Now, with the cultural prejudices gradually melting away, the promptings of the Spirit can no longer be ignored. And it is clear that many Catholic women in many different circumstances are hearing the call.

In 1973 a network of about 80 women who felt called to the priesthood existed in the French-speaking countries of Europe. They decided to preserve anonymity because of the official Church's attitude.[4] A study of 100 women in the USA who felt a priestly vocation was published in 1978.[5] Twenty-seven women called to the priesthood in the German-speaking countries published their testimonies in 1998.[6]

The American study describes the findings of a thorough investigation by trained psychologists and spiritual guides. After rigorous tests and personal interviews, surpassing even those normally applied to male applicants for the priesthood, the researchers concluded that 54% of the female candidates had a mature personality, and 37% a developing personality. Only 9% were rated unsuitable. Moreover, 44% of the applicant women were rated as definitely making effective ordained ministers and 33% probably so. The success of the remaining 23% was deemed less certain. In other words, three quarters of the women who felt called were spiritually, psychologically and pastorally suitable for the ministry of the priesthood.[7]

Not authenticated?

The official line on women's priestly vocations is that they can safely be dismissed on the grounds that they lack the Church's seal of approval.

> A vocation within the Church does not consist solely or primarily in the fact that one manifests the desire for a mission or feels attracted by an inner compulsion. Even if this spontaneous step is made and even if one believes one has heard as it were a call in the depths of one's soul, the vocation is authentic only from the moment that it is authenticated by the external call of the Church.[8]

The Church is, indeed, the authenticator of vocations to the extent that the community of believers plays a role in assessing new candidates. This is why at ordination the bishop asks the people whether they judge the ordinand to be worthy. Nowadays the question is usually answered by the rector of the seminary where the person was trained, but even then he speaks on behalf of the assembled faithful. Also, the bishop's final call does add some kind of institutional approval, but to state that vocations are *only* authentic 'when candidates are externally called' by the Church, makes no sense.

From time immemorial, priestly vocations have been ascribed *to God*. In spite of, and in the middle of, their human origins and human growth, vocations are inspired by the Holy Spirit, we were told. It is God who calls. It is God's voice that youngsters are urged to discern in the stirrings of their heart and in the encouragement of other believers. How may that same pull of God be ignored when God speaks in the spiritual awareness of women? Do we not have a parallel case here to Peter's discerning the Holy Spirit in the faith of Cornelius and his Gentile household? Should the Church, like Peter, not recognise that 'God is no respecter of persons. Could anyone refuse to ordain these women who have received the call of the Holy Spirit as much as we have?'?[9]

Pope John Paul II has spoken of his own vocation as God's mysterious inner voice.

> I am often asked, especially by young people, why I became a priest. Maybe some of you would like to ask the same question. Let me try briefly to reply. I must begin by saying that it is impossible to explain entirely. For it remains a mystery, even to myself. How does one explain the ways of God? Yet I know that, at a certain point in my life, I became convinced that Christ was saying to me what he had said to thousands before me: 'Come, follow me!' There was a clear sense that what I heard in my heart was no human voice, nor was it just an idea of my own. Christ was calling me to serve him as a priest.[10]

'What I heard in my heart was no human voice, nor was it just an idea of my own.' Since men and women are one in Christ and share the same life of the Spirit, how may we declare God's call in women invalid? Is the Spirit not free to call whom she wishes? Does authentication by the Church imply the right to ignore true vocations?

Moreover, if the hierarchy is the sole authenticator of vocations, why does the Church 'not have the power to ordain women', as Pope John Paul II and Cardinal Ratzinger have stated a number of times?[11] If it is the hierarchy, and not specifically God, who is the sole arbiter of whose 'calling' is authentic and whose not, how can the hierarchy maintain that it does not have the authority to ordain women to the priesthood? If the hierarchy is the sole decision maker, how does it not have the authority?

READINGS FROM THE WOMEN PRIESTS WEBSITE

Testimonies of women called to the priesthood:
* Claire Daurelle (France)
> http://www.womenpriests.org/called/daurelle.htm
* Iris Müller (Germany)
> http://www.womenpriests.org/called/muller.htm
* Vivian Rotering (USA)
> http://www.womenpriests.org/called/rotering.htm
* Soline Vatinel (Ireland))
> http://www.womenpriests.org/called/vatinel.htm
* Josefa Münch (Germany)
> http://www.womenpriests.org/called/munch.htm
* Monique (missionary in Africa)
> http://www.womenpriests.org/called/vallin.htm
* Helen Blackburn (Scotland)
> http://www.womenpriests.org/called/blackbur.htm
* Colette Joyce (England)
> http://www.womenpriests.org/called/joyce.htm
* Denise Donato (USA)
> http://www.womenpriests.org/called/donato.htm
* Andrea Mayerhofer (Germany)
> http://www.womenpriests.org/called/mayerhof.htm
* Olive Powell (England)
> http://www.womenpriests.org/called/powell.htm
* Renate Put (Switzerland)
> http://www.womenpriests.org/called/put.htm
* Rosa Maria Miguel (Spain)
> http://www.womenpriests.org/called/miguel.htm
* Alice (USA)
> http://www.womenpriests.org/called/alice.htm
* Ulrike Murr (Germany)
> http://www.womenpriests.org/called/murr.htm
* Anne Brown (England)
> http://www.womenpriests.org/called/brown.htm

21

Unmasking the Intruder

WHEN WE ASK OURSELVES, 'What went wrong? How did the ban on women's ordination manage to inveigle itself into Church practice?', we discover a multiplicity of factors. The pro-feminine attitude of Gnostic sects in early centuries worked against women. The taboo on menstruation raised practical obstacles: it put an end to women deacons in the Byzantine Church.[1] The readoption of Aristotelian philosophy in the Middle Ages did not help, as we have seen in Thomas Aquinas.[2] Male supremacy in the macho cultures of Europe added layers of prejudice. But we must single out Roman culture and Roman law as the main culprits. When the official Church began to adopt the laws and institutions of Roman culture, the fate of women's ministries was sealed. Anchored within a packet of useful organisational material lay the tumour of pagan, anti-feminine bias. Even good things come at a cost.

Roman genius

Even after two thousand years we cannot help but admire the Romans. They established an empire that stretched all the way from Egypt to Britain. It is worthwhile to reflect on their achievements and to appreciate the quality of their skills, so that we can understand why the Church benefited so much from incorporating the Roman system into its Church administration. For Romans were first and foremost administrators.

Unlike the Greeks, who excelled in literature, art and philosophy, the Romans were supremely practical. They knew that political power rested on the strength of the army. Consequently, they expended a lot of ingenuity and engineering skill in shaping their armies into unsurpassed military organisations. Each army was made up of legions, each of which was divided into cohorts and led by officers with precise functions. Soldiers were provided with standard weapons, such as breast armour, a helmet, a sword, a javelin, a shield, and superb sandals. These were mass-produced and of the same quality anywhere in the Roman world. Soldiers were drilled in fighting techniques, but also in all the engineering skills they would require on their military expeditions.

Wherever a legion stopped, it would build a fortified camp, which might soon extend into a real fortress, a *castra*. This again was standardised. The *castra* was always square, with walls and moats of precise specification, and the gate and towers in exactly the same locations. The area inside was laid out according to a predetermined plan: barracks for the soldiers, store rooms for rations, latrines, officers' quarters, war shrines, all in their fixed locations. There were blueprints for every part of the construction project. Timber would be prefabricated somewhere else, then assembled to make either a barracks, a gatehouse or a defensive tower, as required.

Once they arrived at the place of battle, Roman soldiers would quickly build the equipment they needed: an *onega* for lobbing stones or a *ballista*, a large catapult on a stand. They would construct siege towers that rolled on large wheels and that were protected by shields from enemy fire. Such war engines were not carried along. They were put together on the spot in record time according to the accepted design. When Julius Caesar's armies arrived at the Rhine in 55 BC after exhausting marches from Gaul, his soldiers built a 500-metre-long wooden bridge over the river in just ten days. In places the Rhine is 8 metres deep! The Romans could only achieve such a feat because they knew their skills and worked according to predetermined plans.

When the Romans occupied a country, the first thing they did was build all-weather roads. They had learnt that having paved roads allowed them to maintain fewer legions in key locations who could then, in a short time, reach any area of conflict. These roads were extremely well made. Surveyors laid out the straightest route between two centres. The army, with local people pressed into service, would then carve out a path over hills and through forests, lay a foundation of heavy stones, impose a layer of fine sand, then cobbles, then finally flat paving stones, thus ensuring that the road would survive even heavy rains. In first-century Britain, the Romans laid a road network of 10,000 miles. Many of the major roads in England today still rest on foundations laid by the Romans.

The Romans were equally thorough in introducing many of their other engineering marvels. Wherever they governed, they built *villas* for their officials and for veterans of the army, who were often rewarded by grants of land. These villas enjoyed warm-air heating through ducts laid under the floor. They had bathhouses with hot, tepid and cold-water baths. They often enjoyed the convenience of flowing water that was brought from miles away over ingenious aqueducts. Here again mass production and common design prevailed. Bathroom tiles were the same whether used in Gaul, north Africa, Syria or Rome itself. The *amphorae* that held wine or fish-sauce, found in Palestine, Sicily or Britain, are identical.

The Romans applied this tight-knit system of uniform design and centralised control also to political rule. Roman officials governed within clearly circumscribed roles. Roman coins, weights and taxes replaced local customs. In addition, although the Romans tolerated local religions and native superstitions, they saw to it that their law prevailed.

Roman law

Even more than in their engineering projects, the Romans showed their organising genius in their law. Roman law formulated clear distinctions, laid down authoritative rules and prescribed a chain of precedence in rights and powers. Roman law was detailed, specific, definitive. It was born not from philosophy but from the practical need to settle disputes regarding persons, objects or events. Through principles and rules it imposed a very precise hierarchical order of rights, privileges and duties. Roman law was a real gift to judges and administrators because it provided a rather simple tool to impose order on society.[3] Small wonder that present law in practically all European countries is based on Roman law.

The international order brought about by Roman law and Roman rule was known as the *pax Romana* – that is, 'the Roman peace'. It indicated the order and stability within the Roman Empire which made international trade a risk-free enterprise.

The *pax Romana* did have its dark side, of course. The international Roman culture could not be imposed on people of so many diverse racial origins without continuous violence. Not only were military uprisings suppressed, but anything that upset international uniformity in organisation and government was quashed. The whole structure was maintained by taxes levied on the local populations and by an enormous slave force that was constantly replenished by new conquests and by the infliction of slavery as a punishment.

The Church becomes Roman

The Roman Empire in the West disintegrated in the fifth and sixth centuries under pressure from the new nations that invaded Europe. In the East, it continued as the Byzantine Empire until 1453, when the Turks overran Constantinople. The Church, meanwhile, went through its own traumatic experiences. On the one hand, it gained political freedom and made new converts among the young European nations. On the other hand, it suffered greatly from the chaos and destruction in the wake of constant conflict and wars. The Church badly needed to be organised and it is here that the Roman genius found another outlet.

St Benedict (480–547) had seen the moral degradation in Rome with his own eyes. First he lived as a hermit, but then he decided to draw others into spiritual reform. He allowed his mystic insights to be inspired by his Roman charism for management. He drew up the monastic rule that would create an explosion of religious life throughout Europe and that became the backbone for Church reform in all European countries.

Benedict created small communities of like-minded people who were dedicated to both prayer and work. Monks prayed the office together, slept in the same dormitory, and ate in a common dining room at fixed hours, and worked at common tasks in teams. Though he might consult his companions, the abbot enjoyed absolute authority. He acted in God's name. Obedience shown to him was obedience shown to God. The individual monks should learn humility. 'Do not do your own will.' 'Tell the abbot your secrets.' 'Believe yourself inferior and less virtuous than all other men.' 'Do nothing except what is recommended by the common rule.' 'Do not talk if not asked.' 'Do not be noticed in your appearance.'[4]

The rule of St Benedict was copied in numerous other religious congregations of both men and women. Within a few centuries thousands upon thousands of monasteries had been established throughout Europe, creating everywhere mission centres, dispensaries, schools, new agricultural farms; in short, they were the nodes from which Church ministry and spiritual reform could radiate to the local populations. The Church in Europe owes much of its infrastructure to the devotion and commitment of monks and nuns who were helped by an organisational Roman blueprint.[5]

A century after St Benedict, another great Roman, Pope Gregory the Great (540–604) put his stamp on Church administration. Gregory belonged to a patrician family and had served as prefect of the city of Rome for a couple of years before entering Church service. When he was elected Pope, he immediately began to centralise the entire papal administration. He laid down rules on the liturgy and pastoral ministry. He co-ordinated new missionary efforts, such as the conversion of England. He asserted papal authority in face of Byzantine claims. He left a lasting stamp on the way the official Church was run by applying Roman principles and Roman systems of management. He is considered by many historians as the architect of the later medieval papacy.[6]

Meanwhile, in the Latin-speaking countries of the West, the young churches that adopted Roman organisation patterns also adopted Roman rules and customs. Local synods in north Africa, Gaul and Britain laid down rules that applied Roman thinking to Church practice. This came to a head in the early Middle Ages when at universities, Roman law and Church practice were amalgamated into one discipline.[7] The monk Gratian, who taught at the University of Bologna, thus produced the first collection of Church law based on Roman law. It was this collection that was, with some additions, endorsed by one pope after the other as the *Corpus Iuris Canonici*, the 'Body of Church Law' that remained in force until 1918.

Women were hemmed in on all sides in Roman law.[8] The Roman principles that thus became enshrined in Church law and Church practice were:

• 'In many sections of our law, the condition of women is weaker than that of men.'
• 'Women are excluded from any civil and public responsibility and therefore can neither be judges nor exercise any authority.'
• Women are under the tutelage of men 'because of the infirmity of their sex and because of ignorance about matters pertaining to public life'.[9]

All other prohibitions in the Church's lawbook followed from these principles. Women were not allowed to receive communion during their monthly periods. After giving birth to a child they needed to be 'purified' (*churched*) before re-entering a church building. Women were strictly forbidden to touch 'sacred objects', such as the chalice, the paten or altar linen. They certainly could not distribute holy communion. In church, women needed to have their heads veiled at all times. Women were also barred from entering the sanctuary except for cleaning purposes. They were not to read sacred Scripture from the pulpit, preach, sing in a church choir, be Mass servers, or become full members of confraternities and organisations of the laity. And – does it still need mentioning? – women were barred from receiving holy orders.[10]

Cuckoo's egg tradition

In spite of clever *egg mimicry* in the conventional argumentation, opposition to the priesthood of women did not derive from Jesus who made women equal members of the new covenant. It cannot be ascribed to the apostles who declared that there is no longer man or woman in Christ – that 'we are all one'. It cannot be blamed on the Early Church communities who welcomed women as ministers and imparted sacramental ordination to women deacons. *The spurious parent bird that laid the egg was none other than secular pagan prejudice, a prejudice enshrined in Roman law.*

With typical cuckoo hatchling ruthlessness, *the intruder killed off truly Christian initiatives of women's ministries.* Nine centuries of the women's diaconate went by the board. Jurisdictions entrusted to women in the Celtic and Saxon churches were pushed aside. The age-long celebration of Mary's share in Jesus' priesthood was declared a mistake. And, worst of all, the genuine vocations to the priestly ministry in generation after generation of Christian women were denied, stifled, suppressed, usually mercilessly aborted before they could be born.

Church leaders have also demonstrated *a typical host bird bonding to the adopted usurper.* The fattening of the hatchling in the nest through many centuries and its successful nest eviction of rival Christian hatchlings were now hailed as proof of an 'unbroken tradition'. Excuses were found to explain the hatchling's glaring incongruity with Christian principles, its negating the dignity of Christian women. The ritual risk of menstruation was adduced as a justification. Enduring punishment for Eve's sin was blamed. In the Middle Ages much was made of the conviction that women are not fully human and therefore cannot represent the perfect 'man' Christ. In our own time an appeal is made to God's *grand design* according to which Christ had to be male as the Bridegroom and the Eucharist has to be presided over by little male bridegrooms. It is not easy to give up a fat hatchling one passionately wants to believe to be one's own.

The ban on women priests has been unmasked as a pagan interloper, a cuckoo hatchling out of place in a Christian nest. Why allow it to continue its degrading devastation?

READINGS FROM THE WOMEN PRIESTS WEBSITE

The Rights of Women According to **Roman Law**
http://www.womenpriests.org/traditio/infe__rom.htm

Mary Ann Rossi
'The Passion of Perpetua, Everywoman of Late
Antiquity'
http://www.womenpriests.org/theology/rossi2.htm

**Marie-Thérèse van Lunen Chénu and Louise
Wentholt**
'The Status of Women in the Code of Canon Law
and in the United Nations Convention'
http://www.womenpriests.org/body/lunen3.htm

Marie-Thérèse van Lunen Chénu 'Human rights in
the Church: a non-right for women in the Church?'
in *Human Rights. The Christian contribution*, July
1998.
http://www.womenpriests.org/theology/lunen1.htm

22

The Way Forward

THE PRESENT HOLY FATHER and the Congregation for Doctrine in Rome have decided to root out any support for women's ordination in the Catholic Church. They see it as their task to defend what they perceive as orthodoxy. They are under pressure from vocal conservative groups in the Church. They fear disruption and confusion 'if ever the idea of women priests would gain wider acceptance in Church circles'. I have no reason to doubt that they are sincerely trying to protect the Church by enforcing the ban on women priests with ever stricter measures. But, while their motives may be entirely honourable, will their actions really benefit the Church?

The truth of the matter is that, as we have seen, the traditional arguments they rely upon do not hold water. No valid reasons can be found in Scripture to keep women from the ordained ministry. On the contrary, Jesus' full embrace of women in an equal baptism demands openness to the ministerial priesthood for all. Paul asserts this explicitly.[1] Neither can valid objections against the ordination of women be found in tradition. The practice of not ordaining women can clearly be shown to derive from pagan and cultural prejudice, not from a genuinely Christian source of inspiration. In fact, women did receive sacramental ordination as deacons, so that ordaining them priests follows on naturally. Moreover, an appeal to bridegroom imagery fails to convince. But Rome has raised the stakes by appealing to authority.

The ordinary universal *magisterium*?

In their anxiety to 'keep the lid on', the Pope and the Congregation for Doctrine recently declared that the matter 'has already been *infallibly* decided by the ordinary universal *magisterium*'.[2]

The term 'ordinary universal *magisterium*' refers to the concordant teaching of all Catholic bishops together with the Pope, outside the rather

177

rare occasions when the bishops are gathered in an ecumenical council. The First Vatican Council described it in these terms:

> All those things are to be believed with Catholic and divine faith which are contained in the Word of God, written or handed on, and are proposed by the Church either by a solemn judgment or by its ordinary and universal *magisterium* as divinely revealed and to be believed as such.[3]

The Second Vatican Council defined the ordinary universal *magisterium* more precisely and expressed the conditions under which it operates:

> Although the individual bishops do not enjoy the prerogative of infallibility, they nevertheless proclaim Christ's doctrine infallibly whenever, even though dispersed through the world, but still maintaining the bond of communion among themselves and with the successor of Peter, and authentically teaching matters of faith and morals, they are in agreement on one position as definitively to be held.[4]

The Congregation for Doctrine seems to believe that the collective bishops of the world have spoken out on the issue of women priests. How? Rome has not explained, but we can guess. It is a well-known fact that for the past two decades or more, as a condition for acceptance, candidates for the episcopal dignity have been asked by Rome whether they support the ordination of women. Only those who said they did not have been promoted to become bishops. So the majority of bishops today are probably those who indicated opposition to women's ordination.[5] Rome may be convinced that this proves that the 'ordinary universal *magisterium*' supports their view. Hence their claim that it has been infallibly decided. Could they be right?

From the Vatican II text and other texts on which it depends, five conditions can be recognised as being required for infallible teaching by the ordinary universal *magisterium:*

1. *Collegial action.* The bishops must be involved in a collegial exercise of teaching authority.
2. *As 'judges'.* The bishops must be free to express their own considered opinion.
3. *In the service of the faith of the whole Church.* The bishops must listen to the Word of God and the '*sensus fidelium*'.
4. *Regarding faith and morals.* The teaching must concern matters relating to the object of faith.
5. *In a teaching consciously imposed as 'definitive'.* The bishops must want to impose the doctrine as definitely to be held.[6]

These conditions have not been met in the case of the ban on the ordination of women. Were the bishops really *free*, when they were asked for their support? Did they consider the evidence carefully? Did they listen to the *sensus fidelium*? Did they consciously act as a collegial teaching body? Did they want to impose their view as binding on the world Church? None of these conditions seems to be fulfilled. Canon 749 of the Code of Canon Law declares that no doctrine is understood to have been defined infallibly unless this fact has been clearly established.

Consequently, prominent theologians all over the world have rejected the Congregation's claim that the matter has been decided by the universal *magisterium*. Fr Francis Sullivan, who taught me at the Gregorian University in Rome and who is an acknowledged expert on the teaching authority, voiced unambiguous disagreement.

> The question that remains is whether it is a clearly established fact that the bishops of the Catholic Church are as convinced by those reasons [against women priests] as Pope John Paul evidently is, and that, in exercising their proper role as judges and teachers of the faith, they have been unanimous in teaching that the exclusion of women from ordination to the priesthood is a divinely revealed truth to which all Catholics are obliged to give a definitive assent of faith. Unless this is manifestly the case, I do not see how it can be certain that this doctrine is taught infallibly by the ordinary and universal *magisterium*.[7]

Professor Nicolas Lash of Cambridge University spoke plain language:

> Neither the Pope nor Cardinal Ratzinger can *make* a teaching to be 'founded on the written Word of God' simply by asserting that it is so founded. Nor can they by assertion, make it a matter that has been 'constantly preserved and applied in the tradition of the Church'. The attempt to use the doctrine of infallibility, a doctrine intended to indicate the grounds and character of Catholic confidence in official teaching, as a blunt instrument to prevent the ripening of a question in the Catholic mind, is a scandalous abuse of power, the most serious consequence of which will be further to undermine the future authority which the Pope seeks to sustain.[8]

The Catholic Theological Association of America appointed a task force to study the question. On 6 June 1997, the general assembly received the report and endorsed its rejection of Rome's claims:

> There are serious doubts regarding the nature of the authority of the teaching that the Church's lack of authority to ordain women to the priesthood is a truth that has been infallibly taught and requires the definitive assent of the faithful, and its grounds in tradition. There is serious, widespread disagree-

ment on this question, not only among theologians, but also within the larger community of the Church ... It seems clear that further study, discussion and prayer regarding this question by all the members of the Church in accord with their particular gifts and vocations are necessary if the Church is to be guided by the Spirit in remaining faithful to the authentic tradition.

The resolution was adopted in a secret ballot, with 216 theologians voting 'yes', 22 'no' and 10 abstaining.[9] Arguments are not won by tightening thumbscrews.

What next?

I believe that the time has come for those with responsibility to speak out. Because the justification for it fails, the ban against women priests will have to be lifted one day or other, and the longer the Church waits, the more damage will have been done. Even now credibility in the official Church's leadership is fading with large sections of the membership. Women experience the exclusion from ministry as ever more deeply hurtful and discriminatory.[10] Church leadership is wasting valuable time and resources in suppressing a legitimate development that will immeasurably enrich its pastoral ministry. But is retreat from the entrenched position possible?

When I was six years old I was interned, with the rest of my family, in a Japanese prisoner of war camp (from 1942 to 1945). Having experienced its horrors so closely, I am still fascinated by the war. And the older I become, the more I ponder its lessons. Recently I read again a detailed account of the Battle of Stalingrad in 1942. It interested me all the more because one of my missionary colleagues in India, Fr Othmar Reusch, had fought at Stalingrad. He owed his survival to the fact that a bullet had lodged in his spine and he was sent back to Germany on a supply plane. Most other German soldiers were not so lucky.

On 22 November 1942 the 260,000 German troops in Stalingrad were surrounded by overwhelming Russian forces. They lacked food, ammunition and equipment. Their only salvation lay in breaking out from the encirclement, and retreat. But Hitler strictly forbade it, sending a radio message that 'everyone should fight till the last man'. General Friedrich Paulus, the overall German commander at Stalingrad, knew it was a lost cause. What about the people under his command? The famous General Erich von Manstein, who was leading a neighbouring army, advised Paulus to ignore Hitler and break out. Paulus did not. He could not bring himself to oppose authority. Six weeks later, on 30 January 1943, only 90,000 Germans had survived the carnage. Hitler repeated his orders, but

Paulus surrendered. All the remaining German troops went into Siberian captivity, from which few returned.

This was not an isolated case. It was the general picture of the end of the war for Germany. German military leaders by that time realised they were fighting for a lost cause, and most probably disagreed with Hitler. But with few exceptions they allowed Hitler to fight on till three million of their soldiers were killed, till German towns and cities had been totally destroyed by aerial bombardments involving 800,000 civilian casualties, and till half their country was brutally colonised by Soviet Russia. And I am not even talking of all the victims of German aggression in occupied countries!

I have many German friends and I esteem them highly. I do not believe this was a typically *German* phenomenon. I think that we see, in a living parable, what happens when systems with powerful authority structures take over. The Japanese were in a similar predicament, but they were eventually saved when Emperor Hirohito personally intervened on 10 August 1945, ordering his Supreme War Council to accept unconditional surrender. It saved the mainland of Japan from devastation, and, incidentally, also saved my own life. I was seriously ill and our camp doctor told me later that I would certainly have died if the war had lasted another month.

Now all this seems dramatic language and the comparison to the Nazi war machine or Japanese Banzai militarism may seem totally inappropriate. I highly respect the Holy Father and his assistants. I do not want for a minute to imply that, *as persons*, they resemble Hitler and his staff. I am just following the example of Jesus himself who drew valuable lessons from observing 'the children of this world'.[11] And while the Pope is no doubt utterly sincere in pursuing what he believes to be the right course, he does resemble Hitler in the absoluteness of power. Hitler claimed the right over life and death of his citizens. The Pope has an even greater power for he holds *spiritual* authority over the faithful. 'Do not fear those who can kill the body, but cannot kill the soul', Jesus said.[12] Where there is authority, even if it is spiritual authority, there are dangers of suppressing legitimate dissent, promoting a culture of misplaced docile acquiescence among subordinates, ruling by decree rather than by consultation, defending mistaken decisions for the sake of not seeming to lose face – in short, 'of stifling the Spirit'. And these dangers are real.[13]

The need of reform in the Catholic Church does not limit itself to the question of women's ordination. Other important issues are outstanding, such as the ban on artificial contraception; the maintenance of obligatory celibacy for clergy in the Latin rite; the role of the laity in Church administration and in the pastoral apostolate; the legitimate authority of bishops' conferences; ecumenism; dialogue with other religions; recognition for homosexuals; to mention just a few. In all these areas Roman leadership is trying to hold the Church back from fresh approaches. This has led to a crisis about papal authority itself, about its justification as well as about the way it is being exercised.[14]

The Church will need to redress the balance, as I am sure it will in due course. We do need a strong Pope as spiritual leader in an increasingly secular world. But we also need a more democratic way of governing the Church, an openness to the Spirit in the ordinary faithful. It is my hope that the discussion around the ordination of women will be a catalyst that will also usher in other reforms.

Yes, in the past the Church did not ordinarily admit women to the priesthood. This was the unfortunate consequence of the Church's adopting Roman law. On the other hand, public pronouncements by popes have been rare. They date only from 1976 and cover two papacies. The decision can easily be revoked. It is not a big deal, in spite of the mention of 'infallibility' in some documents.

The ban against women priests inflicts serious damage on the Catholic community. It wounds all women in their dignity as daughters of God and members of Christ. It spurns God's call in women who have a vocation to the priestly ministry and deprives the Church of their valuable gifts. By devaluing one half of God's people, it bruises the Church as the sacrament of 'communion with God and union among all people'.[15] It destroys the credibility of the Catholic community and its leaders. All those with responsibility in the Church should speak up now to save the Church from further devastation.

Appendix

Sources of Official Texts Quoted in This Book

1. Fathers of the Church

The translations of texts from Church Fathers are all from the standard *Early Church Fathers Collection* (AD 1–800), in 38 volumes, originally published by T. &. T. Clark in Edinburgh, then republished by Wm. B. Eerdmans in Grand Rapids, Michigan. This collection is now in the public domain and can be accessed at *The Christian Classics Ethereal Library* (www.ccel.org).

2. Medieval theologians

Texts of some of the most prominent theologians have been translated by me from the original Latin, as indicated in the notes.

For texts of Thomas Aquinas, I have followed the translation by the Fathers of the English Dominican Province in 1947, published by Benzinger Brothers Inc. An electronic version can be found for the *Summa Theologica* at the New Advent website (www.newadvent.org/summa) and for the *Summa Contra Gentiles* at the Jacques Maritain Center (www.nd.edu/Departments/Maritain/etext/gc.htm).

As indicated in the notes, for excerpts of writings of medieval canonists I relied on I. Raming, *Der Ausschluss der Frau vom priesterlichen Amt*, Cologne 1973. The translations from Latin and German into English are my own.

3. Documents of Vatican II

For these I follow the translation of *The Documents of Vatican II*, ed. Walter Abbott, America Press, New York, 1966.

4. Recent Roman documents

Inter Insigniores (15 October 1976)
    'Declaration of the Sacred Congregation for the Doctrine of the Faith on the question of the admission of women to the ministerial priesthood', *Acta Apostolicae Sedis 55* (1963) pp. 267–268; *Briefing* 7 (1977) nos 5 & 6.

Commentary on 'Inter Insigniores' (27 January 1977)
    Commentary by the Sacred Congregation for the Doctrine of the Faith, *Acta Apostolicae Sedis* 69 (1977) pp. 98–116; *L'Osservatore Romano*, Thursday 27 January 1977.

Mulieris Dignitatem (15 August 1988)
    Apostolic Letter of Pope John Paul II on the Dignity and Vocation of Women, no 26; *Acta Apostolicae Sedis* 80 (1988) p. 1715; Pauline Books, Boston, 1999.

Donum Veritatis (24 May 1990)
> Instruction on the Ecclesial Vocation of the Theologian by the Congregation for the Doctrine of the Faith, *Acta Apostolicae Sedis* 82 (1990) pp. 1550–1570; *Origins* 20 (1990) 5 July.

Ordinatio Sacerdotalis (22 May 1994)
> Apostolic Letter by Pope John Paul II on Reserving Priestly Ordination to Men Alone, *Origins* 24 (1994) June 9; *L'Osservatore Romano*, 24 November 1994.

Ad Tuendam Fidem (May 28 1998)
> Motu Proprio by Pope John Paul II by which certain norms are inserted into the Code of Canon Law, *L'Osservatore Romano*, 15 July 1998; *Origins* 28 (1998) 16 July.

Commentary on Ad Tuendam Fidem (29 June 1998)
> Commentary by Joseph Cardinal Ratzinger, Prefect of the Congregation for the Doctrine of the Faith, *L'Osservatore Romano*, 15 July 1998.

Notes

Chapter 1: The Discovery

1. The full text was published in *Archief van de Kerken*, 6 August 1972.
2. Cornelius a Lapide, *Commentaria in Scripturam Sacram* (Antwerp, 1616), Paris, 1868, vol. 18, p. 396, see also p. 353.
3. A. D. B. Spencer, 'Eve at Ephesus (Should women be ordained as pastors according to the First Letter to Timothy 2:11–15?)', *Journal of the Evangelical Theological Society* 17 (1974) 215–222; G. P. Hugenberger, 'Women in Church Office: Hermeneutics or Exegesis? A Survey of Approaches to I Timothy 2:8–15', *Journal of the Evangelical Theological Society* 35 (1992) 341–360.
4. G. N. Redekop, 'Let the Women Learn: I Timothy 2:8–15 Reconsidered', *Studies in Religion* 19 (1990) 235–245.
5. 1 Corinthians 11:5; cf. 14:3. 1 Corinthians 14:34–35 is a later gloss.
6. It is interesting to note that, unknown to me, in 1975 the Pontifical Biblical Commission was studying the same question and came to the same conclusion I had arrived at, namely that the exclusion of women from the priesthood could not validly be derived from Scripture; *Origins* 6 (1 July, 1976) pp. 92–96. See also J. R. Donahue, 'A Tale of Two Documents', in Leonard and Arlene Swidler (eds), *Women Priests. A Catholic Commentary on the Vatican Declaration*, New York 1977, pp. 25–35.
7. John Wijngaards, 'The ministry of women and social myth', in *New Ministries in India*, ed. D.S. Amalorpavadass, Bangalore, 1976, pp. 50–82.
8. Wijngaards, *Did Christ Rule Out Women Priests?*, McCrimmons, Great Wakering 1977 (2nd edition 1986); Indian edition, ATC, Bangalore, 1978; Dutch edition, KBS, Brugge, 1979.

Chapter 2: Papal Teaching on Slavery

1. Instruction of the Holy Office, signed by Pope Pius IX, 20 June 1866. *Collectanea de S.C. de Propaganda Fide*, I, no. 1293, 719, Rome 1907 (italics my own).
2. *Gaudium et Spes* no. 29.
3. All these are Aristotle's literal words in his treatise *Politika*, vol. 1; see A.TH. van Leeuwen, *De Nacht van het Kapitaal*, Nijmegen, 1984, pp. 182–205.
4. Aristotle, *Physica*, vol. 1; Loeb Classical Library, 1252 b 8.
5. Aristotle, *Politica*, ed. Loeb Classical Library, 1254 b 10–14.
6. Galatians 3:28.
7. Aquinas, *In II Sententiarum* d. 44, q.1, a.3; *In III Sententiarum* d.36, q.1, a.1 and a.1, ad 2; *Summa Theologica* I–II, q.94, a.5, ad 3; II–II, q.57, a.3, ad 2. Children of

a slave mother are rightly slaves even though they have not committed personal sin! *Summa Theologica* III, Suppl. q.52, a.4.

8. Leander, *Questiones Morales Theologicae*, Lyons 1692; Volume 8, 'De Quarto Decalogi Precepto', Tract.IV, Disp. I, Q.3 (italics my own).

9. Texts in this order: Exodus 22:3; 31:2–6; Leviticus 25:39, 47–55; Exodus 21:7–11. See also Sirach 33:25–30.

10. Luke 17:7–10; see also Matthew 10:24–25; 13:27–28; 18:25.

11. Luke 16:1–8; Matthew 24:42–44; 13:44.

12. Colossians 3:22–25; see also Ephesians 6:5–9; Titus 2:9–10; 1 Peter 2:18–20. Also Philemon was gratuitously interpreted as an endorsement of slavery.

13. Gregory of Nyssa, *Ecclesiastes*, Hom.4; MIGNE, Greek Fathers, Vol.44, 549–550.

14. Juan Ginés de Sepulveda, *Tratado sobre las justas causas de la guerra contra los índios*, Sevilla, 1545; reprint Mexico, 1979.

15. Bartolomé de las Casas, *Unos Avisos y Reglas*, etc.; *El Indio Esclavo; Disputa o controversia con Ginés de Sepúlveda*; all three books Sevilla, 1552; reprinted Madrid, 1958.

16. G.T.F. Raynal, *Histoire Philosophique et Politique des Établissements et du Commerce des Européens dans les deux Indes*, Amsterdam, 1770, IV, livre IX, pp. 169–171; H.B. Grégoire, *De la Traite et de l'Esclavage des Noirs et des Blancs*, Paris, 1815, pp. 21–22; J.M. Sailer, *Handbuch der Christlichen Moral*, II. Sämtliche Werke, Sulzbach, 1830–41, XIV, pp. 196–198.

17. Slavery existed in the Papal States until the end of the 18th century. Slaves were owned by some ecclesiastical institutions as late as 1864. Extensive background material is provided by J.F. Maxwell, 'The Development of Catholic Doctrine concerning Slavery', *World Justice* 11 (1969–70) pp. 147–192; 291–324; *Slavery and the Catholic Church*, Chichester, 1975.

18. Galatians 3:28.

Chapter 3: A Time for Speaking

1. *Ordinatio Sacerdotalis*, Apostolic Letter by Pope John Paul II on Reserving Priestly Ordination to Men Alone, 22 May 1994; *Ad Tuendam Fidem*, Motu Proprio by Pope John Paul II, May 28 1998; *Commentary on Ad Tuendam Fidem*, by Joseph Cardinal Ratzinger, Prefect of the Congregation for the Doctrine of the Faith, 29 June 1998.

2. First Vatican Council, *Constitutio de Fide Catholica*, ch. 4, in *Enchiridion Symbolorum*, ed. H. Denzinger, Freibourg, Herder, 1955 (30 ed.), no. 1795–1800.

3. Second Vatican Council, *The Church*, no. 25.

4. *Donum Veritatis*, § 24, 25, 30.

5. *Gaudium et Spes*, no. 62.

6. *Inter Mirifica*, no. 8.

7. *Acta Apostolicae Sedis* 42 (1950) p. 251.

8. *Communio et Progressio*, Pastoral Instruction on the Means of Social Communication, § 26, 29 January 1971, *Acta Apostolicae Sedis* 63 (1971) pp. 593–656.

9. *Perfectae Caritatis*, no. 14.

10. *Unitatis Redintegratio*, no. 6.

11. *L'Osservatore Romano*, 2 October 1966.

12. Because the term *harijan* has also been applied to prostitutes, it is no longer favoured today.

13. M.K. Ghandi, *An Autobiography. On the Story of My Experiments with Truth*, Navajivan, 1927, passim.

14. Matthew 5:13; Luke 14:34–35.
15. Galatians 2:11.
16. 1 Corinthians 12:27, 29.

Chapter 4: The Focus of This Book

1. Diplomatically hinted at by Phyllis Challoner and Vera Laughton Matthews in *Towards Citizenship – a Handbook of Women's Emancipation*, London, 1928.
2. Joan Morris, *Against Nature and God. The History of Women with Clerical Ordination and the Jurisdiction of Bishops*, London, 1973.
3. Josefa Theresia Münch, 'My Letters to the Pope', translated from the German by Sr. Kira Solhdoost, *The Catholic Citizen*, vol. 72 (1991) no. 1, pp. 18–29.
4. E.g. G. Heinzelmann, 'The Priesthood and Women', *Commonweal* 81 (1965), pp. 504–508.
5. *Interfeminas*, Bonstetten 1964, a joint German-English publication; the book also contained contributions by Mary Daly, Rosemary Lauer, Iris Müller, Josefa Münch and Ida Raming.
6. Haye van der Meer, 'De positie van de vrouw in de Rooms-Katholieke Kerk', *Council Documentation* paper no. 194, 1965; *Priestertum der Frau?*, as manuscript, Innsbruck, 1962, published Freiburg, 1969; *Women Priests in the Catholic Church?*, Philadelphia, 1973. Another Dutch theologian, René van Eyden, published in Dutch and German from the early 1960s; cf. René van Eyden, 'Women Ministers in the Catholic Church?', *Sisters Today* 40 (1968), pp. 211–226 (shortened version).
7. Vincent Emmanuel Hannon, *The Question of Women in Priesthood*, London, 1967.
8. Mary Daly, *The Church and the Second Sex*, New York, 1968.
9. Ida Raming, *Der Ausschluss der Frau vom priesterlichen Amt*, Cologne 1973; *The Exclusion of Women from the Priesthood: Divine Law or Sex Discrimination?*, Metuchen, 1976.
10. Donna Westley, 'A Selected Bibliography', in Anne Marie Gardener (ed.), *Women and the Catholic Church*, New York, 1976, pp. 199–207.
11. Rosemary Radford Ruether, *The Radical Kingdom. The Western Experience of Messianic Hope*, New York, 1970; *Sexism and God-Talk. Toward a Feminist Theology*, Boston, 1983; Mary Daly, *Beyond God the Father: Toward a Philosophy of Women's Liberation*, Boston, 1973; Elisabeth Schüssler Fiorenza, *Der vergessene Partner*, Düsseldorf, 1964; *In Memory of Her*, New York, 1983; *Discipleship of Equals. A Critical Feminist Ecclesialogy of Liberation*, New York, 1993; etc.
12. Elisabeth Schüssler Fiorenza, *In Memory of Her: Feminist Theological Reconstruction of Christian Origins*, New York, 1983; *Bread not Stone: the Challenge of Feminist Biblical Interpretation*, Boston, 1984; *But She Said: Feminist Practices of Biblical Interpretation*, Boston, 1992; Karen Jo Torjesen, *When Women Were Priests*, New York, 1993; Luise Schottroff, *Lydia's Impatient Sisters: A Feminist Social History of Early Christianity*, Louisville, 1995; Anne Jensen, *God's Self-Confident Daughters: Early Christianity and the Liberation of Women*, Louisville, 1996; Ute E. Eisen, *Amtsträgerinnen im frühen Christentum*, Göttingen, 1996; Luise Schottroff, Silvia Schroer and Marie-Therese Wacker, *Feminist Interpretation: The Bible in Women's Perspective*, Mineapolis, 1998; etc.
13. For instance, the *Storia delle Donne in Occidente*, Laterza, Rome, 1991, five large volumes, now in many languages; Hulia Bolton Holloway et al. (ed.), *Equally in God's Image – Women in the Middle Ages*, New York, 1990; Glenna Matthews, *The Rise of Public Woman: Woman's Power and Woman's Place in the United States*

1630–1970, New York, 1992; Susan Hill Lindley, '*You Have Stepped Out of Your Place*', *A History of Women and Religion in America*, Louisville, 1996.

14. Ann Belford Ulanov, *The Feminine in Jungian Psychology and Christian Theology*, Evanston, 1971; *Receiving Woman: Studies in the Psychology and Theology of the Feminine*, Philadelphia, 1981; Carol Gilligan, *In a Different Voice: Psychological Theory and Women's Development*, Cambridge MA, 1982; Charlene Spretnak (ed.), *The Politics of Women's Spirituality*, New York, 1982; Virginia Ramey Mollenkott, *The Divine Feminine: the Biblical Imagery of God as Female*, New York, 1983; Luce Irigaray, *Speculum of the Other Woman*, Ithaca, 1983; Janet Martin Soskice, *Metaphor and Religious Language*, Oxford, 1985; (ed.) *After Eve – Women, Theology and the Christian Tradition*, London, 1990; Demeris S. Weir, *Jung and Feminism: Liberating Archetypes*, Boston, 1987; Mary Grey, *Redeeming the Dream. Feminism, Redemption and Christian Tradition*, London, 1989; Tina Beattie, *God's Mother, Eve's Advocate. A Gynocentric Refiguration of Marian Symbolism in Engagement with Luce Irigaray*, Bristol, 1999; etc.
15. Hebrews 7:1–10,18. About the presbyter-sacerdos shift in Church thinking, see H. Küng, *Why Priests?*, London, 1972; E. Schillebeeckx, *Ministry*, London, 1981.
16. *Presbyterorum Ordinis*, § 4.
17. *Catechism of the Catholic Church*, London, 1994, no. 1548.
18. J. Wijngaards, 'Don't cage the sacred', *The Tablet*, 23 September 2000, pp. 1256–1257.
19. *Lumen Gentium*, § 9–17. H.Holstein, *Hiérarchie et Peuple de Dieu d'après Lumen Gentium*, Paris, 1970; L. Boff, *Die Kirche als Sakrament*, Paderborn, 1971; A. Acerbi, *Due ecclesiologie. Ecclesiologia giuridica ed ecclesiologia di comunione nella Lumen Gentium*, Bologna, 1975.
20. Hermann Häring, 'The Authority of Women and the Future of the Church', *Concilium* 38/3 (June 1999), pp. 117–125; here p. 119.
21. H. Küng, 'The Charismatic Structure of the Church', *Concilium* 4,1 (April 1965), pp. 23–33; G. Hasenhüttl, *Charisma, Ordnungsprinzip der Kirche*, Freiburg, 1969; H.Haag, *Worauf es ankommt. Wollte Jesus seine Zeit-Stände-Kirche?*, Freiburg, 1997; L. Boff, 'The Uncompleted Vision of Vatican II: The Church – Hierarchy or People of God?', *Concilium* 38/3 (June 1999), pp. 31–39; see also the last chapter in this book.
22. See, e.g. Lynn N. Rhodes, *Co-Creating. A Feminist Vision of Ministry*, Philadelphia, 1987; Lettie M. Russell, *Church in the Round: Feminist Interpretation of the Church*, Louisville, 1993.
23. Marianne Bühler, Brigitte Erzner-Probst, Hedwig Meyer-Wilmes and Hannelies Steichele, *Frauen zwischen Dienst und Amt. Frauenmacht und -ohnmacht in der Kirche*, Düsseldorf, 1998.
24. Donna Steichen, *Ungodly Rage. The Hidden Face of Catholic Feminism*, San Francisco, 1991.

Chapter 5: The Mismatch in Vision

1. *Commentary on 'Inter Insigniores'*, no. 40.
2. Ibid. no. 45.
3. John Paul II, Apostolic Letter *Mulieris Dignitatem*, no. 26.
4. John Paul II, Apostolic Letter *Ordinatio Sacerdotalis*, 22 May 1994.
5. *Ordinatio Sacerdotalis*, no 3; *Inter Insigniores*, no. 6; *Mulieris Dignitatem*, no. 27.
6. *Hebrews* 7:16.
7. In fact, it is only in the letter to the Hebrews that the 'priesthood' of Christ is

discussed in explicit terms and contrasted with the priesthood of the Old Testament. See especially *Hebrews* 5:1–4; 7:26–28.

8. More in John Wijngaards, *Did Christ Rule out Women Priests?*, McCrimmon's, Great Wakering, 1986, pp. 64–68.
9. *John* 1:12–13.
10. 1 Peter 2:5–9.
11. Revelation 1:6; 5:10; 20:6.
12. Vatican II, *Lumen Gentium*, no. 10.
13. Genesis 17:9–14.
14. Exodus 23:17.
15. Exodus 20:17; Sirach 26:3; Proverbs 31:10.
16. *Deuteronomy* 24:1–4; *Numbers* 40:2–17.
17. *Galatians* 3:26–28.
18. Vatican II, *Lumen Gentium*, no. 10.
19. Vatican II, *Lumen Gentium*, no. 30.

***Chapter 6:* The Assessment of Believers**
1. Quoted in T. Angelico, *Taking Stock. Revisioning the church on higher education*, Canberra National Education Committee, 1997, p. 20.
2. J.B. Metz and E. Schillebeeckx (eds), *The Teaching Authority of Believers*, Concilium 180, Edinburgh, T. & T. Clark, 1985.
3. Y. Congar, *The Meaning of Tradition*, Hawthorne, New York, 1964, p. 75.
4. These concepts have been worked out beautifully by the Catholic theologians of Tübingen. J.R. Geiselmann, *Lebendiger Glaube aus geheiligter Überlieferung*, Mainz, 1942; *Die lebendige Überlieferung als Norm des christlichen Glaubens*, Freiburg, 1959; *Geist des Christentums und des Katholizismus*, Mainz, 1940.
5. Vatican II, *Lumen Gentium*, no. 12 (my italics).
6. Vatican II, *Acta synodalia* III/1, pp. 198–199; R.R.Gaillardetz, *Teaching with Authority. A Theology of the Magisterium in the Church*, Liturgical Press, 1997, p. 154.
7. Vatican II, *Lumen Gentium*, no. 25. See also J.H. Newman, *On Consulting the Faithful in Matters of Doctrine*, ed. John Coulson 1859, reprint Sheed & Ward, 1961; Y. Congar, 'Reception as an Ecclesiological Reality'. In *Election and Consensus in the Church*, Concilium 77, ed. G. Alberigo and A. Weiler, Herder, New York, 1972, pp. 43–68; Th. Rausch, 'Reception Past and Present', *Theological Studies* 47 (1986), pp. 497–508.
8. These are some of the many responses I received to my website: *www.women-priests.org.*
9. W.V. D'Antonio, *Laity, American and Catholic: Transforming the Church*, Sheed and Ward, Kansas, 1996; 'The American Catholic Laity', *National Catholic Reporter*, 29 October 1999.
10. D. McLaughlin, *The beliefs, values and practices of Catholic student teachers*, Australian Catholic University, Brisbane 1999; see also *Catholic School lay principals: Professional and pastoral issues*, Australian Catholic University, Brisbane, 1996.
11. Figures based on polls reported in national newspapers. In 'non-Western' countries support for women priests seems to be lower: Poland 24%, the Philippines 18%. I have no proper data about Latin America.

Chapter 7: Naming the Culprit

1. Julia Annas, 'Plato's Republic and Feminism', in Osborne (ed.), *Woman in Western Thought*, pp. 24–33; Anne Dickason, 'Anatomy and Destiny: The Role of Biology in Plato's Views of Women', in Carold C. Gould and Marx W. Wartofsky (eds), *Women and Philosophy. Toward a Theory of Liberation*, New York, 1976.
2. G. Homer, *The Didascalia Apostolorum*, the Syriac Version, Oxford 1929, ch. 26.
3. Epiphanius II, *Patrologiae Cursus. Series Graeca*, Migne, Paris, 1857–1866, vol. 43, cols. 497a.
4. C.B. Hale, *Thesaurus Linguae Graecae*, Paris, 1854, col. 2363–2364.
5. Tertullian, *On the Veiling of Virgins*, ch. 9.
6. H. Heumann and E. Seckel, *Handlexikon zu den Quellen des römischen Rechts*, Graz, 1958, pp. 246 and 265. L. Wenger, *Institutes of the Roman Law of Civil Procedure*, Littleton, 1940; F. Schulz, *Classical Roman Law*, London, 1951; M. Kaser, *Roman Private Law*, Oxford, 1965.
7. Ambrosiaster, *On 1 Corinthians* 14, 34.
8. *Decretum Gratiani*, Causa 33, question 5, chapters 11, 13, 15 and 19. *Corpus Juris Canonici*, edited by A. Friedberg, Leipzig, 1879–1881; reprint Graz, 1955; vol. 1, col. 1254–1256.
9. *Decretum Gratiani*, Causa 32, question 7, chapter 18. *Corpus Juris Canonici*, edited by A. Friedberg, Leipzig, 1879–1881; reprint Graz, 1955; vol. 1, col. 1145.
10. Pliny the Elder, *Natural History*, book 28, ch. 23, 78–80; book 7, ch. 65.
11. Jerome, *Letter 22. To Eustochium*, § 37.
12. Dionysius, *Letter to Basilides*, canon 2.
13. Capitulary of Bishop Theodulf of Orléans (760–821), canon 6.

Chapter 8: The Arguments Found in 'Tradition'

1. Translations and analysis published on www.womenpriests.org. I gratefully acknowledge the help of Dr Mary Ann Rossi with the translations of the texts.
2. For data on these authors I am indebted to Ida Raming, *Der Ausschluss der Frau vom priesterlichen Amt*, Cologne, 1973, esp. pp. 79–119; *The Exclusion of Women from the Priesthood: Divine Law or Sex Discrimination?*, Metuchen, 1976.
3. Johannes Andreae, *Novella in Decretales Gregorii IX*, V, fol. 125v.
4. Thomas Aquinas, *Summa Theologica* Suppl. qu. 39, art. 1.
5. Richard of Middleton, *Super Quarto Sententiarum* [commentary on Peter Lombard's Sententiarum vol. 4], Dist. 25, a. 4, n. 1; ed. Bocatelli, Venice, 1499 (Pellechet-Polain, 10132/9920), f. 177–R.
6. John Duns Scotus, *Duns Scoti Opera Omnia*, ed. Vives, Paris, 1894, vol. 24, 'Reportata Parisiensia', Liber 4, Distinctio 25, Quaestio 2, § 19. pp. 367–371 (my italics).
7. Durandus à Saint-Pourçain, *In Petri Lombardi Sententias Theologicas Commentarium*, Venice, 1571, vol. 4, Dist. 25, Quaestio 2, f. 364 v.
8. Richard of Middleton, *Super Quarto Sententiarum* [commentary on Peter Lombard's Sententiarum vol. 4], Dist. 25, a. 4, n. 1; ed. Bocatelli, Venice, 1499 (Pellechet-Polain, 10132/9920), f. 177–R.
9. John Duns Scotus, *Duns Scoti Opera Omnia*, ed. Vives, Paris, 1894, vol. 24, 'Reportata Parisiensia', Liber 4, Distinctio 25, Quaestio 2, § 5. pp. 367–371 (my italics).
10. Quote from the *Codex Iuris Civilis*, I 7; that is, the civil law of the time, based on ancient Roman law (my italics).

11. Henricus de Sergusio, *Commentaria* I, fol. 204v. Source: Ida Raming, *The Exclusion of Women from the Priesthood*, Scarecrow Press, Metuchen, 1976, pp. 83–87.
12. *Inter Insigniores*, § 6.

Chapter 9: Not Created in God's Image?

1. *Commentariun in IV Libros Sententiarum Magistri Petri Lombardi*; Division 25, Article 2, question 1, § d; *Opera Omnia*, Quaracchi 1882–1902.
2. *Summa Theologica* I, qu.93, art.4, ad 1.
3. Huguccio, *Summa*, Causa 33, qu.5, ch.13; Ida Raming, *The exclusion of Women from the priesthood*, Scarecrow Press, Metuchen, 1976, pp. 61–64.
4. *Decretum Gratiani*, Causa 33, qu.5, ch.11.13. *Corpus Juris Canonici*, ed. A. Friedberg, Leipzig, 1879–1881; reprint Graz, 1955: vol.1, col.1254–1256.
5. Epiphanius, *Letter to John, Bishop of Jerusalem* § 6.
6. *De Cultu Feminarum*, book 1, ch.1; *De Virginibus Velandis*, ch.10.
7. *On 1 Corinthians* 14,34.
8. Genesis 1:26–27.
9. J. Jervell, *Imago Dei. Gen 1,26f. in Spätjudentum, in der Gnosis und in den Paulinischen Briefen*, Göttingen, 1960.
10. Genesis 5:1–2.
11. *Wisdom* 2, 23; *Sirach* 17, 1–14. See also: Th. Vriezen, 'La création de l'homme d'après l'image de Dieu', *Oudtestamentische Studiën* 2 (1943) pp. 86–100; L.Köhler, 'Die Grundstelle der Imago-Dei-Lehre', *Theologisches Zeitschrift* 4 (1948), pp. 16–22; H.G.Wood, 'Man Created in the Image of God', *Evangelical Theology* 68/69 (1957), pp. 165–168.
12. Genesis 2:20–22.
13. *Genesis Rabba* 158, 163–164; *Midrash Abkir* 133, 135; *Abot di Rabbi Nathan* 24; *B.Sanhedrin* 39a; R. Graves and R. Patai, *Hebrew Myths, the Book of Genesis*, London, 1964, pp. 65–69.
14. H. Kramer and J. Sprenger, *The Hammer of Witches*, Cologne, 1486, part 1, question 6. Translated by M. Summers, London, 1928, pp. 43–47.
15. 2 Samuel 16:13; Exodus 26:20–35; 27:7; 1 Kings, 6:34; Ezekiel 41:5–26.
16. See also Ph. Trible, 'Eve and Adam: Genesis 2–3', in *Womanspirit Rising*, New York, 1979, pp. 74–83; F. Ferder and J. Heagle, *Partnership*, Notre Dame, 1989, pp. 31–46.
17. Plato, *Symposion*, ch. 14–15.
18. *Genesis Rabba* 55; *Leviticus Rabba* 14.1; *Abot di Rabbi Nathan* 1.8; *B. Berakhot* 61a; *B. Erubin* 18a; *Tanhuma Tazri'a* 1; *Yalqut Genesis* 20; *Tanhuma Buber* iii.33; *Midrash Tehillim* 139, 529.
19. Genesis 2:21–24.
20. The punishment 'he shall rule over you' will be discussed in Chapter 11.
21. Galatians 3:28.
22. K. Kröger, 'An Enquiry into Evidence of Maenadism in the Corinthian Congregation', *SBL Seminar papers* 14 (1978) volume 2, pp. 331–346.
23. 1 Corinthians 11:7–9.
24. Read 1 Corinthians 14:1–33.
25. R.E. Witt, *Isis in the Greco-Roman World*, Ithaca, 1971; see also J.Z. Smith, 'Native Cults in the Hellenistic Period', *History of Religions* 11 (1971/72), pp. 236–249.
26. 1 Corinthians 11:2–16; see J.B. Hurley, 'Did Paul require Veils of the Silence of Women?', *Westminster Theological Journal* 35 (1972/73), pp. 190–220; J. Murphy-O'Connor, 'Sex and Logic in 1 Corinthians 11:2–16', *Catholic Biblical Quarterly* 42 (1980), pp. 482–500; 'St. Paul: Promoter of the Ministry of Women', *Priests & People*

6 (1992), pp. 307–311; E. Schüssler Fiorenza, *In Memory of Her*, London, 1983, pp. 227–230; G. Dautzenberg, et al. (ed.), *Die Frau im Urchristentum*, Frankfurt, 1983, pp. 213–215; R. Schnackenburg, Die sittliche Botschaft des Neuen Testaments, vol. I, Freiburg, 1986, pp. 246–250; etc.

27. Meaning uncertain. Possible explanations offered by J.A. Fitzmyer, 'A Feature of Qumran Angelology and the Angels of 1 Cor 11:10', *New Testament Studies* 4 (1957/ 58), pp. 48–58; M.D. Hooker, 'Authority on her Head: an Examination of I Cor xi.10', *New Testament Studies* 10 (1964/65,) pp. 410–416; A.Feuillet, 'Le signe de puissance sur la tête de la femme' (I Cor. ix.10), *Nouvelle Revue Théologique* 55 (1973,) pp. 945–954.

28. 'Different from' is a better translation of the Greek *chôris* than 'independent from'; see J. Kürzinger, 'Frau und Mann nach 1 Kor 11.11f', *Biblische Zeitschrift* 22 (1978), pp. 270–275; E. Schüssler-Fiorenza, op.cit.; R. Schnackenburg, op.cit.

29. 1 Corinthians 1:11–17.

30. Titus 1:10–13.

31. M. Dibelius and H. Conzelmann, *Die Pastoralbriefe*, Tübingen, 1966, pp. 102–103.

32. 1 Corinthians 11:11–12.

Chapter 10: Not Allowed to Teach?

1. Erasmus, *Laus Stultitiae* (1508), Dutch translation *De Lof der Zotheid*, Utrecht, 1912, pp. 118–119; English translation my own.

2. 1 Timothy 2:12–14.

3. *Decretum Gratiani*, Distinction 23, Chapter 29. *Corpus Juris Canonici*, edited by A. Friedberg, Leipzig, 1879–1881; reprint Graz, 1955; vol. 1, col. 86.

4. *Summa Theologica Suppl.* ,qu. 39 art. 1.

5. Durandi a Sancto Porciano, *In Petri Lombardi Sententias Theologicas Comment-arium*, Venice, 1571, vol. 4, Dist. 25, Quaestio 2, f. 364–v (my italics).

6. *Duns Scoti Opera Omnia*, ed. Vives, Paris, 1894, vol. 24, 'Reportata Parisiensia', Liber 4, Distinctio 25, Quaestio 2, §19, pp. 367–371 (my italics).

7. Richard of Middleton, *Super Quarto Sententiarum*, Dist. 25, a. 4, n. 1, § 9–11; ed. Bocatelli, Venice, 1499 (Pellechet-Polain, 10132/9920), f. 177–R (my italics).

8. *Inter Insigniores*, § 19.

9. 1 Timothy 1:6; 1:7; 4:7; 6:20–21.

10. 2 Timothy 2:14; Titus 1:10; 3:9.

11. 1 Timothy 2:8; 5:14–15.

12. P. W. Barnett, 'Wives and Women's Ministry' (I Timothy 2:11–15): *Evangelical Quarterly* 61 (1989), 225–238; B. Barron, 'Putting Women in Their Place: I Timothy 2 and Evangelical Views of Women in Church Leadership', *Journal of the Evangelical Theological Society* 33 (1990), 451–459; A. L. Bowman, 'Women in Ministry: An Exegetical Study in I Timothy 2:11–15', *Biblical Studies* 149 (1992), 193–213; R. Falconer, 'I Timothy 2,14.15. Interpretative Notes', *Journal of Biblical Literature* 60 (1941), 375–379.

13. A. Padgett, 'Wealthy Women at Ephesus. 1 Timothy 2:8–15 in Social Context', *Interpretation* 41 (1987), 19–31; G. N. Redekop, 'Let the Women Learn: I Timothy 2 :8–15 Reconsidered', *Studies in Religion* 19 (1990), 235–245.

14. E. Schüssler Fiorenza, *In Memory of Her*, SCM, London, 1994, p. 289.

15. Matthew 8:21; Mark 5:13; John 19:38; Acts 21:39–40; 26:1; 27:3; 28:16; 1 Corinthians 16:7; etc.

16. A. D. B. Spencer, 'Eve at Ephesus (Should women be ordained as pastors according to the First Letter to Timothy 2:11–15?)', *Journal of the Evangelical Theological*

Society 17 (1974), 215–222; G. P. Hugenberger, 'Women in Church Office: Hermeneutics or Exegesis? A Survey of Approaches to I Timothy 2 :8–15': *Journal of the Evangelical Theological Society* 35 (1992), 341–360.

17. Ph. B. Payne, 'Libertarian Women in Ephesus: A Response to Douglas J. Moo's article, I Timothy 2:11–15: Meaning and Significance', *Trinidad Journal of New Testament Studies* 2 (1981), 169–197; Redekop, op.cit.
18. 1 Corinthians 11:5.
19. Romans 16:1; 1 Timothy 3:8–12; more about this in Chapter 17.
20. Redekop, op.cit.
21. Genesis 1:20–27.
22. Genesis 1:27.
23. Genesis 3:17–19.
24. G. P. Hugenberger, 'Women in Church Office: Hermeneutics or Exegesis? A Survey of Approaches to I Timothy 2:8–15', *Journal of the Evangelical Theological Society* 35 (1992), 341–360.
25. Barron, op.cit.
26. 1 Corinthians 14:3.
27. Galatians 2:16; 5:1–18; 3:23–28; etc.
28. 1 Timothy 5:23.
29. Matthew 23:8–9; 5:34 and 37; 5:39.

Chapter 11: Carrying the Burden of Eve's Sin?
1. De Baysio, *Rosarium super Decreto*, Causa 27, quaestio 1, chapter 23; Lyon, 1549.
2. De Baysio, 'On account of three reasons a man is said to be the glory of God and not a woman. Firstly, because God appeared more powerful and more glorious in the creation of a man than of the woman, because it is especially through man that the glory of God is manifest because God made him by himself and from the slime of the earth against nature, but woman is made from the man. Secondly because the man was made by God without any intermediate tool, which is not the case with regard to woman. Thirdly because the man glorifies God directly, that is without any intermediary, whereas the woman only glorifies God through the man, because the man teaches and instructs the woman to glorify God.' Ib, Causa 33, quaestio 5, chapter 13.
3. Ibid (my italics).
4. Simon of Cremona, Mitrale V, chapter 11; Ida Raming, *The Exclusion of Women from the Priesthood*, Scarecrow Press, Metuchen, 1976, pp. 58–60.
5. *Decretum Gratiani*, Causa 33, question 5, chapter 19. *Corpus Juris Canonici*, edited by A. Friedberg, Leipzig, 1879–1881; reprint Graz, 1955; vol. 1, col. 1255–1256.
6. Ignatius, *Letter to the Trallians*, ch. 10.
7. Irenaeus, *Against Heresies*, book 5, ch. 21, § 1.
8. Irenaeus, *Fragment* no. 19.
9. Tertullian, *De Cultu Feminarum*, book 1, chapter 1 (my italics).
10. See Chapter 7.
11. St Chrysostom, *Homily* 9.
12. Jerome, *Against Jovinianus*, Book 1, § 27–28.
13. Jerome, *Letter 71. To Lucinius*, § 3.
14. Exegesis in: L.Ouelette, 'Woman's doom in Gen 3,16', *Catholic Biblical Quarterly* 12 (1950), pp. 389–399; G. Duncker, 'In dolore paries filios', *Angelicum* 34 (1957), pp. 18–32; F. de Fraine, *The Bible and the Origin of Man*, New York, 1962; H. Renkens, *Israel's Concept of the Beginning*, New York, 1964; B. Vawter, *A Path*

through Genesis, London, 1957; *On Genesis. A New Reading*, New York, 1977; J.M. Ford, 'Tongues-Leadership-Women', *Spiritual Life* 17 (1971), pp. 186–197; P.K. Jewett, *Man as Male and Female*, Grand Rapids, 1975; biblical theology of the text in: Arlene Swidler, *Woman in a Man's Church*, New York, 1972; Sr Albertus Magnus McGrath, *What a Modern Catholic Believes about Women*, Chicago, 1972; G. Tavard, *Woman in Christian Tradition*, Notre Dame, 1973; R. Kress, *Wither Womankind? The Humanity of Women*, St Meinrad, 1975; L. Russell (ed.), *The Liberating Word: a Guide to nonsexist Interpretation of the Bible*, Philadelphia, 1976; Ph. Trible, *God and the Rhetoric of Sexuality*, Philadelphia, 1978; etc.

15. Deuteronomy 24:16; Jeremiah 31:29–30; Ezekiel 14:12–20.
16. Isaiah 1:18.
17. Acts 10:34; Romans 2:11; Galatians 3:28.
18. *Decretum Gratiani*, Causa 2, question 7, princ.; *Corpus Iuris Canonici*, ed. A. Friedberg, Leipzig, 1879–1881; reprint Graz, 1955; vol. 1, col. 750–751.
19. In the succeeding codes of Church law the reasoning was dropped, but the conclusion stayed. *Codex Iuris Canonici* (1918), can. 968; (1983), can. 1024.

Chapter 12: Deliberately Left Out by Jesus Christ?

1. *Inter Insigniores*, no 9.12.
2. *Ordinatio Sacerdotalis*, no. 2.
3. Titus 2:3–4.
4. 1 Timothy 5:3–10.
5. Ignatius of Antioch greets 'the virgins and the order of widows' (*Philippians* § 15). See also Origen, *Commentary on Romans* 10:17.
6. *Didascalia* ch. 15; G. Homer, *The Didascalia Apostolorum*, Oxford, 1929; my adaptation to modern expression.
7. *Didascalia* ch. 15.
8. See Chapter 10.
9. *Didascalia* ch. 16.
10. The General Council of Trullo (AD 692) endorsed the *Didascalia* in these words: 'It has also seemed good to this holy Council, that the eighty-five canons, received and ratified by the holy and blessed Fathers before us, and also handed down to us in the name of the holy and glorious Apostles should from this time forth remain firm and unshaken for the cure of souls and the healing of disorders' (canon 2).
11. *Duns Scoti Opera Omnia*, ed. Vives, Paris, 1894, vol. 24, 'Reportata Parisiensia', Liber 4, Distinctio 25, Quaestio 2, & 18; pp.367–371.
12. cf. Matthew 5:17–20.
13. Luke 8:1–4.
14. Matthew 18:18; John 20:23.
15. Luke 7:36–50; 7:11–17; 21:1–4; 23:27–31.
16. Mark 5:21–43; 7:24–30; Luke 10:38–42; 8:1–3; John 4:7–42; Elizabeth Schüssler Fiorenza, 'Women Apostles: The Testament of Scripture', in *Women and Catholic Priesthood*, Anne Marie Gardener (ed.), New York, 1976, pp. 94–102; Jane Massyngberde Ford, 'Women Leaders in the New Testament', in *Women Priests*, A. and L. Swidler (eds), New York, 1977, pp. 132–134; Evelyn Stagg and Frank Stagg, *Women in the World of Jesus*, Philadelphia, 1978; Elisabeth Moltmann-Wendel, *The Women around Jesus*, London, 1982; *A Land Flowing with Milk and Honey*, London, 1986, pp. 137–148; Mary Grey, *Redeeeming the Dream*, London, 1989, esp. pp. 95–103; Frank Wheeler, 'Women in the Gospel of John', in *Essays on Women in*

Earliest Christianity, Joplin, 1995; Jo Ann Davidson, 'Women in Scripture', in *Women in Ministry,* Nancy Vyhmeister (ed.), Berrien Springs, 1998, pp. 157–186.

17. Exodus 12:1–14.

18. Joachim Jeremias, *The Eucharistic Words of Jesus,* London, 1966, pp. 46–47; Suzanne Tunc, *Des femmes aussi suivaient Jésus,* Desclée de Brouwer, Paris, 1998, pp. 69–78; Marjorie Reiley Maguire, 'Bible, liturgy concur: women were there', *National Catholic Reporter* (1998), 5 June.

Chapter 13: Not Human Enough to Represent Christ?

1. *Inter Insigniores,* § 26–28.
2. *Summa Theologica Suppl.* qu. 39 art. 1 (my italics).
3. *Summa Theologica,* 1, qu. 92, art. 1, ad 1.
4. Methodius, *The banquet of the ten virgins,* 2. 2, trans. William R. Clark, *The writings of Methodius,* ANCL, 14, Edinburgh, 1969, p. 13; cf. Lucretius, *On the nature of things,* 4. 1037, GB 12, p. 57.
5. Kim E. Power , 'Of godly men and medicine: ancient biology and the Christian Fathers on the nature of woman', *Woman-Church* 15 (Spring 1994), pp. 26–33.
6. Eric Doyle, 'The Question of Women Priests and the Argument *In Persona Christi',* *Irish Theological Quarterly* 37 (1984), 212–221, here pp. 217–218.
7. Galatians 3:26–28.
8. 2 Corinthians 3:18.
9. Romans 8:28–29.
10. Rose Hoover, 'Consider tradition. The case for women's ordination', *Commonweal* 126 no. 2 (Jan. 29, 1999), pp. 17–20.
11. Vatican II, *Sacrosanctum Concilium,* § 7.
12. *Acta Apostolicae Sedis* 35 (1943), p. 202.
13. *In Iohannis Evangelium* VI; PL 35, 1428.
14. *Inter Insigniores,* § 28.
15. Elizabeth A. Johnson, *She Who Is: The Mystery of God in Feminist Theological Discourse,* New York, 1992, p. 153.
16. Thomas Newbold, 'Symbolism of Sexuality: Person, Ministry and Women Priests', in *Women and Priesthood. Future Directions,* Collegeville, 1978, pp. 133–141; here pp. 138–139.
17. *Inter Insigniores,* § 25.
18. *Commentary on Inter Insigniores,* § 88.
19. Ralph A. Keifer, 'The Priest as "Another Christ" in Liturgical Prayer', in *Women and Priesthood. Future Directions,* Collegeville, 1978, pp. 103–110; here pp. 109–110.
20. Marie Augusta Neal, 'Models for Future Priesthood'; Dorothy Donnelly, 'Diversity of Gifts in Future Priesthood'; Arlene Anderson Swidler, 'Partnership Marriage: Model of Future Priesthood'; Leonard Swidler, 'Sisterhood: Model of Future Priesthood', all in *Women and Catholic Priesthood,* Anne Marie Gardiner (ed.), New York, 1976, pp. 103–134.
21. John 15:12–13; 10:11–15; Matthew 20:24–28; John 13:12–16.
22. John 13:35; 21:15–17.

Chapter 14: Not Man Enough to Represent the 'Groom'?

1. *Inter Insigniores,* § 24; *Commentary on Inter Insigniores,* § 81–82.
2. *Mulieris Dignitatem* (15 August 1988) § 10.
3. *Mulieris Dignitatem* § 18–19.
4. *Mulieris Dignitatem* § 29.

5. Joanna Manning, *Is the Pope Catholic?*, Toronto, 1999, pp. 69–70; see also Nancy Chodorow, *The Reproduction of Mothering: Psychoanalysis and the Sociology of Gender*, Berkeley, 1978; Judith Butler, *Gender Trouble – Feminism and the Subversion of Identity*, New York, 1990; Sarah Coakley, 'Creaturehood before God – Male and Female', *Theology* 93 (1990), pp. 343–354.

6. Roger Burggraeve, 'De schepping van de mens als man en vrouw', *Collationes* 3 (1997), pp. 243–281.

7. Mary Daly, *The Church and the Second Sex*, Boston, 1985, p. 149; see also *Gyn/ecology: The Metaethics of Radical Feminism*, Boston, 1978.

8. Mary Grey, *Redeeming the Dream*, London, 1989, pp. 15–19; see also Carolyn Heilbrunn, *Reinventing Womanhood*, London, 1979, pp. 125–170; Jean Majewski, *Without a Self to Deny: Called to Discipleship When We Were Yet Un-Persons*, Chicago, 1984.

9. *Inter Insigniores* § 29–30.

10. Ephesians 5:21–33 (italics are mine). The letter is now commonly attributed to a disciple of Paul.

11. Colossians 3:18–22; Ephesians 5:21–6:9; 1 Peter 2:18–3:7; Titus 2:1–10; 1 Timothy 5:1–6:2.

12. *Isaiah* 61:10; *Exodus Rabba* 15:30; 4 *Esdras* 10:40–43; 1 *QumranIsa* 61:10; *Pesiq* 149a; J. Gnilka, 'Bräutigam – spätjüdisches Messiasprädikat?', *Trierer Theologische Zeitschrift* 69 (1960), pp. 298–301.

13. Philo of Alexandria, *Abraham* 99; *Cherubim* 40–44; *Vita Moysis* 2:69; see R.A. Batey, 'Jewish Gnosticism and the Hieros Gamos of Eph. 5:21–33', *New Testament Studies* 10 (1963/64), pp. 121–127.

14. Ephesians 1:23; 4:1–16; E. Best, *One Body in Christ*, London, 1950.

15. Ephesians 1:9–10; 6:19; cf. 2:11–22.

16. Ephesians 3:4–6, 8–10; A.E.J. Rawlinson, *Mysterium Christi*, London, 1930, esp. pp. 225–244; J.T. Trinidad, 'The Mystery hidden in God', *Biblica* 31 (1950), pp. 1–26.

17. E. Neuhäusler, 'Das Geheimnis ist gross', *Biblisches Leben* 4 (1963), pp. 155–163; J. Cambier, 'Le grand mystère concernant le Christ et son Église', *Biblica* 47 (1966), pp. 43–90, 223–242; J. Gnilka, *Der Efeserbrief*, Freiburg, 1971, pp. 273–294.

18. *Inter Insigniores* § 29–30 (my italics).

19. *Commentary on Inter Insigniores* § 100–102 (my italics).

20. *Mulieris Dignitatem* § 25–26 (my italics); see also *Christifideles Laici* § 51.

21. Isaiah 5:1–7; 27:2–5; Jeremiah 2:21; 5:10; 6:9; Ezekiel 15:1–8; 17:3–10; Psalm 80:8–18; etc.

22. Matthew 20:1–16; 21:33–46; Luke 13:6; John 8:37; etc.

23. John 2:1–10; L. P. Trudinger, 'The Seven Days in the New Creation in St John's Gospel', *Evangelical Quarterly* 44 (1972), pp. 154–158; J. A. Grassi, 'The Wedding at Cana (Jn II 1–11): A Pentecostal Meditation?', *Novum Testamentum* 14 (1972), pp. 131–136; K. T. Cooper, 'The Best Wine: John 2:1–11', *Westminster Theological Journal* 41 (1979), pp. 364–380; R. F. Collins, 'Cana (Jn. 2:1–12) – The first of his signs or the key to his signs?', *Irish Theological Quarterly* 47 (1980), pp. 79–95; V. Parkin, 'On the third day there was a marriage in Cana of Galilee (John 2.1)', *Irish Biblical Studies* 3 (1981), pp. 134–144; etc.

24. John 15:1–7. Cf. 'You are in me'; J. Wijngaards, *The Gospel of John*, Wilmington, 1986, pp. 195–203; M. Vellanickal, 'Divine Immanence in St. John', *Biblebashyam* 1 (1975), 312–332; J. Dupuis, 'Christus und die advaita-Erfahrung', *Orientierung* 41 (1977), 168–172.

25. Tina Beattie, *God's Mother, Eve's Advocate. A Gynocentric Refiguration of Marian Symbolism in Engagement with Luce Irigaray*, Bristol, 1999, p. 64.
26. H. U. von Balthasar, *Wer ist Kirche? Vier Skizzen*, Freiburg, 1965, p. 24; Hedwig Meyer-Wilmes has called von Balthasar's reflections 'male daydreaming that comes closer to ecclesiastical soft porn than to a theological treatise on the Church'; 'Vater Gott und Mutter Kirche', in Marie-Therese Wacker (ed.), *Theologie feministisch*, Düsseldorf, 1988, p. 150.
27. H. U. von Balthasar, *Elucidations*, trans. John Riches, London, 1975, p. 150.
28. Beattie, op. cit. p. 65.
29. Galatians 3:28; *Mulieris Dignitatem* § 25.
30. About the 'bridegroom' argument, see also: P. Lakeland, *Can Women be Priests?*, Dublin, 1975, pp. 64–65; C. Stuhlmueller, 'Bridegroom: a Biblical Symbol of Union, not Separation', in *Women Priests*, Leonard Swidler and Arlene Swidler (eds), New York, 1977, pp. 278–283; J. R. Donahue, 'Women, Priesthood and the Vatican', *America*, 136 (April 2 1977), pp. 286–287; R. Radford Ruether, *Sexism and God-Talk*, London, 1983; D. Coffey, 'Priestly Representation and Women's Ordination', in *Priesthood. The Hard Questions* ed. G. P. Gleeson, Dublin, 1993, pp. 79–99.
31. J. Morgan, *Women Priests*, Bristol, 1985, p. 171.
32. Kelley A. Raab, *When Women Become Priests*, New York, 2000; see also Mary D. Donovan, *Women Priests in the Episcopal Church: The Experience of the First Decade*, Cincinnati, 1988; Sue Walrond-Skinner, *Crossing the Boundary: What Will Women Priests Mean?*, London, 1994; Hilary Wakeman (ed.), *Women Priests: The First Years*, London, 1996; B. Brown Zikmund et al., *Clergy Women: An Uphill Calling*, Westminster, 1998.
33. 'Symbolica theologia non est argumentativa'; Thomas Aquinas, I *Sententiarum* prol. Q.1; dist. 11, q.1. ; I am indebted to René van Eyden for this reference.

Chapter 15: Verdict on the Presumed 'Tradition'

1. *Dei Verbum*, § 9–10.
2. Denz. no 423; 430; 468; 714; in H.Denzinger, *Enchiridion Symbolorum*, Herder, 1965.
3. *Matthew* 16:19; see also 18:18; *Mark* 16:16.
4. For other examples read: Matthew 7:4; 23:24; 5:29; 5:34–35; 24:36; 12:30 (contrast with Mark 9:40!).
5. *Lumen Gentium* § 16.
6. *Matthew* 8:5–13; John 4:7–26; Luke 10:29–37; Matthew 15:21–28; Mark 7:24–30; Romans 2:6–16.
7. Pseudo-Ambrose, *On I Corinthians 14:34*; Gratian, *Decretum Gratiani*, Causa 33, question 5, ch. 19; Huguccio, *Summa*, Causa 33, qu. 5, ch. 13; Thomas Aquinas, *Summa Theologica* I, qu. 93, art. 4, ad 1.
8. Richard of Middleton, *Super Quarto Sententiarum*, Dist. 25, a. 4, n. 1, § 11; John Duns Scotus, *Opera Omnia*, Liber 4, Distinctio 25, Quaestio 2, § 19.
9. Guido de Baysio, *Rosarium super Decreto*, Causa 27, quaestio 1, ch. 23; Gratian, *Decree*, Causa 33, qu. 5, ch. 19.
10. See Chapters 5 and 12 above.
11. See Chapter 12.
12. *Disdascalia*, ch. 15.
13. Thomas Aquinas, *Summa Theologica* I, qu. 92, art. 1, ad 1.
14. *Letter 74a*. See Letters 71:3 and 73:13.

Chapter 16: **Genuine Tradition**

1. Matthew 13:52.
2. 2 Corinthians 3:3; compare especially Jeremiah 31:31–34.
3. *Stromata,* book 6, ch.15,131, 4–5.
4. *Antirrheticus,* III, 7.
5. Augustine, *De Spir. et Litt.,* 14, 23 and 17, 30; Thomas Aquinas, *Summa Theologica* I–II, q. 106, a. 2. See *ST* I–II, q. 106, a. I, sed cont.; a. 2, ad 3 III, q. 42, a. 4, ad 2, q. 72, a 1l; *Comm. in 2 Cor.,* c. 3, lect. I; *In Hebr.,* c. 8,lect. 3 end.
6. See Yves Congar, *Tradition and Traditions,* London, 1965, pp. 494–508.
7. J. Ratzinger, 'On the Interpretation of the Tridentine Decree on Tradition', in *Revelation and Tradition,* by K. Rahner and J. Ratzinger, London, 1966, pp. 50–68.
8. John Henry Cardinal Newman, 'A University Sermon Preached on the Purification', § 11 & 13; *University Sermons,* Oxford, 1843 (italics are mine).
9. Pius IX, dogmatic definition in *Ineffabilis Deus,* 1854, Denzinger no 1641.
10. Giorgio Otranto, 'Note sul sacerdozio femminile nell'antichita in margine a una testimonianza di Gelasio I', *Vetera Christianorum* 19 (1982): 341–60; trans. Mary Ann Rossi, 'Notes on the Female Priesthood in Antiquity', *Journal of Feminist Studies* 7 (1991), no. 1, pp. 73–94. Karen Jo Torjesen provides valuable background information to women's leadership in Christian communities: *When Women Were Priests,* New York, 1993.
11. Ute Eisen, *Amtsträgerinnen im frühen Christentum,* Göttingen, 1996, pp. 193–209; see also Dorothy Irvin, 'The Ministry of Women in the Early Church: The Archeological Evidence', *Duke Divinity School Review* 2 (1980), pp. 76–86.
12. 'Vita Sanctae Brigidae' in Th. Messingham, *Florilegium Insulae Sanctorum seu Vitae et Acta Sanctorum Hiberniae,* Paris, 1624, ch. VI, p. 193ff.; see also J.H. Bernard and R. Atkinson (eds), *The Irish Liber Hymnorum,* vol. II, London, 1898, pp. 41, 192–193; W. Stokes, *The Martyrology of Oengus the Culdee,* London, 1905, p. 67; L. Hardinge, *The Celtic Church in Britain,* London, 1972, p. 190.
13. L. Duchesne, 'Lovocat et Catihern, prêtres bretons de temps de saint Melaine', *Revue de Bretagne et de Vendée* 7 (1885), pp.5–18.
14. H.E. Lohman and P. Hirsch, *Die Sachsengeschichte des Widukind von Korvei,* Hannover ,1935, p. 127. The reading is confirmed in various manuscripts, see p. 127 note d.
15. G. Fabricius, *Originum Illustrissimae Stirpis Saxonicae,* libri septem, Leipzig, 1597, vol. I, p. 27; vol. II, pp. 100–105; vol. V, p. 551. The Quedlingburg Annals, preserved in the museum of Dresden, were lost during the bombardment of 1945. Much can be confirmed, however, from F. E. Kettner, *Antiquitates Quedlinburgenses,* Leipzig, 1712.
16. Sr Telchilde de Montessus, *Insignata Abbatium,* unpublished manuscript at Jouarre, France, 1962; cited with other data in Joan Morris, *Against God and Nature,* London, 1973, pp. 130–139. Morris's book was published in the USA as *The Lady was a Bishop: The Hidden History of Women with Clerical Ordination and the Jurisdiction of Bishops,* New York, 1973.
17. 'The Gospel of Mary', § 17; *The Nag Hammadi Library,* J. Robinson (ed.), San Francisco, 1988, pp. 526–527.
18. Elisabeth Schüssler Fiorenza, 'Mary Magdalen, Apostle to the Apostles', UTS Journal (April 1975), pp. 22–30.
19. See Chapter 10.
20. J.H. Emminghaus and L. Kuppers, *Maria Magdalena,* Recklinghausen, 1964; E. Duperray (ed.), *Marie Madeleine dans la mystique, les arts et les lettres.* Actes du

Colloque international, Avignon, 20–22 juillet 1988, Paris, 1989; Susan Haskins, *Mary Magdalene: Myth and Metaphor*, New York, 1995; Margret E. Arminger, *Die verratene Päpstin*, Freiburg, 1997; W. Eggen, 'Mary Magdalene's Touch in a Family Church', *New Blackfriars* 78 (1997), pp. 428–438; E. de Boer, *Mary Magdalene: Beyond the Myth*, New York, 1997; *Mary Magdalene and the Disciple Jesus Loved*, New York, 2000; Theresia Saers, *Een Alabaster Kruik*, Tilburg, 1998.

21. J. Ansor, 'The Female Transvestite in Early Monasticism', *Viator* 5 (1974), pp. 1–34.
22. P. Loose-Noji, 'Temptation and Redemption: A Monastic Life in Stone', in Holloway et al. (ed.), *Equally in God's Image. Women in the Middle Ages*, pp. 220–232.
23. Raymund of Capua (fourteenth century), *The Life of St Catherine of Siena*, Harvill Press edition, London, 1960, pp. 33–34, 108–109.
24. From an avalanche of publications, see Fiona Bowie and Oliver Davies, *Hildegard of Bingen*, London, 1990 (excellent bibliography); Juliana of Norwich, *Showings*, New York, 1978 (good introduction by Edmund Colledge and James Walsh; Mary Grey tells me that Juliana carried real pastoral responsibility for a wide area). See also: Sheila Rowbotham, *Hidden From History: Rediscovering Women in History*, New York, 1976; Renate Bridenthal and Claudia Koontz (eds), *Becoming Visible: Women in European History*, Boston, 1977; P. Dronke, *Women Writers of the Middle Ages: A Critical Study of Texts from Perpetua (+ 203) to Marguerite Porete (+ 1310)*, Cambridge, 1984; Gerda Lerner, *Women and History*, Vol. II. *The Creation of Feminist Consciousness: From the Middle Ages to Eighteen-seventy*, Oxford, 1993.
25. M. Eliasova, 'Davidek Of Czechoslovakia', *NewWomen NewChurch*, 22 (1999), pp. 7–8.

Chapter 17: Nine Centuries of Women Deacons
1. *Inter Insigniores*, § 5–8.
2. Council of Trent, *On the Sacrament of Ordination*, ch.2 and can. 6; Latin text in *Enchiridion Symbolorum*, Denzinger-Schönmetzer, Herder, 1976, no. 1763–1778.
3. The manuscript was translated into Latin and published by John Morinus, Antwerp, 1695; pp.55–57.
4. The Greek term is *euchologion*.
5. In this rite the copyist sometimes speaks of the 'bishop', sometimes the 'archbishop'. The original text carried 'bishop', as we know from other manuscripts, but because this *euchologion* was transcribed for an archbishop, the scribe wrote 'archbishop' whenever he remembered to do so.
6. See Vatican Manuscript 1872; John Morinus, in *Commentarius [sic] de Sacris Ecclesiae Ordinationibus*, publ. Kalverstraat, Antwerp, 1695; pp. 78–81.
7. Evangelos Theodorou, 'Die Weihe, Die Segnung der Diakoninnen' (in modern Greek), *Theologia* 25 (1954), pp. 430–469; 'Das Ambt der Diakoninnen in der kirchlichen Tradition. Ein orthodoxer Beitrag zum Problem der Frauenordination', *Una Sancta* 33 (1978), pp. 162–172.
8. Jacob Goar, in *Euchologion sive Rituale Graecorum*, Paris, 1647, pp. 262–264; with notes on pp. 264–267.
9. The Council of Trent, *On the Sacrament of Ordination*, Canon 4, Denzinger no. 964.
10. Pope Innocentius III, *Letter to the Bishop of Brixen*; F. Solá, '*De Sacramento Ordinis*', in *Sacrae Theologiae Summa*, ed. J.A. de Aldama et al., vol. IV, Madrid, 1956, pp. 710–713.

Chapter 18: The Reality of Women Deacons

1. *Ante-Nicene Fathers*, Series II, Vol. XIV; Council of Nicea, can. 19.
2. About Paul of Samosata, see: Eusebius, *Ecclesiastical History* VII 27–31; G. Bardy, *Paul de Samosate*, Paris, 1929; H. de Riedmatten, *Les Actes du procès de Paul de Samosate*, Fribourg, 1952; G. Kretschmar, *Studiën zur frühchristlichen Trinitäts-theologie*, Tübingen, 1956; G. Downey, *A History of Antioch in Syria*, Princeton, 1961.
3. *Ante-Nicene Fathers*, Series II, Vol. XIV; Council of Orange, can. 26.
4. Council of Calchedon, canon 15.
5. Also known as the Quinisext Council. *Ante-Nicene Fathers*, Series II, Vol. XIV, Council of Trullo, canon 14.
6. Aimé Georges Martimot, *Les Diaconesses. Essai historique*, Rome, 1982, p. 155.
7. *The Testament of Our Lord* (fifth century), I § 19, 40; J. Cooper and A. Maclean (eds), Edinburgh, 1902; James of Edessa (sixth century), *Canonical Resolutions*, § 24; A. Lamy, *De Syrorum Fide et Disciplina, Louvain*, 1859, p. 127.
8. John Telo (ninth century), *Canonical Resolutions* § 36 & 38; Assemani, *Bibliotheca Orientalis*, vol.II, 'De Monophysitis' § 10.
9. An ancient rule in the *Statuta Ecclesiae Antiqua*, ch. 12. Deaconesses had ceased to exist in the West at the time of the *Statuta*'s redaction. So 'widows or nuns' was substituted for 'deaconesses' in the text.
10. An ancient Copt ritual from Egypt; H. Denzinger, *Ritus Orientalium*, vol.I, Würzburg 1863, pp. 192–214; see also Ritual of Jacob of Edessa, pp. 279–288.
11. *Apostolic Constitutions* 3,15 (fourth century).
12. *Apostolic Constitutions* 3,16.
13. *Stromata*, Causa 15, qu. 3, beg.
14. *Summa*, Causa 27, quaestio 1, ch. 23.
15. *Summa Theologica Suppl.* qu. 39 art. 1.
16. From *Commentarium in IV Libros Sententiarum Magistri Petri Lombardi*, Div. XXV, art. II, qu. 1, § m-n.
17. Much more historical information about women deacons in: Anne Jensen, *Gottes selbstbewusste Töchter: Frauenemanzipazion im frühen Christentum*, Freiburg, 1992; Kyriaki Karidoyanes Fitzgerald, *Women Deacons in the Orthodox Church*, Holy Cross, Brookline, 1998, esp. pp. 28–58.
18. K. Arnt, *Die Diakonissen der armenischen Kirche in kanonischer Sicht*, Vienna, 1990; E. Synek, *Heilige Frauen der frühen Christenheit*, Würzburg, 1994; U. Eisen, *Ämtsträgerinnen im frühen Christentum*, Göttingen, 1996, esp. pp. 154–192.
19. *Romans* 16:1.
20. As attested to by St Ignatius of Antioch (died AD 110), *Trallians* 7:2; *Smyrnaeans* 8:1.
21. *Stromata* 3, 6, §53.
22. *1 Timothy* 3:8–12.
23. J. Daniélou, *The Ministry of Women in the Early Church*, Leighton Buzzard, 1974, p. 14; see also N. Brox, *Die Pastoralbriefe*, Regensburg, 1969, p. 154.
24. *Letters* X, 96:8; G. Lohfink, 'Weibliche Diakone im Neuen Testament', in G. Dautzenberg et al. (eds), *Die Frau im Urchristentum*, Frankfurt, 1983, pp. 332–334.

Chapter 19: The Devotion to Mary as Priest

1. Jean-Jacques Olier, *Recueil*, manuscript in Saint Sulpice, Paris, Rue du Regard, p. 64.
2. F. de Salazar, *In Canticum*, vol. 2, p. 40.
3. See Chapter 14.

4. *Mulieris Dignitatem*, § 27; *Letter to Women*, § 11, *Origins* 25 (1995), p. 5.

5. John Paul II, 'Address to the Cardinals and Prelates of the Roman Curia', *L'Osservatore Romano*, 23 December 1987.

6. René van Eyden in a letter to me.

7. Joanna Manning, *Is the Pope Catholic?*, Toronto, 1999, p. 72.

8. For further discussion, see: Rosemary Radford Ruether, *Mary, the Feminine Face of the Church*, Philadelphia, 1977; Elizabeth Johnson, 'The Symbolic Character of Theological Statements about Mary', *Journal of Ecumenical Studies* 22 (1985), pp. 312–335; 'Mary and the Female Face of God', *Theological Studies* 50 (1989), pp. 500–526; Marina Warner, *Alone of All Her Sex – The Myth and the Cult of the Virgin Mary*, London, 1990 (1985); Edward Schillebeeckx and Catherina Halkes, *Mary: Yesterday, Today, Tomorrow*, London, 1993; Else Maeckelberghe, *Desperately Seeking Mary: A Feminist Appropriation of a Traditional Religious Symbol*, Kampen, 1994; Maurice Hamington, *Hail Mary? The Struggle for Ultimate Womanhood in Catholicism*, New York, 1995; George H. Tavard, *The Thousand Faces of the Virgin Mary*, Colleville, 1996; Tina Beattie, *God's Mother, Eve's Advocate*, Bristol, 1999.

9. The Fathers' views on Mary's priestly dignity are documented in Hilda Graeff, *Mary. A History of Doctrine and Devotion*, London, 1965, pp. 101–202; and Réné Laurentin, *Maria, Ecclesia, Sacerdotium*, Paris, 1952, pp. 21–95.

10. St Thomas of Villanova (1486–1555), 'Concio I in Purificationem', *Opera*, Manila, 1883, vol. 4, p. 397.

11. *Summa Theologica Moralis*, Venice, 1477, IV, Tit. 15, c. 3, § 3.

12. *The Foot of the Cross*, London, 1857, p. 399.

13. Albertus Magnus, *'Mariale Super Missus Est' in Opera Omnia*, ed. A. and A. Borgnet, Paris, 1890–1899, vol. 37, pp. 84–87 (translation my own).

14. I. Marracci, *Sacerdotium Mysticum Marianum* (ca.1647), passim; F. Maupied, *Orateurs Sacrés*, Paris, 1866, vol. 86, p. 228.

15. F. C. de Salazar, *Canticum*, vol. 2, pp. 92, 94–95.

16. A. Vieira, 'Sermon on the Rosary', in *Maria Rosa Mystica*, Lisbon, 1688, pp. 78–80a; A. Nicholas, *La Vierge Marie d'après l'Évangile*, Paris, 1858, p. 295.

17. J. le Vasseur, *Diva Virgo*, Paris, 1622, ch. 22, pp. 171, 176; F. Bourgoing, *Vérités et excellences de Jésus Christ*, Paris, 1636, vol. 2, Méditation 19, § 3, pp. 183–184.

18. A. Vieira (1608–1697), 'Sermon on the Rosary', in *Maria Rosa Mystica*, Lisbon, 1688, p. 81.

19. L. Laplace, *La Mère Marie de Jésus*, Paris, 1906, p. 404.

20. Pope Pius X, *Acta Sanctae Sedis*, 9 May 1906.

21. *Acta Apostolicae Sedis* 8 (1916) p. 146.

Chapter 20: **Women with a Priestly Vocation**

1. *Story of a Soul*, ed. G.M. Day, London, 1951, p. 187. Read also the perceptive analysis of this passage in M. Furlong, *Thérèse of Lisieux*, London 1987, p. 95.

2. The text is quoted by E. Doyle, 'The Ordination of Women in the Roman Catholic Church' in *Feminine in the Church*, M. Furlong (ed.), London, 1984. p. 40.

3. *La Croix*, Wednesday, 15 December 1999, by André Baffert and Georges Duperray, priests of the Lyon diocese.

4. 'Dans les Églises, des Femmes aussi sont ministres' ['In the Churches, women too are ministers'], *Actes du Seminaire*, Femmes et Hommes en Église, (68, rue de Babylon, 75007 Paris), 1996, pp. 82–85.

5. F. Ferder, *Called to Break Bread?*, Mount Rainer, 1978.

6. *Zur Priesterin Berufen* ('Called to be a Woman Priest'), ed. I. Raming, G. Jansen, I. Müller and M. Neuendorff, Thaur, 1998, pp. 205–213.
7. F. Ferder, *Called to Break Bread?*, Quixote Centre, Mount Rainer, 1978, esp. pp. 17–80.
8. Commentary by the Sacred Congregation for Doctrine on *Inter Insigniores*, 1977, § 107; *Acta Apostolicae Sedis* 69 (1977) 98–116.
9. Compare *Acts* 10:34–47.
10. *Los Angeles Times*, 14 September 1987.
11. *Ordinatio Sacerdotalis*, § 2, 22 May 1994; *Responsum ad Dubium, 28* October 1995.

Chapter 21: Unmasking the Intruder
1. Blastares, orthodox theologian, fourteenth century, *Patres Graeci* vol. 144, col. 1174.
2. See Chapter 13.
3. D. Daube, *Forms of Roman Legislation*, Oxford, 1956; *Roman Law: Linguistic, Social, and Philosophical Aspects*, Edinburgh, 1969; H.F. Jolowicz and B. Nicholas, *Historical Introduction to the Study of Roman Law*, Cambridge, 1972; W.W. Buckland and P. Stein, *A Textbook of Roman Law from Augustus to Justinian*, Cambridge, 1975; A. Borkowski, *Textbook on Roman Law*, London, 1997.
4. D. Parry, *Households of God, the rule of St. Benedict with explanations*, London, 1980, pp. 42ff. ; see also: H. van Zeller, *The Holy Rule*, New York, 1958; A.C. Meisel and M.L. Del Mastro, *The Rule of St. Benedict*, New York, 1975; L.J. Lekai, *The Cistercians: Ideals and Reality*, Kent, 1977; A. de Vogüé, *Reading Saint Benedict. Reflections on the Rule*, Collegeville, 1980.
5. I.C. Hannah, *Christian Monasticism: A Great Force in History*, New York, 1925; D. Knowles, *Christian Monasticism*, London, 1969, pp. 35–36; C.H. Lawrence, *Medieval Monasticism*, New York, 1984.
6. F.H. Dudden, *Gregory the Great, his Place in History and in Thought*, London, 1905; B. Colgrave, *The Earliest Life of Gregory the Great by an Anonymous Monk of Whitby*, Cambridge, 1985; R.A. Markus, *Gregory the Great and his World*, Cambridge, 1998.
7. M. Conrat, *Geschichte der Quellen und Literatur des römischen Rechts im früheren Mittelalter*, Leipzig, 1891, reprint Aalen, 1963; F. C. von Savigny, *Geschichte des römischen Rechts im Mittelalter*, Heidelberg, 1850, reprint Bad Homburg, 1961; P. Vinogradoff, *Roman Law in Medieval Europe*, Oxford, 1929, reprint New York, 1969.
8. Jane F. Gardner, *Women in Roman Law and Society*, London, 1986; Antti Arjava, *Women and the Law in Late Antiquity*, Oxford: Clarendon, 1996.
9. *Corpus Iuris Canonici*, edited by A. Friedberg, Leipzig, 1879–1881; reprint Graz, 1955, passim.
10. The Code of Canon Law of 1918 lifted two prohibitions: communion during menstruation and women singing in a church choir. The others remained in force. *Codex Iuris Canonici*, ed. Herder, Freiburg, 1918; see canons 118; 709, § 2; 742, § 1 & 2; 813, § 2; 845; 968, § 1; 1262, § 1 & 2; 1306, § 1 & 2; 1342, § 2; 2004, § 1. The present Code of Church Law (of 1983) allows women to read, serve or preach at Mass only by 'temporary deputation' (can. 274 § 2–3); it bars women from receiving an ordained ministry (can. 1024), and therefore also from holding any form of jurisdiction (can. 219 § 1; 274 §1).

Chapter 22: The Way Forward

1. Galatians 3:28.
2. *Ordinatio Sacerdotalis*, 22 May 1994; *Responsum ad Dubium*, 28 October 1995.
3. Vatican I, *Dogmatic Constitution on the Catholic Faith*, Denzinger-Schönmetz no. 3011.
4. Vatican II, *Lumen Gentium* § 25.
5. Catholics who are not academically trained may fear that bishops who have promised not to promote the ordination of women as a condition of their admission to the episcopacy, will not be able to change their position once they realise that the ban against women priests is based on faulty evidence. Bishops, however, know from their study of moral theology that a promise, even if made under oath, ceases to be valid if (a) a substantial error affected their knowledge regarding the object of the promise, or (b) if an error affected the purpose of the promise (e.g. what is good for the Church), or (c) if the promise was made under fear, or (d) if the object of the promise has become impossible or harmful. The promise ceases *ab intrinseco*, as Thomas Aquinas taught: 'Whatever would have been an impediment to the making of a promise if it had been present, also lifts the obligation from a promise that has been made.' *Scriptum super IV libros Sententiarum* dist. 38, q.1, sol. 1 ad 1; D. M. Prümmer, *Manuale Theologiae Moralis*, Freiburg, 1936, vol. II, 'De Voto', pp. 326–348.
6. The various conditions are explained more fully in: K. Rahner, *Commentary on the Documents of Vatican II*, New York, 1965, pp. 210–211; 'Magisterium', *Sacramentum Mundi*, Herder and Herder, New York, vol. III, pp. 356–357; F. A. Sullivan, *Magisterium. Teaching Authority in the Catholic Church*, Gill & MacMillan, Dublin, 1983, pp. 101–104; R. R. Gaillardetz, *Teaching with Authority, A Theology of the Magisterium in the Church*, Liturgical Press, Collegeville, 1997, pp. 167–176, 219.
7. F. Sullivan, 'Infallibility doctrine invoked in statement against ordination by Congregation for the Doctrine of the Faith', *The Tablet* 23/30 December 1995, p. 1646. Among his other books see: *Magisterium: Teaching Authority in the Catholic Church*, New York, 1983; *Creative Fidelity: Weighing and Interpreting Church Documents*, New York, 1996.
8. N. Lash, 'On Not Inventing Doctrine', *The Tablet*, 2 December 1995, p. 1544.
9. Report 'Tradition and the Ordination of Women'. See also E. A. Johnson, 'Disputed questions: authority, priesthood, women', *Commonweal*, vol.123, 26 January 1996, pp. 8–10; G. Greshake, 'Response to the Declaration of the Congregation for Doctrine regarding the doctrine proposed in the apostolic letter *Ordinatio Sacerdotalis*', *Pastoralblatt* 48 (1996), pp. 56–57; A. E. O'Hara Graff, 'Infallibility complex: Have we heard the final word on women's ordination?', *U.S. Catholic*, vol. 61, April 1996, pp. 6–11; S. C. Callahan, 'Is black white? Letter to Cardinal Ratzinger concerning infallible teaching and ordination of women', *Commonweal*, vol. 123, 9 February 1996, pp. 6–7; R. R. Gaillardetz, 'Infallibility and the Ordination of Women. A Note on the CDF Responsum ad Dubium regarding the Authoritative Status of Ordinatio Sacerdotalis', *Louvain Studies* 21 (1996), pp. 3–24.
10. See J. Manning, *Is the Pope Catholic? A Woman confronts her Church*, Toronto, 1999.
11. Luke 16:8.
12. Matthew 10:28.
13. 1 Thessalonians 4:19.
14. H. Küng, *Infallible? An Inquiry*, Collins, London ,1971; SCM, London 1994; B. Tierney, *Origins of Papal Infallibility*, Brill, Leiden, 1972; P. Chirico, *Infallibility:*

The Crossroads of Doctrine, Michael Glazier, Wilmington, 1983; J.M.R. Tillard, *The Bishop of Rome*, Michael Glazier, Wilmington, 1983; P. Granfield, *The Papacy in Transition*, Gill, Dublin, 1981; P. Granfield, *The Limits of the Papacy: Authority and Autonomy in the Church*, Crossroad, New York, 1990; L.M. Bermejo, *Infallibility on Trial: Church, Conciliarity and Communion*, Christian Classics, Westminster, 1992; P. Dentin, *Les privilèges des papes devant l'écriture et l'histoire*, Cerf, Paris, 1995; P. Collins, *Papal Power*, HarperCollins, Australia, 1997; M. Fiedler and L. Rabben (eds), *Rome has Spoken . . .* , Crossroad, New York, 1998; E. Stourton, *Absolute Truth*, London, 1998; J. Manning, *Is the Pope Catholic?*, Toronto, 1999.

15. Vatican II, *Lumen Gentium* § 1.